AF539981

YOGA PHILOSOPHY

YOGA PHILOSOPHY

Editor-in-Chief
Swami Chidatman Jee Maharaj

ANMOL PUBLICATIONS PVT. LTD.
NEW DELHI - 110 002 (INDIA)

ANMOL PUBLICATIONS PVT. LTD.
H.O.: 4374/4B, Ansari Road, Daryaganj,
New Delhi-110 002 (India)
Ph.: 23278000, 23261597
B.O.: No. 1015, Ist Main Road, BSK IIIrd Stage
IIIrd Phase, IIIrd Block,
Bangalore - 560 085 (India)
Visit us at: www.anmolpublications.com

Yoga Philosophy

First Published, 2009
ISBN 978-81-261-3620-9

PRINTED IN INDIA

Printed at Mehra Offset Press, Delhi.

Contents

Preface

India colourful and vibrant, a land as diverse as its people. A mosaic of faiths, cultures, customs and languages that blend harmoniously to form a composite whole. One of the world's oldest living civilizations—which gave to the world—the concept of zero, the primordial sound Aum..., Yoga and Buddhism.

She is old. She is young. The two diametrically opposite, different yet unique and dynamic faces of India coexist even at this turn of the millennium. With a history of heritage, learning and civilisation dating back to almost 5000 years or perhaps even more, the modern India presents itself as an ideal country. From snow clad mountains to breezy sparkling blue sea side. From arid deserts with shifting sand dunes to lush green country sides. From ancient relics and architectural ruins dating back into antiquity to modern cities, India has it all.

To the north it is bordered by the world's highest mountain chain, where foothill valleys cover the northernmost of the country's maximum states. Further south, plateaus, tropical rain forests and sandy deserts are bordered by palm fringed beaches. Its southernmost tip is the meeting point of three Oceans.

India is a land of staggering contrast with a mingling of the tradition and modernity that is an unique experience to be in India. One will forever remember the stay in this wonderful Homeland-a land truly of mystery and enchantment. Only India can offer such an astonishing variety of contrasts.

She has given birth to numerous spiritual leaders and founders of some of the popular religions of the present day world. India probably has the most religious diversity in any country. It's the birthplace of Hinduism, Buddhism, Sikhism and Jainism and is among the few places to have a resident

Zoroastrian population. India with her veritable treasure trove of culture, mysticism, philosophy, art, music and architecture to name a few. Much of India's classical music is devotional and the North Indian Hindustani and South Indian Carnatic streams are distinct and both have a complex 'raga' framework. The legacy of dance in India is tremendous. The classical dances of India are numerous such as Kathakali of Kerala, Bharatnatyam of Tamil Nadu, Kuchipudi of Andhra Pradesh, Manipuri and Odissi from Orissa are the prominent dance forms in this country that sways to an altogether novel beat. The Yakshagana, nautanki and puppetry are ancient folk forms that live on till date. The earliest specimens of Indian painting are the ones on the walls of the Ajanta Caves dating back to 2nd century BC. The Mughals had a huge impact on Indian art. The influence of Persian art brought placid garden scenes, illustrations from myths, legends and history into Indian art. Word craft, handicrafts, architecture and sculpture all contribute to this rich and varied domain. Indian literature, both in English and in the vernacular, is ever more popular around the world.

The book aims at presenting perspectives of different aspects of Indian culture. It has topics on Indian classical music and dance, painting, ayurveda and yoga which are traditional and indigenous system of physical and mental wellbeing, language, philosophy and excellence achievements by Indian in the different branches of science and social sciences. It also includes our ancient religious and classic literature.

It is hoped that this book will be welcomed by the general readers as also scholars who are interested in the Indian heritage.

—Editors

1

The Great Indian Philosophy of Yoga

The outlook of one's life depends upon one's conception of reality. The structure of the universe decides our relationship with things. What is known as a vision of life is just the attitude which the individual is constrained to develop in regard to the atmosphere of the universe. Such an exalted conception of the totality of experience may be designated as the philosophy of life. It is, thus, philosophy which determines human conduct and enterprises of every kind in the social field as well as in one's own person. Not merely this; the psychological pattern of the apparatus of perception and inference and the like is also conditioned by the relationship that obtains between the universe and the individual. As such, it can be safely said that psychology and ethics are rooted in metaphysics.

It is often held that the programme of human life may be carried on with an amount of success without straining one's consciousness to the distant depths of the structure of the universe. People mostly prefer to live on the surface and move with the current of the river, with the least effort involved in the vocations of their personal and social existence.

But, it is not difficult to notice that a sort of merely getting on with life through the vicissitudes of history is not only soulless in its effect, by which the spirit of existence gets converted into a lifeless skeleton, but life, in the end, whether psychological, social or physical, would be impracticable if action is not fixed upon its proper relation with the environment of the entire pattern of life. Even as the working arrangement and the day-to-day performance of administration is based on a Governmental Constitution, along the lines of which contemplated programmes are carried on smoothly, life's enterprise would not be a possibility if the same is not rooted in a standard picture of the whole pattern of existence which directs and determines the nature as well as the details of activity.

Hence it is necessary to bestow a further thought on the facile formula of the commonplace of mankind that one can go on with the urges of life always in the direction in which the winds of the world blow, because without a stable ideology and a lofty idealism, no movement is conceivable. If this is the aim behind all enterprises and programmes, no worthwhile action of any kind would be possible without it, even in contemplation.

It is not that the activities of life are to be psychological meditations in an academic sense, or in the way in which people wrongly try to understand philosophy. Often, the erroneous notion goes that philosophy is an abstract thought process which idealises life into an ethereal and, perhaps, an unknown something, while life is concrete and substantial.

It is surprising that the world of matter should be taken as a solid substance while the ideas are regarded as airy nothings, even in the light of the astounding discoveries of modern researches in the field of science, which have swept off matter from the region of solidity, and matter appears to be evaporating into an undivided continuum of what is sometimes called a space-time extension, transcending the notions of a three-dimensional distance and a time process divided into the partiteness of past, present and future.

There is something more about this interesting discovery. If the continuum mentioned is indivisible by the very nature of its impartite and non-durational structure, naturally it would follow that the individual observer of things cannot stand outside the continuum. The consequences of this deduction are, again, startling, while being obvious. The observing individual merges, as it were, into the vast indivisibility of the continuum, and the events of the universe knowing itself and the individual knowing himself, as well as the individual knowing the universe, cannot be separated from one another. It would appear that the universe, in this analysis, is itself a measureless conflagration of intelligence, knowing itself, and nothing outside it can be noticed as an object of sensory perception or psychological cognition.

We find ourselves entering into the bottom of an ocean of force and existence which is inseparable from intelligence, and to know the universe would be the same as to know one's own Self. In the act of Self-knowledge, the universe is known at once, and the knowledge of the universe, on the other hand, is the knowledge of the Self.

In this circumstance of a new vision that we seem to be confronting before us, our personal and social life should be, indeed, a mirror-like clarity, which would include the type of relationship that we should adopt with other people in our day-to-day existence. What we call the ethics or morality of human relationships as well as of personal behaviour amounts, from the above analysis, to a conscious participation in the pattern of things in general, which is only the face of the brooding Spirit of the Cosmos as a whole. Love becomes spontaneously unselfish.

Love, then, cannot be directed exclusively to any person or thing, or to an isolated ideal, but becomes a spring of joy arising from the recognition of the fullness of existence. Hatred of any kind gets abolished from the surface of life by the very fact of the unity of procedure and purpose involved in the structure and programme of creation. Human history can transfigure itself into a saga of the dramatic evolution of the particulars to the Universal through the various levels and degrees of its manifestation.

What people have been dreaming of as the glorified ideal of *Rama-Rajya,* or the Golden Age of *Satya-Yuga* of divine and eternal perfection, would not, indeed, be a far-off object to be realised. It was a perennial message which Plato proclaimed with the conviction of a genius when he declared that no peace on earth can ever prevail unless philosophy goes with administration, and administration with philosophy. We have a glorious day ahead. Humanity! Be prepared to extend it a warm welcome.

Prefatory

We are all here for the fulfilment of a purpose. It may not be that everyone will be entertaining a uniform idea of what this purpose is. You must have attended schools. You must have passed through various stages of education. You are educated persons, and learned in many respects. You have studied well. You have lived in the world. Now you have come to another place to study something else.

So, most of us are likely to have the idea that we are going to pursue another 'course of studies', just as we have already studied something else before: "If today I study physics here, I will study chemistry somewhere else, and for biology I will go to a third place." This idea can be in the minds of many of us, that we are here to study some subject with which we are not acquainted up to this time. It may be Yoga, a very well-known term these days. It may be Vedanta, it may be religion, it may be spirituality, it may be the art of God-living, and what not. Thus, it becomes a kind of subject among the many which are useful to people in one way or other.

At the very outset, it becomes necessary that we have to decondition our minds before we attempt anything positive and worth the while. We are not going to study any subject in the ordinary sense of the term. We do not study philosophy here, for, that one can study anywhere else, in a college or university. You have professors and learned men. That would not be a difficulty but here we are not to get acquainted with a branch of learning, if that is your definition of education. This is something quite different, a kind by itself, of which an idea occurred to many stalwarts of yore, both in the East and the West. The latest example of this category, at least to my mind, was Swami Sivananda, the Founder of this Institution.

One cannot say that they were not educated persons, but their education was different from the type into which people get initiated usually as learned persons, lecturers, professors, etc. We have to reorient our way of thinking, with some effort, in order to fathom the intentions of these Masters. It requires an effort because we are born into a world of certain prejudices which die very hard. The purpose of these sessions that we are contemplating to hold here is to get over these preconceived ruts of thinking; the purpose is to bring a right-about turn in the very art of thinking. More properly, we may say we are attempting to learn a way of thinking which is a little different from the usual way of the world. The normal way of thinking is well known: "I belong to America, I belong to India; I am a man, I am a woman, I am a businessman; I am a teacher, I am rich, I am poor, I am happy, I am unhappy, this is good, that is bad." These are well-known ways of outlook in anyone's life.

This, then, is the atmosphere in which we are living in the world, and we work hard every day, whatever be the work we do in the various fields of life, to adjust ourselves to these so-called chaotic presentations before us that we call life. All your day is spent in adjusting yourself with the conditions of the world. If it is cold, you put on your coat. If it is hot, you throw off your *bunian.* If you are hungry, you eat some food. If you are tired, you lie down. If you are angry, you show your teeth. Well, so many things occasion different conditions in our minds - the psychological circumstances and we have to adapt ourselves to these sources of the influx of environmental conditions. All effort is only this much—somehow to adapt ourselves to the world-conditions, whether they are geographical, political, social, or family circumstances. We work very hard. Every one of you is working hard. But what for? In what direction? What is the purpose? We are impelled by a peculiar urge from within us to work. Otherwise, there is a sub-conscious threat felt from within towards the very extinction of our existence. We may die if we do not work. Our existence can be abolished by the powerful conditions of life outside.

The adaptations that we make with life outside vary from person to person. That is why what I do may not be what you do every day, and what you do may not be what another does. It does not mean that everyone is doing the same thing, in the same manner, everywhere in the world, in spite of the fact that everyone does something. Now, the necessity to do something is common to every person. Everybody feels a necessity to 'do', whether it is in a factory or a chapel or a temple or a shop. Everybody *does* something. The variety in doing arises on account of there being a variety in the condition of one's own psychological being. Your actions depend on your mental structure; so activities have connection with psychology. Everyone is active but in different ways. The necessity to be active can be explained only by the impulsion from one's psychological structure. If you study your mind, you can know something about the need that you feel in regard to work in the world.

Why should you do any work? You know it very well. Each one knows the answer. The world is a hard job before us, and we have perforce to go hand in hand with the laws of the world. We cannot regard it as a stranger, as an outsider, as something not connected with us. Our sorrows are our maladjustments with the world, with life, with everything. The rectification of the maladjustment is attempted by work, activity, enterprise, project, planning, etc. All these plannings and projects, of every kind, in life are methods of personal adjustment with the requirements of outward life. I mention to you a few of these interesting factors which have to be considered before we endeavour to find out what it is that we are supposed to do finally, why we are existing at all, why we are breathing and eating and getting on, somehow, in the world. What is the purpose behind it all?

There is something which keeps us restless and anxious, whatever be the things we do. The practice of our vocations in life has a psychology behind it. That is why there is variety in the circumstances of life. There is this picturesque world before us of colours and sounds and movements evincing different kinds of emotions and reactions from each different person. Life is activity. It is work. The moment you think of living in the world, you think of 'doing' something. And this doing, again, as I mentioned, has vital relationship with the needs of your inner personality - the mind, if you want to call it that way. We shall try to think of what this mind is, in a little detail, after some time. For the time being, we may be satisfied with this thing called mind, with which we are almost familiar, which is the thing that limits and streamlines our activities. Activities have a psychology behind them. Every practice of any kind has a mental condition preceding.

The question may pose itself: Why should the mind think in the way it thinks, and drive us in a given direction, towards the performance of some work, towards engagement of ourselves in some activity? The 'how' of the activity of mind is called psychology. How does it work? What are the various branches of the movement of the psyche? The study of the details of the variegated patterns and activities of the mind is psychology. A very vast subject it is, the study of the mind. Unless this is known, you cannot be fully conversant with the techniques of activity in the world, and you would be doing things without sufficient success. Activities will then be like pursuing the will-o'-the-wisp; a wild-goose chase, a going through blind alleys, with no idea as to what will happen in the future, unless there is a correct knowledge of the background of these activities, which is human psychology. Unless you know your mind, you cannot know the nature of the works that you have to do, and the purpose towards which the works are directed.

But, why does the mind work in this manner? Why should I think in the way I am thinking just now? Why do you think in the way you are thinking? What is this devil working inside us, separating one from the other and demanding that one should think in this way and another should think in another way? Why should it be like that? Why should you think in that way and I should think in this manner? Why not think together in the same way? What is the difficulty? This 'why' raises a problem which goes beyond the field known as psychology.

Normally, this field is called philosophy. The 'why' of a thing is studied in philosophy. The 'how' of a thing is studied in psychology, and the 'what' is the actual daily routine of activity. In our approach to anything, even the smallest item, even the most insignificant so-called addendum to our life, we have to be scientific in our approach. And what is the meaning of being scientific? It is taking the first thing as the first thing and the second thing as the second thing and not mixing up one with the other. You should not start with the second thing while the first thing has been ignored. To be able to conceive the consecutive series of any kind of movement is to be scientific.

But if you are oblivious of the series and miss a link in the chain of the development of thought and activity, then, you would not be scientific. And it is practically the same thing as to be logical; to be logical is also to be scientific, though there is a little difference in the significance of these terminologies, with which we need not concern ourselves at present. To be systematic, to be patient, to be observant, to be accessible to rectification, to be tending towards more and more generalised forms of ideas, to attempt at an exceeding of the limitations of body, community, individuality, etc. - these are certain characteristics of a scientific attitude, the logical approach to things. Philosophy is the study of life with reference to 'ultimate causes', and not merely the 'immediate antecedents'.

We are here to bestow some serious thought on the essentials of what we may generally call life, which condition the outward varieties with which we are connected. The outward details are expressions of inward essentials. The type of food that I eat depends upon the kind of hunger that I have, and the way in which the physiological organs operate, and the liver, the pancreas, the intestines, etc., work. So is the case with every kind of inward tendency, mental or psychological. A serious contemplative attitude is to be bestowed upon the factors which go to constitute the structure of the whole of our life, which includes the geographical aspect, the astronomical aspect, the political aspect, the social aspect, the personal aspect, etc. You will find that you are connected to various factors even when you are sitting here near your desk. You are seated here with a little desk in front of you, but you are many things just now. You are an American, a British, a male, a professor, a hungry man; you have anxiety about your future, you have a desire to achieve something, and many such unimaginable things are conditioning you. It does not mean that you are always thinking, "I am a German, an Indian, American," etc., but the idea is not rooted out from the mind. It is there at the background.

How can you forget that you are a woman or man, or that you are coming from such-and-such a country, that you are a national of such-and-such a place? You may not be brooding over this always, but it is there at the back of every kind of thought that is generated by your mind and every approach or outlook which may be there in your mind in regard to life. So, what is it that you are after? It is not study of philosophy, psychology or economics in the traditional sense of the term. You are trying to go into tho deepest roots of the various branches of study you call economics or psychology or philosophy, or whatever it is, all which are the outward expressions of an inward need.

The whole effort of ours seems, somehow, to be released of the shackles which restrain us like prisoners within the four walls. You know what these shackles are. Each one of you knows what your bondage is. They are the bonds which do not allow you freedom unless you have an adequate knowledge of the way in which you have got into this bondage. You have problems of visa and passport and economic conditions and family relationships and bodily limitations. All these are shackles. You cannot be free like that so easily. But who has put us into this situation of suffering and is keeping us ever restless and unconscious of a future? We are worried about the past, restless about the present, and anxious about the future. Thus, it becomes obvious that we are not merely students of some branch of learning, enabling us to earn our bread. Rather, we are after something which will keep us sober in our minds, and give us peace, if you would like to call it so, under every circumstance. What we lack is not so much bread as peace of mind.

It does not mean that a person who has plenty to eat is a person with sobriety or peace of spirit; nor is it true that a person who is physically starving has no peace of mind. What we are after is quite different from what people generally think they are after in the work-a-day world. We also belong to the work-a-day world; it is true. We are not out of the world. We are on the earth, but being on the earth, being in the world, we are after a serious search for something which is not merely bread, and a building, and a comfortable social and physical life. These are accessories to something else which we are truly seeking. Many of you may not be in a starving condition. You are not beggars. You may have an adequately satisfactory arrangement for your daily meal. You have a proper place to sleep at night. You have clothing. I do not think we have so much difficulty about these matters, which are the physical realities of life. But what is it that you do not have? That is important.

There is something which speaks within us in a language of anxiety. Something is not all right, though you have everything in the physical or social sense. You are respectable people in society. You have a financial status of your own; everything is well, so far as it goes, but you are not happy, really speaking, for a reason which you have not yet found time to go deep into. We are so busy with the enormous flood of the atmospheric conditions outside that we have been prevented from even finding time to think, let alone the capacity to think.

Whether we have a capacity to think correctly or not is a different subject. Have you time to think? That also is not there. Very busy indeed, is everyone. And there is therefore the need to learn also the art of finding time to think in the proper way, because your life is nothing but a mental life and if the mental life is ignored, your physical and social life is not going to make you free. You know very well how important your mind is. There is no need to go on speaking about the nature of the mind and the importance of its working.

With all the comforts and the glories of physical life, if the mind is not in peace, of what avail is this glory of the earth? You may be a king or a queen. Well, wonderful, but the mind is not working. What do you say to this? And you know what it means. There cannot be a greater hell than that. Well, then, the mind is working, but in the wrong direction. That, too, is very unfortunate. What you seek is, therefore, something which is the precondition of your physical needs and social relationships. Hence, the subject that we shall take up in these sessions, with which I am personally supposed to be concerned now, would be a series of approaches towards the causes of the effects which our inner and outer lives are.

Our life, whether it is inner or outer, consists of a series. It is not a solid substance. Our existence is not like a hard stone which is immovable and motionless. It is a flux, a series of tendencies, movements, enterprises, etc., which get practically bifurcated into the inward and the outward phases. Life in itself is neither inward nor outward. It is everywhere. But for convenience's sake we make this distinction of being inside and outside, just as we say we are inside the room. But this 'inside' idea arises on account of the wall around. If the wall were not to be there, we would not say that we are inside. We are just on the surface of the earth.

But because there is a consciousness of walls on the four sides, there is also a consciousness of an inside and conversely a consciousness of an outside. There is really no such thing as inner life and outer life, just as there is no inside or outside really, unless there is a wall which separates the inside from the outside. But we always speak of an inner life and an outer life as if they are really there. This bifurcation or gulf, so-called, between our inner life and outer life is due to a wall that seems to be there between what we call the inner and the outer. This wall has also to be seen, as to what it is.

Here we have walls made of bricks. But, what is this wall which makes us feel that we have an inner life as distinguished from an outer life? Everything has to be clear before we start doing anything. Yes; we have to see that everything is clear, and there are no doubts and obsessions in the mind. I began by saying that you should decondition yourself first and abandon all conditioned habits. Do not say: "I have read the Upanishads already." Well, you forget the Upanishads for the time being, forget the Gita, forget the Bible, forget your nationality, forget that you are anything whatsoever. But remember that you are a spirit that is seeking solutions to certain serious problems which are universally harassing the minds of everyone. The basic problems are the same everywhere, though the outward expressions of the same are different.

The daily difficulties that we confront in our life are not the same. But the basic root-cause will be found finally to be one and the same thing. We think as human beings. That is the essential way of thinking. But, outwardly, one may think as a man, and another may think as a woman; one thinks as a professor, another thinks as a rustic in the field, etc. These are outward forms of outlook. But there is what is called a common denominator of normal thinking, which is the human way of thinking. We do not think as a dog or a cat, and we do not move like a tree towards the sun. We do not think as the non-human species. We think as human beings only, and we cannot think in any other manner. This is a great limitation on us, again, in the way we think.

I have mentioned certain of the limitations which prevent us from generalised thinking, but the human way of thinking also is a bondage. That is why you have been told many a time that the intellect is a barrier. You must have heard from people that the intellect is an obstacle in higher pursuits, because the intellect is an endowment of the human being. It is not present in an earthworm or a centipede. They have some other instincts of their own. And we have a peculiar structure within us we call intellect, reason, etc. We have been told a hundred times that this is an obstacle. But why is it an obstacle when it is the only faculty we have in the end? It is an obstacle because it is present only in a human being and we cannot find it elsewhere. The way of thinking or the outlook of the different species will be different. And in order to be able to enter into a more generalised form of the outlook of life we should not be wedded too much to our own endowment called the intellect. Though it is an aid, it is not enough.

It is a prerogative of the human species only, but the truths of life are not merely human. There are many more things in the world than human values, and we should not be under the impression that we are gods ruling over this world. We have, at times, a pride, which takes us off from our feet and makes us feel that we are angels walking on this earth, looking down upon subhuman creatures. They are all nothing before us, as if they do not exist at all. We are the masters. The world belongs to us. The earth is the property of the human being. When we have such feelings, we say, 'this land is mine'. How does it belong to you? God knows! Anyhow, you have a feeling it is yours. The man that is in us works in an imperious manner. And that humanness in us, while it is a great virtue in many respects, is also going to be a great hindrance in the last resort. Our human character is one link in the chain of the development of the various species of life in creation. There are, also, superior faculties higher than human reason, which belong to superhuman realms of being.

You know that the world is not made up of human beings alone. There are others below us and above us. We are in the middle hanging somewhere on the rope that stretches from the earth to the heavens. We are on a long journey. We are not stationed in this world as permanent proprietors of properties here. We are not owners of anything. We are in a moving flux, as I said. We are on a perpetual journey onward, and we cannot, as a great master said, step into the same water of the river the next moment, because the next moment we step into another water of the same river.

Thus, too, the next moment we are not living the same life. Every moment we are in a new life into which we perpetually enter, and the so-called continuity of our personality which makes us feel that we were yesterday the same thing that we are today, and the hope that we shall be tomorrow exactly what we are today, is due to a limitation of the way in which the mind works, the way in which we get tied up to one set of connotations in this movement. The habit of the mind is to look through a small hole or an aperture. The vast expanse of life, of which we are a small part, is out of the range of our perception, due to certain structural defects in the mind.

That is why we feel that we are the same person every day without knowing that we are changing every moment and are heading towards something different altogether until a catastrophic change will take place, when the mind will know that real change has occurred. And that catastrophe is called death. Every moment we are dying, but we are not aware of it because of the capacity of the mind to adjust itself to this little change every moment. And perhaps if our mind were in a position to adjust itself even to that so-called change called death, we would not know that we are dying. We would not even know that something has happened, just as we do not know that we are today different from what we were yesterday. But the mind is not so made. It is so much conditioned to this body that the severance of it from this body looks like a complete severance from existence itself.

There is a continuity, which is life, of which we are a part, and we are not just X, Y, Z, or A, B, C, sitting here; it is not like that. If we open our eyes to fact, we will be surprised that we have been living a fool-hardy life up to this time, and now the time has come when we have to be serious. Our time is short, and there is so much to learn, and a lot to achieve. Obstacles are too many, and we have no time to wool-gather, sleep or while away our time as if there is eternity before us. We cannot take things lightly. Life is precious. We cannot take it as a joke. Every moment of time is as gold because every moment is nothing but a little loss of this span of our life. Every bell that rings tells us that we have lost one hour. It is not a happy thing that we are hearing. Tenacious has to be our effort at gaining insight into that which we seek.

Be humble. Be patient. Do not try to be big, but be small, until you almost become a nothing, which is better for you than to be a large thing in the world, a cynosure of all eyes. There is hope, and so be always confident that you will get what you need. Always remember three things:

1. Be clear as to what you want;
2. Be sure that you will get what you want; do not be hesitant. Assert: 'Yes, I am certainly going to get it', and
3. Start with that effort just now. Do not say 'tomorrow'. 'Everything is clear to me now, and I shall start at it.'

If these three maxims are before you as your guiding lights, you will succeed always, and with everything.

The Human Predicament

Make three columns: 1, 2, 3. In the first column, write the Heading: "What do you want?" In the second column, "Can you achieve it?" In the third column, "What is the way to it?"

Now, take the first item. "What do you want?" What are you in search of? What do you wish to know? All these questions imply almost one and the same thing, and are attempted and answered in the system of studies usually known as "Philosophy". So put this under column No. 1, which comes under philosophy.

Then, comes the second column. "Can you achieve this goal or knowledge, of search, of aspiration, of asking?" The analysis of your own capacities in this great search of that which you seek or want, comes under what is known as "Psychology". This is under No. 2.

Then, is the third section. "What is the way?" Taking for granted that you have the capacity, the equipment, the endowment, which is requisite, what is the methodology that is to be adopted? This is the "practical" aspect of your search. Thus, there is a "philosophical" aspect, a "psychological" aspect and a "practical" aspect of the whole subject. This is to make a broad division of our approach to the entire question of life in its completeness.

Properly speaking, the subject of philosophy is concerned with the nature of Truth, or Reality. It is quite obvious that we are not after unrealities, phantoms or things that pass away; we are not in search of these things. We require something substantial, permanent. And what is this? What do you mean by the thing that is permanent, which is the same as what you call the Real? The search for Reality is the subject of philosophy.

Then we come to the second issue, the individual nature, the structure of our personality, the nature of our endowments. An analysis of the entire internal structure of ourselves as individuals in search of anything is comprehended under the various branches of psychology and even what we call "psycho-analysis". They all are subsumed under this single head of an internal analysis of the individual.

Now, we have the third thing, under the third column - the way to the achievement of this ideal, the Reality; the methodology, the practice of it, is what we are concerned with essentially. This is what we generally hear of as "Yoga". Yoga is practice, though it is preceded by certain philosophical and psychological studies and discussions.

What is this Reality which we are in search of? What do we mean by the Real? Well, if we put a question generally to a layman, there will be an immediate answer, "What I see with my eyes, is the real." And what do "I see with my eyes"? "The World." This is the reality. The world in which we live is the real thing; that is the object which we regard as real. It is permanent. "It was there even before I was born; it is now, and it may be there, even when I shall pass away. The world is my reality and I cannot conceive of any other reality."

In the section on psychology, I may ask you a question, "What are you?" A simple answer will come forth, *viz.* "I am such and such," "so and so," "a person," a usual reply. If you are asked, "Who are you", you know what sort of answer you will give. It is quite clear. Perhaps you will imply as an underlying current of your answer that you have a mind, an intellect, a reason, a thinking power - that is all. One cannot go beyond these simple definitions of oneself. And if you are asked, "What are you supposed to do? What is the practical aspect of your life?" - here too, you have a very simple, offhand answer. "We have to work, for the maintenance of ourselves, in relationship to this world, in the context of the atmosphere of human society, and various other factors."

This is a prosaic and naive approach of the common person in regard to the problems of life, the duties of life and the values of life, but these are to touch the subject only on the surface, even as we can have a very inadequate and unscientific diagnosis of the illness of a person by merely looking at the body of the person, or by just passing the hand over the body of the individual, without investigating into the internal complications which give rise to the discomfort of disease. We are impelled to search for things on account of a discomfort we feel in life. Otherwise, there would be no impulsion for search in respect of anything.

Dissatisfaction is regarded as the mother of all philosophy. Philosophy is the child of a recognition of the inadequacies in life. There are many kinds of dissatisfaction. We can write a book on what dissatisfaction means, because we are dissatisfied with everything, practically. It is difficult to imagine that we can be satisfied with anything permanently, or even for an elongated period. We cannot be satisfied with summer for a long time. We cannot be satisfied with winter for a long time. We cannot be satisfied with any atmosphere for a long time, and so on are our grievances.

There is an ingredient of dissatisfaction in the very structure of our existence in this world. This is something very strange. How is it that we should be kept restless and longing throughout our life? Each one of you, just for a few seconds, withdraw your minds and contemplate your lives from the time of your birth, or at least from the time you can recollect yourselves. Were you satisfied at any time? You were always asking for something, and if you obtained that thing, you would ask for another thing. If you get the second thing, you ask for a third thing.

Now, where is this quest going to end? Is a person going to be satisfied with anything at all? How is it that we are under the grip of the demon, as it were, of endless asking, an asking for that of which we have no clear knowledge in our minds? We are demanding endless things, in a variety of ways, constantly, throughout our lives, because it has not yet become clear to our minds as to what we want finally. We are only experimenting with situations: "Perhaps this is what I want, perhaps that is what I want"; and when we go to these things, we realise that these were not the things that we sought to have.

It is like experimenting with various medicines and finding that none of them will suit our illness. We have been experimenting with persons, with things, with professions and the various other facets of our longings. They have not satisfied us. Even today, we are not satisfied - neither you, nor I, nor anybody else. It is impossible to imagine a condition of complete satisfaction, where we will have to say nothing, where, perhaps, we have to think also of nothing, where everything is obtained for ever. The state of obtaining all things is, indeed, beyond even the stretch of imagination. We cannot imagine whether such a state is possible, that is, to have all things that we need.

It looks, many a time, that we have to pass away from this world in despair with everything. If we read the history of the minds of human beings, if there is any such thing as a history of psychology of human nature as such, we will be surprised to observe that it is impossible to pin-point even one individual who has left this world with genuine satisfaction, save those few who are the salt of the earth. There has always been a gap, an unfinished something with which the person had to quit. Everyone goes with something left incomplete. It will never be finished. This is the seamy side of things, the unhappy facet of life, which seems to be the outer picture of this world painted before us.

But we have also a peculiar solacing and satisfying inner core, which always eludes our grasp. There is something in us, in each one of us, which escapes our notice every moment. We can never visualise it with all our effort, and yet there is that mysterious and tremendous something which keeps us somehow hoping for the possibility of success in the end. This peculiar something in us, which keeps us positively hoping for the practicability of our enterprises in life, and expecting a victory at last - that is the glory of our personality.

Man has remained a wretched suffering individual in this world, it is true, but he is also a glorious something, a majestic and incomprehensible mystery, a combination of two contraries, as it were, which is just the miracle of man. Every human being is a miracle by himself. It is not possible for us to know ourselves wholly. If it had been possible, we would not be in search of things and running about here and there.

There is a peculiar eluding difficulty on account of which we are in search of things and yet are not able to get anything; with all the search, we seem to be receiving nothing in the end. Yet, we cannot withhold this quest. This is another peculiarity. On the one hand, it appears that we are going to get nothing, because we have got nothing up to this time, after so many years of suffering. If, for the last twenty-five, thirty or forty years of search and effort we seem to have achieved nothing, what is the guarantee that we are going to gain anything satisfying in another ten years? Perhaps they will also pass in the same way as the last twenty-five or thirty years have gone. "Impermanent and joyless, verily, is this world (*Anityam, Asukham*)."

The Portals of Enquiry

We go back to where we stopped, viz, the ways in which we try to probe into reality. Obviously, we have three ways or three avenues of observation and we cannot think of a fourth method. We look outside and try to see what is there; we look inside and try to find out what is within us; also, often, we look up and wonder at what is above us. This has been the attitude of all investigators, whether in the field of science, philosophy or religion.

Fundamentally, we noticed that there is the usual objective approach of science which is remarkable for its achievements these days, and which almost goes about as a gospel. We have to see how far it has succeeded before we can enter into a contemplation of other methods and ways of approach. What is science doing? What is the way of the specialist in the field of observation and experiment? Whoever tries to discover truth by observation and experiment is a scientist, and we try to do that in our own humble way in our attitude to things in the world. We look at the world. All our business in life is objective, external and material for the most part. We see the oceans, we see the wind blowing and we see the stellar system; we see the five elements - Earth, Water, Fire, Air, Ether. What else can we see in the world? There was a time when our specialists in the field concluded that the world consists of the five elements, and we cannot see anything else. We are also acquainted with the advances made later on, further to these main observations of the five elements merely.

We have the great advancement of physical science, which has gone deep into the structure of matter, by which we mean all the five elements - Earth, Water, Fire, Air, Ether. All these constitute matter in its essentiality. Physics goes into the structure of matter. What is matter made of? Of what is it constituted? Primarily, we say matter is only five elements, but we have seen that further experiments are performed, and have noticed that this solid earth is porous, a well-known fact. The earth is not an indivisible mass. Water is porous; air is porous. Even fire is a continuity of processions of energy. So, none of these four visible elements is really the hard or impartite thing that it appears to be. All these are complex substances and not compounds. A compound is indivisible; a complex is divisible. These elements are divisible and are not an indivisible substance. This was discovered later on.

So, our original observation was not correct, *viz.*, that there are solid elements. Now, if matter is divisible, into what is it divisible? It is divisible into molecules. These are the chemical substances. All these, including our own bodies, are reducible to certain chemical elements. There are only bundles of chemical molecules to which our bodies can be reduced and to which anything on the earth can be reduced. The molecules are chemical in their nature, but these chemicals are also constituted of finer particles called 'atoms'. They are more difficult to apprehend than the chemical substances. Scientists as well as philosophers have given varying opinion about the nature of atoms.

There were people who thought that the Earth-atoms are different from the Water-atoms, and the Water-atoms are different from the Fire-atoms or the Air-atoms. We had in India at least some schools of thought which believed in the atomic structure of matter, but also held at the same time that the atoms vary one from the other. The Earth-atom is different from the Water-atom, etc. But this was not the finality of the discovery.

We, today, are told, again and again, that there is no intrinsic difference between one atom and another atom. The so-called difference is not due to the inner structure of the atom but because of the arrangement of the constituents of the atom. So, Earth differs from Water, Water differs from Fire, etc., not because their atomic essentiality varies but because they are arranged in different patterns constitutionally.

But all this is what is known as classical physics. We may safely say, this is the physics which brought us down to the time which is a little later than what they call the Newtonian Era, when classical physics reached its climax and it was decided, once and for all, that matter is contained in space, space being regarded as a receptacle for the material contents. The great discovery that Newton made was the law of gravitation, the pull of the material parts in regard to one another due to the mass and the distance of these parts of matter.

But, we have come today to the twentieth century, beyond half of it, and people are dinning into our ears the greater discoveries of a strange picture that is before us of even the world of matter, of which even Newton would be surprised if he were to be alive today. There are not even atoms. There is only a continuity of energy, so that we cannot know where is earth, where is water, where is fire, where is air, where is ether. We are not here to discuss science, and mention is made of all these only as a kind of preliminary introduction to the ways in which science has been moving in a search for reality. Our interest in this regard is philosophical.

Where has it brought us finally? Where are we standing after all this discovery? Are we more informed about the nature of truth, today, than we were at the time when we were told that there are only five elements in their gross form? Are we better off today socially, philosophically, religiously, ethically, or spiritually, merely because of the fact that we have discovered a continuum of energy in the Universe instead of the gross five elements? The crux of the matter is something which eludes our grasp. We are not in search of what matter is constituted of That is not our interest.

It avails us of nothing, if we know what another possesses. You may possess anything, and what does it matter to me? Why should I go on enquiring into your property, your bank-balance, your relations in the world, etc.? What does it matter to me, whatever you are, unless there is some connection of these informations with my life which I am attempting to understand?

How are we benefited by these discoveries? If the world is a continuum of energy, what does it matter to us? Let that be. Are we better off? Well, we know well that we are in the same condition in our personal lives and social lives, in our aspirations and in our searches today, as our ancestors must have been centuries back. Where, then, is the difficulty? And it has somehow been missed. This is the defect of a purely scientific approach of the experimental type.

The advantage of scientific discoveries has been a rapid technological development in this age. We have fast-moving aeroplanes and subtle submarines, and gadgets of every kind. All are discoveries, inventions made as a consequence of the knowledge that people have gained today of the components of matter. But, finally, it has kept us in a state of unhappiness and anxiety, because of the ostensible fact that our lives are not connected with these discoveries.

There is, to put it in a more technical form, an epistemological gulf between the seer and the seen. The knowledge pattern remains the same today, as it was a few thousand years back. And what is the knowledge pattern we are referring to? The student has to be very attentive here, because this is a little novel theme and perhaps a little difficult to comprehend, because here is the essence of the whole problem.

Our life is inseparable from our experience. What we call life is nothing but experience, and this is important to remember. And experience, whatever be the nature of it, is inseparable from a consciousness of that experience. There is no experience without a consciousness of it. We are aware that we are undergoing a process or are in a state of experience. If the awareness is absent, we cannot be said to be in a state of any experience at all. To have no experience is to have no awareness of what is happening.

Now, our life being identical with a conscious experience, and our search for reality being observational and experimental in the scientific fashion, we have to find out how the panorama of external nature, as it stands before us from the point of view of science, is connected with our personal life.

The world is as unmanageable today as it was many years back. Merely because we say that there is a continuum of energy in the universe, instead of the five elements, we have not bettered the things. It means the same thing, finally. Why is it the same thing, and why cannot there be a difference? Because our disconnection from the world remains today the same thing as it was before. Our sorrow is due to the dispossession of ourselves from things we call real or reality. We cannot control the earth or the water, the fire or the air. And the vast space outside is enough to take one's breath away.

Likewise, today, we cannot control the atoms or the electrons or the energies or the forces that be, because we are outside them. Our life, to repeat again, is a function of consciousness, and so long as our consciousness is not en-rapport with the reality that we are in search of, we are not in possession of that reality, and so long as we are not in possession of it, we have practically nothing to do with it. It is like a treasure that belongs to somebody else, about which we have only a theoretical information and with which there is, practically, no relationship. Our disconnection from reality - let us be contented just now with the scientific definition of reality as external objects, the world that we see - is also our weakness. Our strength enhances as we gain more and more control or possession of reality.

The more do we possess reality, the more is the power that we wield. And what is possession? To possess an object, to possess anything for the matter of that, is to be invariably connected with it, in an inseparable manner. We have a power over the limbs of our body. I am giving one example of what power means, and what power does not mean. I can lift my hand at my will; there is no difficulty about it. Even if the leg of the elephant is very heavy, the elephant can lift its leg. The elephant can lift its whole body, though even a hundred people cannot lift an elephant. Perhaps, I may not be able to lift your body, but you can lift your body. You may not be able to lift my body, but I can lift my body. What is this mystery? Wherefrom comes this strength by which I can lift my body and walk? The reason is that my consciousness is one with my reality, which is this body; it is not outside. But you cannot lift my body, nor can I lift your body, because your consciousness is disconnected from my body, and mine from yours. The analogy is simple, and clear enough.

The reason is that power is identical with the union of consciousness with its object. The content of consciousness should not be outside consciousness, if real power is to be there. As long as the content remains outside, consciousness loses control over it. So, no scientist can control the universe or have any reasonable or appreciable relationship with it, because the scientist remains a puppet in the hands of the powers which he has discovered and of which, he, now today, realises, is an inseparable part. But, with all these defects of science, it has awakened us to one important truth, that to know the world is to know our own selves. One would be surprised how science can teach this truth; yes, it has somehow stumbled upon this fact - by a chance, we may say.

We cannot know the universe unless we know ourselves. While this is true, the reverse also is true, at the same time. We cannot know ourselves truly, unless we know the whole universe. The one is the same as the other. Now, how does science lead us to this conclusion? The secret is the discovery of an indivisible continuum of nature, outside which no individual, nothing, can exist. The space-time continuum which scientists speak of today, in the relativity cosmos, is inclusive of yourself and myself and all things. We cannot stand outside it. We are an eddy in this ocean of force which is called the space-time continuum, and so, how can we know it unless we know ourselves, since we are a part of it? Also, it becomes more obvious on account of the fact that to know is to have an awareness of the fact; and awareness is an essentiality of our being. Our being and our consciousness of our being are the same; they are not two different things.

The moment we say that we exist, we imply we are conscious that we exist. The existence of things is inseparable from the consciousness of the existence of things. In as much as it has been decided that existence is a continuity, inseparable in its meaning, with no gulf whatsoever, to know the universe would be to have a consciousness of the universe. But in what manner? Not in the form of the consciousness of the world that we have today. I am having the consciousness of a mountain in front of me; that is not the consciousness we are referring to. As consciousness cannot be separated from the existence of things, and inasmuch as the existence of things has been identified with a continuity and a wholeness of process or energy, the revelation would imply a strange conclusion which will startle us beyond our wits.

It would imply that to know anything would be the same as to be cosmically conscious. We cannot know anything in this world, unless we are universally awakened. Neither can we know ourselves, nor can we know even a particle of sand on the bank of the river, unless we are omniscient. And what religion calls God is nothing but this state of consciousness, where knowledge is identical with being. This is not the subject of science or physics, but it has landed us in this conclusion willy-nilly, by a mathematical force of logical deduction. This is a great benefit that science has given us, with all the horrors that it has created on the other side due to its technological aberrations.

But, science is not over with this, for we have been thinking only of physics up to this time, and physics is not the whole of science. Students of science know that there is something more about it. There is what is called life. Living beings are different from inanimate matter. The world of physics and chemistry is different from the world of life or living beings. In addition to astronomy, physics and chemistry which deal mostly with inorganic matter, we have the science of biology which studies living organisms and tries to find out what life is.

Here, we have something of a very interesting nature to observe. What is biology? What is the study of life or living beings, and why is it called a science? It is a science because we identify science with the process of observation and experiment. And what is it that the biologists have observed and experimented with? The functions of life are their field, but one cannot observe life. I cannot see with my eyes the life in the people sitting in front of me. I can only see movements and symptoms of the presence of life. So, even biology, as a science, has been able to proceed only up to the point of observation of symptoms of the existence of life, but not life itself. We cannot see life with any apparatus or instrument.

But how do we know that living bodies are different from dead bodies, that a tree is different from a stone? We have this knowledge because there are certain indications of the presence of life in what we call living bodies. These indications are not present in what we know as matter. Here, again, is a defect in the process of science. We have already standardised the symptoms of life. Only if such-and-such a symptom is observable, we call it life. We have passed judgement like this. We have concluded that to regard a thing as living, it must have these characteristics. If they are not there, we regard that thing as inorganic. But this is a prejudice of the scientific method. This is its defect.

Why should we standardise the symptoms of life? This standardisation arises again and again on account of certain definitions which we form in our own minds. The mere discovery of certain movements in the world of matter cannot be equated with a discovery of the secret of life. The question has been put: How did life originate? This is an age-old question. Geologists and astronomers tell us that this earth has come from the Sun. It is practically accepted as a fact. It may be true. Once upon a time, there was no earth.

The earth is a chip of the boiling mass of the Sun and, due to a whirling motion of the Sun, as some people think, or, due to a tremendous friction created in the body of the Sun on account of the proximity of another star passing near it, a piece was cut off from the Sun. This is the theory of the creation of this planet.

There are two theories put forth, the one thinking that there was a digression of the movement of the Sun in a tremendous velocity on account of which a chip was cut off, and the other holding that a gravitational pull exerted by another star coming near the Sun cut off a portion of it, which ran off into empty space in a great speed, with boiling contents, fire in its essence. The fire cooled into liquid, which solidified itself into earth, gradually; this is the story.

But where is life? We cannot see living beings in this state of affairs where there is only fire and water or even inanimate earth. People tell us that life must have come from some other planet. Well, this looks like the old story of the wolf and the lamb. "If you have not disturbed the water, your grandfather must have done it." Our question is: How did life originate? Merely by saying that it has come from another planet, we have not answered the question. For, again, the question would be: How did life originate there? Then we would say that it has come from a third planet. No one can say how life came about. It is a mystery even today.

How can living beings originate from the hot masses of stars? There are cases of germs manufacturing themselves from stagnant water, insects coming out from a dunghill, etc. How does this become possible? It is said that scorpions are born out of dung. This is one doctrine. Well, scorpions have life, and dung has no life. How can life come from non-life? So, biology has a dark screen in front of it finally, and the discovery of life, somehow, becomes an inference rather than an observation.

Many people think that biology is not an exact science, while physics and chemistry are exact sciences. Biology is not an exact science because some inference is involved in its processes, and it is not enough to have merely experiments and observations. But what is this inference? We go deep into biology. We should remember that we are discussing the objective approach of science to find out where it has taken us, and where it has made us to halt, and what are its shortcomings, and why it cannot help us finally.

In the same way as physics, chemistry and astronomy have landed us halfway, biology, too, seems to leave us somewhere in the middle and is unable to take us further, because the nature of life is inscrutable. We do not know what life means. When we say, "I am alive," what do we mean actually? Perhaps, we mean that we are moving. Can we say that a bullock cart is a living being because it is moving? Is a motorcar living? By 'life' we mean something different from mere motion.

It is a difficult thing to answer the question. What is life? When I say, "I am living, I am alive," I mean something quite different from a mere motion of the body. What is the essence of the biological research? Here, we somehow take a different turn of approach altogether and are forced to accept that life is a purposiveness in being; it is to be teleologically conscious.

We are characterised by purposive movements and not merely aimless movements as in the case of a motorcar or a bullock cart, which can simply go anywhere and in any way. Our movements are purposive, directed, filled with an aim, and this is what is meant by teleological movement. Now, that this, also, is not a very satisfactory answer will be noted when we consider the issue further.

When I say, "I am living, because I have a purposive existence, and not merely an aimless motion," I have to explain what I mean by purposiveness. It is interesting to see how we go from step to step into greater difficulties. What do we mean by a purposive existence?

It would mean, at least in outline, the consciousness of an aim in front of oneself. Now, again, we see where we are moving, dangerously. From science, where have we come? To be conscious that there is an aim before us is to be purposive. Life is, again, inseparable from a state of consciousness. And biology, also, takes us to the same thing on which physics landed us, in the end.

Somehow we cannot escape the dilemma of it being impossible for us to be without the principle of consciousness, in whatever we do, in whatever direction we move. The basic sciences - astronomy, physics, chemistry and biology - have a common thing to say, finally.

In the end they tell us the same thing and by this proclamation of a truth, which is beyond their own jurisdiction, they, as sciences, are exceeding their limits. Science becomes philosophy.

The Search Within

It requires to be emphasised again - because it is easily forgotten - that our studies are not a mugging up of information from books. We are not inmates of a school where we are students in the classroom and animals outside. This is not our aim. Let alone the possibility of living as animals, each one trying to pounce on the other. It is not even enough if we live merely as human beings. There is no need for instruction that we should not be animals, but it requires an instruction to tell us that it is not enough if we live merely as human beings.

There is always a distinction between our laboratory life and our public life. We are scientists in the laboratories, but commonplace persons in the shops, in the railway stations, and the bus-stands. This is the outcome of our learning in colleges, in universities, in institutions. Wherever we are, we are fed up with this kind of life, and that is why we are trying to find a little time, if it is possible, to think in a different manner. It is easy to study.

There are countless schools in the world and the result of all the studies is an upsurge of emotions and feelings in the minds of people, a veritable warfare perpetually threatening to take place, so that it is difficult to say if one person, at least, sleeps soundly in the night, with freedom from all anxiety. We have seen this, and we know this, and we are in the midst of this atmosphere. We are tired of it to the core and we realise that there is a basic error in our way of living and thinking, due to which all our studies look like a blank. These have led us nowhere.

To find out where the mistake lies, we are here not to study the Upanishads or the Bible. We may read the scriptures a hundred times; we would be the same persons. Nothing will change in our personality. It is not study in that sense that we are thinking of here. We have enough of people who have studied more than many of us. But there has been no desirable effect of these studies, except that we carry a burden on the head of a lot of information, and often of some rubbish which keeps us in a state of a fattened egoism and an empty soul.

If we are not able to be serious in regard to our own selves, how can we be serious in regard to the world outside? Who would like to go deliberately into the pit of hell? This possibility is there, on account of our missing the point in the life that we live. What do we see? We see people outside. Do we see people in the same way as anybody else sees? Even a pig sees people and we also see people outside us. But is there a difference between the pig seeing and our seeing? If there is no difference, it should be a travesty of affairs, that we should call ourselves cultured, educated.

If our eyes are made like pig eyes and if there has been no transformation in the values of life with our studies, and we live in the same way as anyone else lives, then, it is high time that we should retrace our steps from our advance in the pursuit of the so-called studies and strike a retrospective view of what is wrong with us. We need not be under the impression that our studies are inadequate and therefore we are unhappy. We might have studied very well; nobody denies that, but those studies had evidently no meaning, no purpose, no substance in them.

After a bath given to the elephant, the elephant remains the same, with dust thrown on its body. Likewise, it is obvious that the perspective of life has not changed, for it cannot easily change as long as we see with our present eyes and cannot have another eye. If it is possible for us to see things with another eye altogether, other than the two eyes that we have been using right from our childhood, then our attempts may yield a value and a meaning.

But if we persist seeing with the same two eyes, naturally we will see the same things. If we use the same telescope or the same microscope, we will see the same thing as before. But can we change this telescope or the microscope and see things differently, in the way they are really stationed, and not in the way they appear through the instruments of our eyes? We have to be honest to our own selves, for it is easy to deceive ourselves. It may be a little difficult to deceive others, but we can very easily go out of the track, due to the vagaries of the mind.

Our purpose in undertaking these studies, if they are to be worth the while, is quite different from the studies which people generally undergo through textbooks and in classrooms of institutions devoted to the several arts and sciences of the world. Ours may look like a classroom, from the point of view of its physical structure, but it is not supposed to be merely that. We are supposed to get up from here with a new spirit in our minds. But if the spirit is the same as the one that came an hour before, drooping and sinking and complaining and seeing ugliness and animosity and the diversities which are common to human perception, which has the undercurrent of even animal values, then we should be sorry for ourselves and not at the world that is.

This was a point of view which was emphasised before, *viz.*, that we should be cautious with regard to ourselves, and it is useless to be merely observant of what is happening outside in the world. There is a maladjustment and an upsetting of the sense of values in our own minds, due to which we are in a very unenviable position. We are in search of facts and truths and realities, and we have not found anything of this kind. Everything is moving, everything is passing, everything is changing, and our ideas about things also change. We have discovered nothing of value or reality in the world.

We have tried our best to probe into the nature of things outside in the world. We have seen nothing, we have only hit our heads against the walls. We have stones and trees in front of us, not values which are worth considering and which are going to do us any good in the true sense of the term.

We noticed that this external search lands us in a failure, finally, because of the simple reason that the things we see are outside of us. A thing that is really 'outside' cannot come in contact with us, because we have already dubbed it as an 'outsider'. A thing that is external to us cannot become a part of our knowledge.

What is knowledge? It is an assimilation of the object into the consciousness. If I assimilate you in my consciousness, I know you, but if you stand outside as a stranger to me, as an object which is totally independent of me, I cannot know you. All knowledge is participation in the content thereof. Participation implies our capacity to enter into the nature of the object and the capacity in the object to enter into the nature of our being, our knowledge; that is mutual assimilation of the nature of things. If I stand outside you totally and you stand outside me wholly, there would be no concourse between the two. I cannot know you and you cannot know me.

This is what has happened to the scientific observations of modern times. If science is an observation of objects, regarding them as objects having nothing to do with the subjects which observe them, then, science cannot give us knowledge. It can only give us descriptive information, the length and the breadth, the weight and the mass, the form and the colour, etc., of an object. I cannot know you, even if I know your height and weight, your girth, colour, shape, geometrical feature, or the chemical structure of your body. All these I may know, yet I would have not known you.

To know you physically, chemically and biologically is not to know you, because physically, chemically, and biologically, one would be the same as the other. The same substance is in each person, each thing - the earth, water, fire, air and ether are the components of the physical body of each and every individual in the world, so that to study one body would be equal to studying any other body. Why are there many people and many things, if everything is equal in bodily structure? The scientific observation is tentatively useful for our physical and social life, but it is not real knowledge; by it nothing can be known, not even one atom, truly if it is 'outside'.

This world outside is a fantastic world. It has a tremendous, fearsome significance, for anything that is outside is a source of fear, anxiety and insecurity. There is a great saying in the Upanishad that fear is caused by duality. Our fear is because there is another outside us, and as long as there is an 'other', we will have to be in a state of sorrow caused by the fear. And the fear is born of the fact that there is something independent of us, vying with us in reality and claiming equal status with us. There may be even one grain of sand there, but we cannot tolerate its presence, if it is outside us. We feel irksome that something is there totally alien.

Suppose you are in the midst of a society where people are aliens; you feel very uncomfortable. You have to get out from that place and go to an atmosphere where people are more friendly. You like friendliness and not 'foreign' characters. And what is friendliness? It is a tendency to assimilation of the one into the other. Friendliness is a social word, a term signifying the inclination of an individual to enter into the being of another. You have not actually entered into the being of another, no doubt, but there is a tendency, at least, and that is called friendliness. We have an aptitude to enter into our kith and kin. We might not have taken even the first step, but we have a desire, nevertheless, to take that step in the direction of our becoming a part of the friend's being. That is love, that is affection, that is friendliness. But if that tendency is absent, we wish to withdraw our being from others' being. That is the opposite of love, affection and friendliness. So, the tendency of friendliness is also the tendency to unite oneself with the desired object of perception.

All love longs for the union of the subject with the abject. It cannot really unite itself, and that is why loves are frustrated for various reasons. It is not possible for us to get into union with anything, ultimately. But there is a desire to be united with things. That desire is what we call love and unselfishness. The desire to exceed ourselves into the region of another is love. We do not want to be locked up in our own bodies; unselfishness is the desire to go out of our bodies and enter into the bodies of other things.

We cannot achieve this purpose easily. We cannot enter into the body of anything, but we have a desire. This desire is what is called love and love indicates the possibility, under given circumstances, of such a union. Under certain conditions the union is actually effected. This is what we are going to study. Under what conditions is it possible for us to unite ourselves with things? Normally, this is not possible, because the structure of the physical world is such that it will not permit this union. There is what we call space which will not allow the unity of any two objects. There is the time factor, there is causality, there are social prejudices and personal ambitions, all which cut the ground from under one's feet at the very outset.

But that it should be certainly possible is proved by our own urges inside and our longing to achieve this aim. We have tried our best to conquer nature, to know nature, to become one with nature, to harness the powers of nature and be in union with nature. Science has made this attempt but has not succeeded, because, unfortunately, nature has always managed to remain as an outside object to the scientific observer. Like the horizon that recedes the more we go near it, the objects of the scientist - call them electrons or whatever they are - recede and elude the grasp of the observer. Nobody has understood what an electron is even today, because it is outside, and how can anyone know it?

Here we are with inconclusive researches of the objective approach of science. We have not found reality in science. We have not found it anywhere in the world. Then what is the way out? As we noticed, we can look at things from three angles. We look outside. We look inside. We look above. These are the three ways of looking at things. Now, we have already looked outside and found nothing, at least nothing satisfactory.

Let us look inside and see what is there. This is the subjective approach, quite the other side of the objective method of science. What do we see when we turn our gaze within? We see ourselves. Let us close our eyes and see what is there. We do not see anything outside; we see our personality and begin to wonder what it is made of. What am I? The search for an answer to this question is the subjective approach of psychology.

Now, let us see what comes out of this search. Are we going to be landed in the same unfortunate situation of the external approach, or does something else come out? We see the body when we look inside ourselves. We see the physiological and anatomical structure of the body, the skin and the bones, the flesh and the marrow, the blood and the various biological features of the physical body.

If I ask you, "Who are you?" you will say, "I am the son or daughter of so and so, the brother or sister," and something like that would be your definition of yourself. By all these definitions you mean that you are a body; that is all. It means nothing else. Otherwise, how are you a son or daughter of some body? It has no meaning except in the sense that you are a body. But let us see whether we are able to see only this much, and nothing further.

Are we living only as bodies and nothing else? Let us give everything to the body and see if we are satisfied. We have our breakfast and lunch and we have dinner, and we have a good sleep. What else do we want for the body? We will be given all these things, food and clothing and a house to live in. These are the things that the body requires, and the body is happy. But do we say that we are satisfied with this alone? No, these are not the things that people require merely. It is not just food and clothing and shelter that we need. They may be the requirements of our body. They may be necessities, no doubt, but these are not enough.

People with all these things are still searching for some other thing. There are people - we call them well-to-do people - who have got all these physical amenities. But they are still in search of some other relief. The reason is that their physical needs have not satisfied them, because they are not merely physical bodies. They have something else within them, which also needs a certain type of food, as the body requires material food.

What are we, then, other than the body? If we go deep into the body, we will find nothing there, except physical structure. By an amputation, or an operation on the physical body, one will see nothing inside the body, except the physical matter only in some layer. It is when we probe into a different state of our existence, through which we are almost daily passing, that we will be able to discover some other element of personality in us than the physical body, *e.g.*, dream. In dreams, our physical bodies do not take part and yet we have an independent existence in dream, just as we have an independent existence in the waking condition. Now, did we exist in dream? Yes, we did exist. What was there? Not the physical body. What else? Well, very strange, we do find something else there. We had only the mind.

That we existed as a mind in dream is obvious. This does not require much explanation or commentary. We had joys and sorrows in dream, similar to those we experience in waking. We were exactly the same in dream as we were in waking, for all practical purposes of experience. We saw things, we encountered various phenomena, we were happy or unhappy, in the same way as we had such experience in the waking condition. So, it means that we can have, even independent of the body, the same kind of experiences as we have with the body, through the body, in terms of the body. The bodily existence or non-existence is not going to make a difference to the experiences of another layer of our personality which can independently exist and with which we can identify ourselves.

The phenomenon of dream demonstrates that we are more than a body and we can exist without the body. In dream we existed without any connection with the body, and we passed through all the experiences of waking independent of the body. The body was used only as an instrument, but it was not our real personality.

What are we, really? What do we discover when we probe into our own selves? We realise that we are a mind rather than a body. This is the reason why we are not satisfied even if we have plenty of money, a lot of food and clothing, large gardens and palatial buildings. With all these physical comforts, we cannot be satisfied, because we are not merely a physical body - a son, a daughter. We are a mind; that is why we are unhappy. It is not the body that is unhappy or is dissatisfied. It has everything - it eats well, it sleeps well; what is the difficulty with the body? Why is it that we are still unhappy?

The unhappiness comes from the mind and not from the body. All our difficulties are mental, not so much physical. Such emphasis is laid on this mental life of man that, it appears, compared to it, physical comfort is almost nothing. If our mind is satisfied, we will not bother much about physical amenities.

There are various avenues of mental satisfaction which can overwhelm the requirements of even the physical body and this, again, does not require much of an analysis or study, for everyone knows what it means. If we are immensely happy for some reason, which state has lifted us up from the physical level, we forget our breakfast, and lunch, and sleep, and everything else. Satisfaction is a mental condition.

We are happy for reasons other than physical, and in some other world are we then. That world is a psychological world, a mental realm. If the mind is satisfied, the physical world can give us not much substance. We are all, in fact, searching for something psychical, intellectual, emotional, volitional, rational. If our reason is satisfied, the physical needs almost amount to a zero, but with all the physical amenities, if the reason is dissatisfied, they amount to a zero again. We are rational beings, rather than physical bodies.

This is an interesting observation that we make when we go deeper into our own personalities. We are minds, we are intellects, we are emotions, we are wills, and we are reasons. Until we satisfy the psychic nature of ours with its requirements, the physical world cannot make us happy with all the goods that it has. Nothing that is material can give us entire satisfaction. Material satisfaction is set at naught in a second by mental dissatisfaction. It is useless to harp upon physical needs too much, under the impression that they are the causes of our sorrows. The physical conditions are not the sources of anxiety. Our mental structure has not been provided with its needs, its requirements. The mind longs for some thing, in the same way as the body needs some thing, and the mental needs are more significant, more important than the physical ones.

The ego is a part of the psychic world. Our sense of individual being is not a physical sense. It is a psychic centre. "I am so-and-so, I am such-and-such - this kind of assertion is not a physical act. It is not the body making this affirmation. When you are annoyed, you say, "What do you think I am?" You look up; gazing at the other. "What do you think you are?" These arrogant statements arise not from the body; they are arrogations fuming up like a volcano from the psychic individuality within. It asks for food in the same way as we ask for bread for the body. The food of the ego is what people are asking for, and the ego has not been able to obtain it, with all the foods that one has physically, materially. The ego is starving, and so we are unhappy.

Man wants to swallow the whole world, if it could be possible. Behold the audacity of a dictator, a terrorising despot, or an out-and-out egoistic, self-affirmative person. People whose ego is at its heights would like to masticate the world and digest it, so that they alone exist and other things do not exist before them. The desire of the ego is to destroy the world, because the affirmation of the ego is equivalent to an intolerance in regard to the presence of other egos. One ego cannot be the friend of another ego. It wants to destroy the other, somehow, and therefore one is irksome, much agitated if one sees another person like oneself. One wants to put down that person by some hook or crook. One cannot tolerate a person equal to oneself. The other must be inferior always; that is the glutting glory of the ego.

We may not be consciously feeling that the ego is there at all. But it is present as a secret urge. We are yet to see why the ego is operating in this manner. Why is this ego operating in this manner that it cannot tolerate an other than itself? What is the devil that is working inside? What is the harm if another person also exists? But this is not possible for some important reason, which is outside the vision of ordinary observation. For some strange reason the ego cannot bear the sight of other egos. It cannot tolerate the presence of even the world outside; it wants to control it and subdue it and make it its own, superintend over it, and wants to be a master. This is the desire of the autocrats, the dominating rulers, the despots, the apotheosis of ego.

We have a tremendous world inside us. And it is not so simple as that. We are not the little persons we seem to be. We have a hidden submarine content inside our personalities. This is to give a short outline of the psychic world which is our area of functioning, and of which we are citizens. We are not citizens merely of this physical world. We are also inhabitants of the psychic world. Thus, this is a psychic relationship of ours with other people, due to which we are, either this way or that way, related to this person or that person, positively or negatively, with pleasure, pain or indifference attending.

We are denizens of a psychic world and not merely of a social world of Indians and Americans, Russians and Japanese, etc. We are in a different world inwardly and that world is as much real as, if not more real than, the physical world. With the bare analysis that we have made, we can realise that the physical world is, before this psychic world, far less significant than the credit it receives. If the psychic world is well, the physical world follows suit with it. The physical values lose much of their significance before the insistances that are psychic, rational, intellectual and emotional. Perception, inference, doubt, memory, love, hatred, attachment to life, fear of death, are all phases of the psychic individuality.

This is an aspect of psychology, which reveals itself when we analyse ourselves deeper than our physical personality. The physical body is made up of the five elements - earth, water, fire, air, ether. All are that, I am that, and every one is that; even the tree is made up of these five elements, and the stone is that. Everything is just the five elements. So, materially or physically, no difference can be observed among things. But we see difference among people. This has to be attributed not to the shapes of the bodies, but to the minds which are different in each individual. I do not think as you think, and you do not think as I think. That is why we are two different persons. The psychic raw material makes all the difference, and is responsible even for the physical differences.

The difference is not in the physical body, because the bodies are identical in structure. The same flesh, the same blood, the same chemical compounds are present in every body, but there is a difference in the structure of thinking. The whirling of the mind is in different directions in different cases, the current of the movement of the mind varies in different individuals, because of the purposiveness with which the minds move - an observation that we made in regard to living bodies - and, this changes even the nature of the physical components.

The purposiveness or the intensive urge from within the psyche of an individual distinguishes it from others and from inanimate matter.

There is a purpose behind the growth of even a tree; it moves in a particular direction and with an aim behind it. Every living being has an intention in the performance of its varied functions and inasmuch as the intention varies from individual to individual, there are different individuals. We are different persons because we are different minds. And why are we different minds? Because a mind is nothing but a particular pattern of thinking. As the pattern of thinking varies, the mind varies, and therefore, people vary.

And what is this pattern of thinking? It is a particular direction which the psyche takes, just as a river may take a particular direction. Because of the variety in the direction of the movement of the psyche, there is difference in the intention. The direction and the intention are practically the same, because when the intention is of a particular mode, the mind moves in the same direction. Why is there difference in intention? Why should not all people think in the same way, in the whole world?

Why should we all think differently? Where is the necessity? What is the harm if we all think identically? This is not possible for the same reason which keeps one's ego intolerant of other egos. The ego which works in an affirmative manner intolerant of the presence of other egos is also the reason behind the variety in the intention behind the psyche which keeps everything always apart. I am 'I', you are 'you'. "I mind my business. You mind your business." This is the world. Is there a solution, a remedy for this malady?

The Psychology of Knowing

We observed that our inner world is constituted of the psyche; it is a mental world, and that is the real world of ours, of which we are citizens primarily. We are nationals of a psychic world, more properly than the way in which we belong to the physical world of social beings. Our psychic apparatus is a complicated structure, because it has connections with almost everything in the world. It is like a main switchboard. We are not so much detached from things as we appear to be. There is a subterranean relationship between our inner contents and the whole cosmos outside.

The moment we begin to enter the realm of Yoga practice, we also start operating upon our cosmic relationships. This is something important to remember. At present we believe that we are isolated individuals with no connection whatsoever with others. But meditation is adventure, which opens up a new vista before us and surprises us with our relationships which were not apparent in our waking work-a-day life.

Our mind is not made up of any simple substance. It is rather a process than an entity. It may be compared to electric energy, if we would like to associate it with something known to us. We cannot say that it is a substance, or a body, or something existing in one place. It is almost like a fluid. At present it pervades our entire body. That is why our thinking is connected with every part of the body.

The whole body thinks, as it were, because of the pervasion of the body by the mind. This mind which is not an entity or a substance like physical objects, and appears to be a moving process, is our inner working faculty. We live a psychic life, rather than a physical life. Our joys and sorrows are psychic and not physical. Our activities, also, are psychic. Physical activities are no activities if they are divested of the psychic content. It comes to this finally, that the mind is everything.

The whole world is nothing but mind operating in mysterious ways, in its wondrous relationships of variegated types. Western psychology particularly distinguishes between three aspects of the psyche:(1) Understanding, (2) willing, and (3) feeling. But in Eastern psychology, a further diversity of this content has been noticed. It has infinite varieties of expression but in the main outline we may say that our psyche consists of many functions on account of which it takes various names. Even these aspects of nomenclature as understanding, willing, and feeling are the outcome of the different functions that the one psyche performs.

When the psyche decides, by a clarity of grasp, upon a particular situation, we call it understanding. And the affirmation which follows the decision that is taken on the basis of the understanding of the situation is the will. Then something more significant takes place. When we understand that a thing is such-and-such, and we also decide to act upon this situation in a particular manner, our whole being reacts in a given proportion.

That reaction is emotion. There is a welling up of our whole personality in regard to the existent situation outside. We begin to feel, and not merely will or understand. Now, this activity of the psyche, in the form of understanding, willing and feeling, is rooted in what is usually known as the ego-principle. The ego is the faculty of self assertiveness or self-affirmation. As a matter of fact, it precedes all other functions. Before we can understand, will or feel, we have to be sure that we exist. This certainty of the fact of our existing as an individual is the activity of the ego.

The word *ego* gets translated in various ways. When we generally speak of an egoistic person, we mean thereby a proud person, for instance. But the ego does not and need not necessarily mean 'pride'. Pride is only a gross outer expression of it. Its essentiality is something subtle, far more invisible than the outer expression as the so-called pride of the individual. The ego is a sense of individual being, our confidence that we exist as an individual independent of other individuals. The conscious confidence in us that we are isolated individuals, quite different, in every way, from others, is the ego-principle in its essentiality.

What, then, is the ego? It is a consciousness of our individual existence, isolated from other individuals. And this self-assertiveness concretises itself in various levels of our life. There are different kinds of egos. There is a metaphysical ego; there is the psychic or purely volitional ego; there is the physical ego; there is the social ego; and, finally, it becomes the political ego. All these are expressions of a single impulse from inside to affirm oneself as distinct from others, to dominate over others, to absorb others into oneself. This desire to be distinct from others is the disease of man. It is a primary evil and Yoga psychology calls this principle of the ego, 'Ahamkara'. This word, 'Ahamkara', is very interesting in its connotation. In the Sanskrit language, 'Aham' means 'I', 'Kara' means, 'one who does'. One who causes everything to feel that it is, is the ego. It is that 'which is developed from' the sense of 'self-consciousness'.

The ego does not rest quiet merely by an affirmation of itself. It becomes grosser, when it operates in external life, until it reaches the most concrete of its expressions.

The ego exists originally as a principle of awareness, a simple consciousness that one is. That is why it is then called the metaphysical ego. It simply 'is', but 'is' as distinct from others. The consciousness of "I am" is the primordial empirical and it is the philosophical ego. Then, this simple principle of self-affirmation in its primary capacity of isolation begins to operate as the psyche which starts to think objects outside. It does not merely think of itself as an isolated being. It has become something worse now. In the beginning, it was content with being only aware of itself. Now it wants to be aware that 'others are'.

So, there is a further consequence following from the affirmation of oneself. If "I am", others also are, as distinct from me. This distinction between oneself or one ego and others expresses itself as distinction between physical personalities. The physical ego is the bodily ego which identifies itself with the bodily encasement.

The 'I-amness' is not merely a consciousness of 'my being'. It is also a consciousness of others' being. It is a specific affirmation of this body as the 'me' and a distinction drawn between this body and other bodies.

Then there are the various social distinctions extending to almost endless details. We cannot even count how many social distinctions there are. There is a great variety of the differences that we draw between one and the other in our social life and we need not go into the forms of these, because they are all obvious. Then there is the worst form of the ego, which intends to exercise authority, power, by way of political manoeuvres, which may begin with one's family management and end in a desire for world-government by oneself, until the farthest limit of it is reached, wherein it seeks to affirm itself to the exclusion of others. One of the important features of the ego is not merely self-affirmation and distinction of self from other selves, but a resentment of the presence of other selves.

This follows as a consequence of the structure of the ego. The self-affirmation of the ego is charged with a deep impulsion towards survival of itself at the cost of anything whatsoever in the world. If we believe in the doctrine of the survival of the fittest, the ego says, "I am the fittest, and, so, I alone should survive, and nobody else". Naturally, if every ego has this sense of the fittest in itself and if each one is the fittest, the consequence is battle and the wars that history records.

These wars are nothing but the conflicts of egos, each ego wishing to assert itself as the fittest, whether it is an individual ego or a group of egos. These create a chaos of circumstance and if one goes into the inner secret of the sorrows of life, one will realise that all these are rooted in the ego principle. Understanding, willing, feeling, and the other psychological functions are the rays of the ego, which is the parent of all these manifestations.

We have heard that Yoga is 'union', a common definition that is given in all textbooks. But union with what, and who is to be in union with which substance, or reality? This cannot be made clear unless we know the basis of this definition itself. In our study of the objective world, we concluded that in the farthest analysis of the universe outside, we come face to face with the reality of the perceiver getting involved in the perceived, inasmuch as nature is a whole, a complete continuum, and the bifurcation of the seer and the seen is foreign to the structure of Nature. Nature in its wholeness may not even be aware that there are such things as the seer and the seen, even as we cannot say that the right hand is the seer of the left hand or the left hand is the seer of the right hand in one's own body. These appellations would not apply to an organisation of parts which belong to a whole, in an inseparable manner.

Under the circumstance that in the end a distinction between the seer and the seen cannot be drawn, because of the fact that such a distinction does not exist, and also under the circumstance that the distinction between the seer and seen is really made in practical life, there is a contradiction between practical life and life as it really is.

Our present way of living is far removed from the truth of life in its essentiality. We make a marked distinction between the seer and the seen by the operation of the psychic apparatus. The mind thinks the object; the object is outside the mind, which means that the object seen is different from the mind that sees it. We are so sure that this is the case that we work in the world with the certainty that the world is outside the mind, that the seer is completely cut off from the seen.

But this is not going to be a lasting conclusion in the event of a further analysis of the deeper structure of life. Reality is quite different from what we see with our eyes or even what we think with our minds. What we see with our eyes is not reality, and what we think and understand is also not reality. So, Yoga, when it is defined as union, should naturally be understood in the sense of the union of the seer and the seen, because the seer and the seen cannot be isolated. If they are really different, there cannot be a knowledge of the seen by the seer. In this connection there is an important theme discussed in philosophical circles, known as "The theory of knowledge".

How do we know the world? How are we aware that things are? This is a vast subject which takes us into deep waters. We cannot easily explain how we are aware that the world is there at all. This awareness takes us by surprise; we suddenly become aware that there is a world. The way in which we become aware of the world is comparable to the way in which we wake up from sleep. We are fast asleep, where we are oblivious of everything. When we wake up, we have only a general awareness of our having woken up. We become aware that there is no sleep, sleep has gone, and there is a general awareness without knowledge of details of either this or that particular fact. After this, the general awareness concretises itself. We begin to feel that we are; we become conscious of our own self, after some time. But we will not be much aware of the things outside, the table and the chair etc.; even the windows and the doors we will not see properly, because we have just woken up from sleep. We do not know even the exit from the room, sometimes, because of the deepness of the sleep. There are deep-sleepers who often perch upon the window, thinking it is the door, and hit their head against it; so deep was the sleep.

Well, the point is that we become aware of ourselves first; only later we know things outside. After we become aware that things are outside, we become also aware as to what those things are. From a general knowledge of things, we reach to the specific knowledge of things. "It is not merely some things in a featureless bareness that are in front of me, but this is a chair, this is a table, this is a wall clock, this is a person." Then, the awareness becomes more specified. "This is my son, this is my daughter, this is my friend, this is so- and-so," etc. Then it becomes further more expressed in the form of an impulse to action with regard to the things seen. This is also, in a way, the process of the creation of the world.

What happened cosmically must have been something like this individual phenomenon that we pass through every day after we wake up from sleep. The point at issue is, how do we become conscious of the world? We become conscious of the world by an expansion of our consciousness gradually from our selves outside. What is this 'outside'? The so-called 'outside' is the world, really speaking. The world is not constituted of mountains and trees, human beings, cows and asses.

These are not the world. The world is an 'outsideness' of things, the externality, the so-called 'thingness' in all things, a peculiar separation of one thing from another, and this feature becoming a content of our consciousness. The consciousness of externality is the world. If this externality were not to be there, there would be no world.

If there is no space between you and me, we would not see each other, and space and time go together. If the one is, the other also is there. So, the space-time structure is the world. What we call the world is nothing but space-time. If this were not to be there, there would be no externality of perception, and if the externality were not to be there, there would be no world-experience. World-experience is nothing but externality of experience. If we are to somehow divest ourselves of the consciousness of externality of every kind, we will 'enter' into the world at once, and the world will 'enter' into us. The whole problem is of the externality of space-time, and we are given here a lot of information in the theories of knowledge of the various schools of philosophy, as to how we become aware of things outside.

The things are not really outside; that is the point. That they are not outside should be clear from the analysis of Nature itself. Things form one organic whole. We cannot say that our leg is outside our body, notwithstanding the fact that we are seeing it. Merely looking at things cannot be regarded as a proof of their externality, because I see even my fingers, but I do not say that they are outside me.

The outsideness of a thing arises on account of a distinction between the consciousness of the seer and the existence of the seen. We begin to feel that our consciousness is different from others' being. When we speak of the distinction between the seer and the seen, we actually mean a distinction between beings in their essentiality. But, how does one know that another being exists? The space or the time content between us cannot be the cause of this perception. An undercurrent of consciousness is necessary. If there is not going to be a secret connection of consciousness between me and you, I cannot know that you are sitting in front of me.

The wind that is blowing on my face through the fan that is moving cannot be regarded as the cause of my awareness that you exist. The wind has no consciousness; it cannot make me know that you are. Nothing that is visible to our eyes, as that which exists between me and you, can be considered a cause of my knowledge that you are. There is nothing, practically, between you and me, there is only empty space. How do I know that you are there? This is a strange phenomenon. My eyes, physically constituted as they are, are spatially cut off from your physical existence. You are not sitting inside my eyes. How do I know that you are and how do you know that I am here? Nothing that is visible to the eyes can be regarded as a cause of the perception of an object.

We may say, there is the mind, and we have finally to bank upon this aspect of our being. The mind is thinking that we are. But, then, where is the mind? Where is it situated? Mostly, we think that it is inside our body. My mind is inside my brain or at least within my body; it cannot be outside. Now, if my mind is inside my body, naturally it cannot be of any help to me in my knowing that you exist, because you are outside me, at least a few yards away from me, and the mind is inside my body; it has not gone out.

But if you say that perhaps the mind is going out and is touching the bodies of others, and then it becomes aware, it would be curious that the mind can exceed the border of the body. Why speak of people before me? I know even that there is a sun shining in the sky, 93 million miles away from me. Does it mean that the mind is extending 93 million miles outside my body? If we accept this doctrine that the perception of the object is due to the operation of the mind and the mind has to touch that object in order that one may become aware of the object, then the mind should reach the stars, which are several light-years away. This is a revelation, indeed.

If this is a fact, the mind is not our mind merely, it is a mind that reaches up to the distant space, the stars, or whatever it is; if we do not accept this theory, we cannot explain how we are aware that the stars are shining in the sky. This is a tentative answer to this pressing pragmatic question. But more important than this issue is the thing that follows. What is mind? Is the mind capable of knowing that things exist outside? We have said so much about the mind, but what is mind? What is it made of? Provisionally accepting the position that the mind knows objects, we have to attribute the mind with some sort of consciousness because knowing an object is the same as being aware of the object, and if the mind is aware of the object, it is conscious. It cannot be an inert substance.

The mind has to be charged with some kind of consciousness, in the same way, perhaps—to give a prosaic example - as a copper wire may be charged with electricity. We need not say that the wire is the same as electricity; the two are quite different things. But the wire is filled with the flow of electricity, on account of which we call it a live wire. If the electricity were not to be there, it becomes an ordinary wire, on which we can hang a wet cloth for drying. It is to be accepted that the mind has to be endowed with some consciousness. If that also is not conceded, the chance of knowing anything does not arise. It should follow that the mind is inseparably connected with consciousness. It has to be pervaded by consciousness, and, so, my being aware that you are in front of me is due to the movement of consciousness towards you, even in the intermediary space between you and me.

This conclusion that consciousness is not limited to the body but is also outside the body follows from another interesting analysis that we can make. We cannot set a limit to consciousness. We cannot say that consciousness is here and not there. Because, to be conscious that consciousness is limited, consciousness has to be outside the limit at the same time. Who is to know that consciousness is limited? It is consciousness itself that knows. The awareness of the limitation of awareness is also a function of awareness. So, the boundary that is tentatively set to a state of awareness is also a content of awareness. One cannot be conscious that there is a limit to consciousness, unless consciousness has exceeded that limit. To imagine that there is division between two parts of consciousness would be to assume that there is consciousness even midway between the two assumed parts of consciousness. Otherwise, who is to be aware that there is a gap between two parts of consciousness? The awareness of a gap between two parts of consciousness is also awareness and, therefore, there cannot be a gap in consciousness, which means that consciousness is indivisible.

If consciousness has no parts, it is indivisible, and so all-pervading. It is infinite in its nature. The presence of the infinitude of consciousness is the reason behind the mind being aware that there are objects. But where comes the question of an outside if there is a pervasion of all things by consciousness? There is an error in the perception of externality in things. If the consciousness that knows things is indivisible, and exists everywhere as subject and object, there must be definitely some mistake in our seeing or apprehending things as if they are outside us. This mistake is introduced into our perception by the operation of space and time.

Meditation is the art of transcending space and time. The moment this is effected, we enter into an infinitude of consciousness. By the various techniques of meditation, we overcome the barrier that is created between us and the objects by the action of space-time. The moment we think of an object, we think of it as it is existent in space and in time. The methods of Yoga are the ways of defying the operation of space-time and effecting a union between the subject and the object, the seer and the seen, in their essentiality. In their outward forms, they are distinct; names and forms differ, but the essentiality of the things does not so differ. The content does not vary, only the shape differs. Thus in all processes of the practice of Yoga, one thing alone is aimed at, *viz.*, the union of consciousness with being.

There is a single Yoga, ultimately, taking forms on account of the difference in the structural patterns of minds. Just as one would like a sweet dish, another a saltish dish, etc., but it makes no difference to the fact that all partake of food for a common purpose, likewise, the essentiality behind meditations is the same, though the outer focus differs due to the needs of the minds of the individuals in the different stages of evolution in which they find themselves. Yoga is union, yes. It is the union that is necessary for beholding things as they really are and for outgrowing the erroneous awareness of the apparent duality of things. Our weaknesses, physical or psychological, are the outcome of our dissociation from things.

Strength is the necessary consequence of a union of ourselves with things. Energy is abundant in Nature. The universe is full of power; it has infinite resources. It is never poor. It is always rich. There is no poverty in the world in its true nature. But we look poor socially, physically, mentally, in every way. We are helpless beings and forlorn. This situation arises because we have blocked the avenues of the entry of forces of Nature into ourselves by the activities of the sense-organs. The senses are our enemies, if at all there are enemies anywhere, because they present us with a picture of the world which is not really there. The friends and foes that we see in the world are the concoctions of the ego and the sense-organs. The five elements we see are also the reports given to us by the five senses. There are no five elements; there is one element only everywhere, appearing in different densities of expression.

The world is seen or known in five different ways because of the five ways in which the senses work. To give an example, electric energy is common everywhere. But, when it passes through a refrigerator, it cools; when it passes through a stove, it heats; when it passes through a railway train, it moves. The various functions of electric energy are due to the instruments through which it is made to operate; likewise is Nature.

It is neither sound, nor touch, nor colour, nor taste, nor smell. There are no such things as that in Nature. But our senses abstract certain features of Nature and then become cognisant of these specified features and one sense tells us that it is smell, another that it is colour, and a third something else. If we had a hundred sense-organs, perhaps, we would have seen a hundred things in the world. Now we have, thank God, only five senses, and we see only five things. If we had only one sense, we would have seen only one thing. The sense-organs create a quintuplication of perception, where there is only a uniform reality.

Firstly, the senses deceive us into the belief that things are outside. Then there is a further deception into the belief that there are five different objects. That objects are outside is mistake enough; that there are five different things is a worse form of it. In our practices known as Yoga, we have, therefore, to tackle the sense-organs first, which multiply perception into a fivefold operation, and then the mind which tells us that the world is outside us. The whole of Yoga hinges upon the operation upon the senses and the mind in such a manner as to enable us to overcome the awareness of externality and its outcome as the fivefold perception through the senses. The task is undertaken either directly or in the reverse order, as is one's predilection. Thus, Yoga leads us to a kind of operation which is not merely individualistic.

It is a common affair of all people. There is no such thing as my Yoga or your Yoga. We are all in the same boat. Our problems are common stock. We are in the same difficulty and we have to seek for the same remedy. Yoga is a common need that will be felt by every individual. It is neither a religion, nor a creed; it is a need of life, as the breath we breathe. Yoga is the science of existence. It neither belongs to the West nor to the East. It is neither Hindu, nor Christian, nor Muslim. It is not any religion at all. It is the very fact of the essential structure of human existence.

The Preparations for Yoga

We have heard it said that there are many kinds or types of Yoga. This idea of a variety in Yoga arises on account of a sectional thinking, into which we perforce have introduced ourselves as the result of our mental structure. Really, the Yogas are not many, just as we cannot say that the rays of the sun are many, though they appear to be so due to a peculiar projectional structure of the mechanism of this emanation.

We have observed that there is an objective way of thinking and also a subjective way, the connection between which is what we call knowledge, or perception. Our knowledge of the world, or the knowledge of anything, is a reaction set up between the subject and the object. Unless these two are there in juxtaposition, there will not be knowledge; there will not be any kind of experience. Every experience is a reaction between the percipient subject and the perceived object, whatever be the nature of that object, physical or otherwise.

Now, we can think in three ways and so there are supposed to be three Yogas, the well-known systems of Karma (action), Bhakti (devotion) and Jnana (knowledge), in which schools like that of Kundalini Yoga, Tantra Yoga, Japa Yoga, and even Patanjali's system of Yoga, and various methods of self-analysis, get subsumed.

We have to recall to our memories that when we go deep into ourselves, we find the very same things that we discover when we go deep into anything outside. That which is deeply within us is also deeply within everything in the world. Even as, at the bottom of the crests of the ocean, we find the same base of the ocean, which is at the back of every other crest also, likewise, we will discover a common reality underlying every individuality.

There is a substance which is equanimously present as the background of particulars, and Yoga is the process of the gradual withdrawal of consciousness from particulars to the generals, until the highest common factor is reached. The particularised attention paid by consciousness in respect of any thing is to be withdrawn into the more general background of it, and the more it goes near to the general background, the more does it approximate to the ideal of Yoga. This withdrawal, to repeat again what was noticed earlier, can be either inward, outward, or transcendent.

There are three kinds of withdrawal. But how is it possible to withdraw oneself in three ways? We are generally accustomed to the idea that withdrawal means going into one's own self in an individual sense, but it need not necessarily mean that. One can withdraw oneself even into an object by a peculiar adjustment of consciousness and in that technique of objective withdrawal, the object ceases to be an object any more. Here consciousness assumes a different position by an adjustment of itself with the object in a novel way. In fact, Yoga is a gradual attempt of consciousness to convert every object into a subject; and the more do we succeed in transforming the object into the subject, the more are we said to be advancing in Yoga.

The greatest problem in life is involvement in objectivity, externality, the conditioned attitude of the mind by which it segregates itself from all things which it thinks, or visualises. The world of objects is a connected whole; this is the doctrine of Yoga. The world is not constituted of isolated parts as it appears to the outward senses of perception. The recognition of this inward connectedness of things in the form of the universe is the endeavour of Yoga. Inasmuch as we are accustomed to think only in terms of objects and we cannot think in any other manner, we have to take the stand of the object first, and that method is the way of Karma Yoga and Bhakti Yoga, and partly of the Yoga of Patanjali, and the initial stages of even Jnana Yoga. Everything starts with the concept of the object; only the notion of the object varies according to the different systems of practice, the notion getting widened gradually, in an ascending degree.

Before we start seriously any kind of practice in the direction of Yoga, we must be well up with the requisite preparations. The achievements in Yoga are a gradual evolution, a systematic advance and not a sudden jump. It is not a revolution that we are setting up. There is no revolutionary process in Nature. Everything grows slowly, stage by stage, without missing even one link in the process of development, as we have grown from babyhood to the adult stage. How beautifully does a tree grow from the seed! How many years does it take? There is no abrupt skipping from the seed to the fruit.

So is Yoga a gradual developmental process of the 'wholeness' of our personality towards an achievement of All-Being. We have, therefore, to be cautious that the necessary preparations are made. We cannot suddenly conceive of the goal without being aware of the preparatory stages. Apart from the techniques to which we shall refer a little later, five of the requisites may be noted with advantage among many others: 1. Place, 2. Time, 3. Method, 4. Regularity, and 5. Whole-souled devotion to the Ideal.

You must have a place which is suited to the practice. You must also have a time chosen for the practice. You should have a method which has to be adopted continuously, without changing it every now and then. Then the practice must be regular and there should be no break in it. And, lastly which is perhaps the most important aspect of it, you must have a whole-souled love for the practice. It is said in the Yoga scriptures that one loves Yoga as the mother loves the child and thinks of it the whole day and night, and there is no other thought in the mind except that. "How shall I get it?" This ardent longing from the heart is itself half of the success in the practice, and everything else comes afterwards.

The cooperation from your deepest feelings is the affection that you have for Yoga. You do not approach it with suspicions or doubts in the mind. It is absolutely certain that you are going to achieve the goal. This conviction should be there at all times. If the calculations are correct, the mathematical problem should yield the required result. You cannot doubt whether the calculations will give the result or not. The system of mathematics is so exact that there cannot be any suspicion about it.

Yoga is a highly technical and systematic subject, and if the methods adopted are correct, there should be no doubt, whatsoever, as to the possibility of the achievement of the end. The time that you take in reaching the goal depends upon the extent of the intensity of the practice and the emphasis that your feelings lay upon it, the extent to which you are in communion with the ideal which you are trying to contemplate.

We take into consideration, first of all, the place. Everyone knows what this actually means. One has to be located in a place which is conducive to the practice. Now, what do you mean by saying 'conducive to the practice'? There are certain necessities: geographical, climatic, social, political, physical and the like, which are associated with the selection of a place. Beautiful suggestions are given to us in such scriptures as the Svetashvatara Upanishad, for instance, as also in the Bhagavad-Gita and the Yogavasishtha. The place should be pleasing to the inward sense of spiritual quest. You should be lifted up by the very atmosphere in which you are. That is why people go to sequestered places. The more are you away from centres which have an atmosphere of clash of personalities and egos, the more can you be in tune with Nature.

When you go for a walk, you go alone and not with another person. You will feel happier when you walk alone than when you go with another person; else, there would be two egos walking. And one ego never wholly agrees with another ego. You may be thick friends, but notwithstanding it, you are still two persons and not one person. The very fact that you are two persons shows that there are two egos and one has to adjust oneself in an artificial manner to the presence of the other. You cannot be natural when you are in the presence of another person. You cannot utter a word which will not be pleasing to the other. You cannot have a gesture made which is not to the taste of the other, and so on. But if you are under a tree you can do anything there, because the tree has no ego like the human being.

The birds, the animals, have no egos like men and they do not bother about what you do, what you say, what you think, etc. Choose a place which is free from tensions arising from the presence of egos. This is the reason why we go to monasteries, temples, convents, and such other sanctified localities. Also it is said that elevated places are more convenient than others, because of the electro-magnetic influences which high altitudes are supposed to produce. The tops of mountains are regarded as very conducive. Places which are near vast areas of water, or near the ocean, are electro-magnetically more suggestive. This is the discovery of ancient sages. There is also a discovery that cloudy weather is more conducive to meditation than clear sky because of the presence of electric forces that are generated in the sky during the movement of clouds. These are minor matters, not very important things, but they are things to be remembered, as they are helpful.

Times which are suggestive of an automatic withdrawal of the mind from external activities are to be preferred. Night time is generally, and obviously, helpful because of an automatic tendency of the mind at that time to withdraw itself into subjectivity. When we speak of time for the practice of Yoga, or meditation, what we actually mean is not merely the hour of the day, such as eight o'clock, etc., but a fixed time. There is a cyclic movement of everything in Nature.

This system of cyclic movement applies not only to the external world of astronomy but also to the internal world of the psyche. If we start taking our meal at a particular hour and we continue taking it at the same hour, we will start feeling hungry at the same time and not at other times, because of a cyclic effect in Nature which generally gets associated with the way of thinking, and affects sympathetically the physiological functions.

Hence it is necessary that one should fix a specific time for contemplation, studies, etc., whatever the nature of the practice- not that one starts meditating today in the morning and tomorrow in the evening and the day after at midnight, etc. Such anomalies will create a kind of jarring effect and not yield a harmonious contribution to the practice. The time should be fixed, whatever the chosen hour be.

There are some people who are anxious to get up very early in the morning. They force themselves into waking up into a consciousness of meditation imagined at a particular time which is suggested by scriptures, etc. This may not have the desired result following. No kind of force should be exerted upon the mind. It may be that early morning is good for certain reasons, but in the beginning one will not be able to adjust oneself to that hour, because one is not used to that life. It is better to take things easily as an art and not as a sort of labour or an imposition that has been inflicted upon the mind. Joy should be the touchstone of the practice and not uneasiness, pain or regret.

Yoga is a process of rejoicing. It is not a suffering. It is a movement through happiness. From one state of joy, we move to another state of joy. It is not that Yoga starts with sorrow, or that it is a kind of prison-house into which we are thrown. We have sometimes a feeling that Yoga is a torture, a suffering, to the normal life of man. Sadhana means a fear, and indicates an unnatural seriousness. This is so, often because people have created a picture of awe and sternness about Yoga, an other-worldliness about it, dissociated from the natural likings of the human being. Our desires are, no doubt, obstacles to Yoga. But they are 'our' desires; this much we must remember, and they are not somebody's. So, we have to wean ourselves from these desires gradually and not make it appear that we are peeling our own skin. Such a drastic step should not be taken, and it is not the intention of Yoga.

You have to draw up a systematised programme: what is the thing to be done first, what is the thing to come next, what is the third item to be taken up, etc. The thing that is to be done after three days should not be done today, and so on. Have a graduated programme of the practice according to your own capacity. This suggestion is general and is not intended as a particular instruction to each and every person without distinction, because interests vary.

You have to maintain your own spiritual diary, to put it in the way of Swami Sivanandaji Maharaj. You can have a diary of your own according to your need and capacity, the stage of your mental evolution, the studies that you have made, the aptitude of your mind, the technique that you are going to adopt, etc. Have a positive attitude towards the practice.

Just as a sick person feels happy when he is in the process of moving towards health, Yoga, as a process of one's growing towards healthier and healthier conditions of personality from states of illness, makes for a state of happiness. When one becomes healthier, one also becomes happier. Suppose you have high temperature, and the temperature comes down gradually; as it comes down, you feel greater relief, a satisfaction which arises from within, automatically and spontaneously. So is the case with Yoga. It is your mother. She will not torture you. She takes care of you. Even one thousand mothers will not equal Yoga in tending the child with affection. As is the affection that Yoga has for you, so should be the affection that you must have for Yoga.

Why is it that Yoga has such love for you? You will be wondering what is this consideration that Yoga has for you. Yoga is not a human being. Yes; but it is more than a human being. Yoga is not a word that we utter. It is a surprising revelation to us.

The great thing that is called Yoga is God Himself conceived in our minds, according to our own manner; and our love for Yoga is nothing but our love for God, love for Reality, love for the Absolute, love for 'That which is'. If that Being has no love for us, what else can care for us? Not all the humans put together can have such concern over us as this great Reality has. It wants us more than we want It. All the worlds conceivable will not equal the positive affectionate reaction that this Mystery exerts upon us at every moment of time.

Feel happy: "I am in proper position with Reality. God is seeing me." This is a fact. That God sees you is not merely a doctrine; it is a truth and there cannot be a greater truth than this. Every atom is looking at you. The whole world is awake and is conscious as to what is happening. The world is made up of love and not enmity, hatred or dissociation; it is affection that the world is made of. It is made of love, and there is nothing else here.

Love is the essence of things. You want things, and everything wants you. Feel this, assert this. Chant Mantras, recite Slokas, read scriptures which awaken you to this consciousness of the presence of the divine love exuberant in everything, even in the air that you breathe, the sun that shines, the rain that falls, the atmosphere that is around you, the people that are in society. All are centres of affection, really. They appear to be otherwise sometimes on account of a misconstruing and miscalculation of fact that we make in our perceptions.

The world is, therefore, a Yoga by itself; things are in a state of Yoga even now, and they are going to be in a state of Yoga always. One is only going to realise this truth. We are getting awakened to this presence which is already there and we are not going to manufacture Yoga after some time. It is not that Yoga is not here now and it is going to take place afterwards. It is not a product artificially to be concocted with the effort of the human being. Yoga is an eternal truth. The great central Absolute is perpetually there; it was not different, it is not different, and it will not be different in the future. We have only to wake up from sleep and see what is there.

So, Yoga is not a creation of something which is not now and is to be there after some time. It is rather a consciousness into which we rise as we wake up from deep sleep and become aware of the world outside. When we wake from sleep, we are not creating the world outside; it is already there, but we become aware that it is there, a fact which was not known to us when we were in sleep. Yoga, when it is said to be a gradual developmental process, is really a development and enhancement of the consciousness of reality, an increase into a depth of the awareness of things and the lessening of the gap that appears to be between us and the world.

The point, then, is that you should have a fixed place, and it would be good that a person is in one place for a period of some years; in the initial stage it may be one year, two years or three years. Later on it can be even for a lifetime. Do not be drifting from place to place like a tourist; that is not the way of Yoga. You must be in one place for a protracted period, as far as possible.

The time, also, should be selective. You have your own convenient time, not necessarily four o'clock in the morning. If it is four o'clock in the morning, and that is convenient, very good; if it is not, let it be six o'clock. Whatever the time be, you are to be comfortably woken up from your sleep, and have no other engagements.

What is the time that you have to fix for Yoga? The time when you will not be distracted by attention to other activities in life. Suppose you have to catch a train after half an hour; that would not be the time for meditation, because there is a distraction. Or you have to meet some official in the government, or there is a case in the court, etc.; these would be unsuitable occasions.

At least for the next three hours after you commence Yoga, there should be no engagements for the mind. Let the conscious mind and the subconscious mind tell you, "Yes, for the next three hours you are not going to be disturbed by anything." Well, then, sit up for Yoga.

The early morning hours are supposed to be good for a peculiar reason. You are not much conscious of your subjectivity which has been in sleep, and you are also, then, not acutely aware of the world outside.

The time can also be the last hour of the night. An hour before you go to bed is a very useful one. The last few minutes that you spend before you sleep should be the time for the most noble thoughts. And who knows that one will get up in the morning tomorrow? This is a well-known fact. The last thought will determine one's next birth. What we shall be after this life is over is conditioned by our last thought. And why should we entertain distracting thoughts when we go to bed? It is always good to think of the most sublime things possible at the time of retiring. Read a passage from the Bhagavad-Gita, the Sermon on the Mount, or the Dhammapada, or whatever is to your liking - something which will transport you, enrapture you, catch you by the spirit, and flood you with the joy of divinity. Let that be the thought at the time one goes to bed in the night.

And, well, if it is God's will that we are not going to wake up in the morning, let it be. But we shall get up in the very atmosphere which is in harmony with the last thoughts with which we went to sleep. Therefore, it is important that people should not spend the last hours of the day in clubs, hotels, cinemas, etc. It is a bad habit, highly distractive, very injurious to psychic health. One should never go out of one's room after sunset, as far as this is practicable. People have a habit of going to shops in the night. And you know what you see in the shops, the market place and the streets. It is all confusion, chaos, noise, distraction. The last hours of the day should be spent in such a way that you are alone to yourself studying elevating scriptures of Yoga and thinking noble and lofty thoughts which are to the advantage of your own soul.

The place and the time are to be chosen according to your convenience, under the guidance of a Teacher. It is important that you should have a guide until you are able to stand on your own legs, till you are confident that you can do everything for yourself, when you have no doubts in your mind, when everything is clear and you are not going to have any kind of difficulty on the path. Until that time, you require a guide. You may call him a Guru, a friend, or a philosopher. Whatever be the way you regard the guide, such a one is necessary because the world is full of mysteries, and you do not know what it contains.

Every step is a new step, and it will take you to the unknown. The path of Yoga is difficult to tread because the further steps cannot be visualised at the initial one. You can see only one step at a time and when you are taken by surprise by a phenomenon to which you are not accustomed, you will not know how to adjust yourself to that situation. That is why guidance from a competent master, or teacher, is necessary - help from one who has already trodden the path. He will help you even in these small matters like place, time, and the like.

Then comes the method. The method that you adopt should be uniform. You should not take to different Gurus. You should not go on changing your techniques of meditation. There should be only one system, even as you drive a nail into the wall at the same spot, and then it goes inside by hammering again and again, and you do not hit it at ten places, which will be of no avail. To find water, you dig in the same place, and not go three feet down in a hundred places.

So also do you tap the source of reality at one spot and go deep into it, and you will find there what you seek. But if you merely scratch the surface at different places, you will not find anything; no treasure will come forth. You have dug the earth three feet down in one thousand places, and you have found nothing because you have gone to various places unnecessarily. Dig deep at one place. This is the uniformity that you have to adopt in the method of practice.

What is method? This touches the process called initiation. You might have heard that a disciple, a student, gets initiated into the mysteries of Yoga. Initiation is the prescription of the technique or the method of meditation. You will not be able to choose it for yourself always, because you may have doubts as to whether 'this is good, or that is good', and so on. A competent teacher will tell you, considering your psychological make-up, what would be the proper method of practice for you. This is known as initiation into Yoga.

The prescription of the method is important. Just as a physician gives a prescription, and you go to the same doctor and follow the same prescription - you do not go on changing the doctors or the prescriptions every day, for that is not the way of curing the illness—so do you persist in the adoption of a single technique, the prescription given by your Teacher. The method is selected according to the nature of the student, the circumstances in which the student is placed in society, etc., and so it varies from person to person. You cannot have a general method for everyone.

Then there is regularity. You must be honest about things. You should not make a joke of Yoga. It is a very serious matter. Just as you do not take lunch at different times on different days, for that would spoil the tummy, you must take to the practice at the same time every day, and that is regularity. You should not miss this concentration even on a single day. Suppose, you take your meal today, and tomorrow you do not have it, and the day after tomorrow you take it again, and the practice continues; you know how it affects your health. Even if you are in a moving train, the meditation should not cease. Swami Sivanandaji Maharaj used to do Sirshasana even in moving trains in order to teach it to the interested passengers. He had a system. Every day he used to do Asanas. Likewise, even if you are in travels by some occupation of yours, you must be able to find a little time to withdraw yourself into concentration some time, because the cyclic order of Nature, and the cyclic method with which the mind works, have a connection with the effects of all processes and activities.

At a particular point there is a connection of factors and they are ready to contribute to success. Just as the gastric juices begin to secrete themselves at a particular hour of the day and cause hunger in the stomach, so does the hunger of the spirit manifest itself under specific conditions. You must take advantage of this structure of the mind according to which it asks for a thing at a particular time. Hence, keep to regularity. If you start sitting for meditation at a particular time, sit at that time alone every day, unless something unavoidable intervenes. Normally, one must be able to stick to an appointed time.

Then, lastly, you should have a surging affection and love for the practice of Yoga. You must have made a decision: "This is my goal. I have been born for this purpose only. I have nothing else desirable in life." When this conviction comes, everything shall come. This decision of yours is the great love that you evince to God. We do not merely shake hands with Yoga. There is a real communion established with this great

Reality, from the bottom of your soul. If this love is there, God will love you as His own, and there will be nothing that you lack in this world.

The Metaphysics of Meditation

As all the works that we do in life aim at the fulfilment of a purpose, Yoga tends towards meditation. There is likely to be a prevalent notion among students and seekers of Truth that meditation is a kind of activity like many other activities in life. Instead of going for shopping, you go to the meditation hall. Instead of doing one work, you do another. It becomes a question of choice of activity, rather than a change in the quality of activity. When you tell the mind that it has to do meditation, it is not likely that it will always be in a state of rejoicing exhilaration. If you carefully probe into your sub-conscience, you will discover this strange attitude from within.

You will find yourself, to some extent at least, in a state of tension. It will look that some duty is being imposed upon you. The mind is afraid of the word *discipline* because of a peculiar meaning that is attached to it. And that meaning is the frightening factor in discipline. Meditation is a discipline in some respect, of course. We do not like discipline or systematization of anything, because it appears that, thereby, we are going to restrain the mind from its usual proclivities. The restraining of a desire is a pain to the mind. It is not a joy; and if Yoga, spiritual practice or meditation is going to be any attempt to restrain the usual longings of the mind, certainly, the mind is not going to be happy. There will be an undercurrent of anxiety and resentment, in spite of the fact that the logical intellect accepts the necessity for meditation and spiritual life.

Man is not made up merely of logic. The mind can set aside all logic in a second if it comes to its attention that the logic goes counter to its deepest desires. Logic goes to the dogs, and rational investigations will cut no ice, before the pressure of instinctive longings, the desires of the heart, the normal ways in which the mind works. This difficulty can also be regarded as an obstacle to any tangible success in the practice of Yoga. There are various kinds of battle going on within us. There is a war that is always being waged inside our own minds. It is true that we are like a house divided against its own self.

We live in two worlds at the same time, the one pulling us in one direction, the other in another direction. Who can deny that we have desires and that these desires are not always desires concerning God? We have simple tentacles which connect us with the different avocations of life and the sentiments which become part and parcel of our existence. There are certain things which we can never forget, in spite of our efforts. Who can forget that one is an Indian national, a British, an American, and so on? We cannot get out of the idea that we are born of some parents, that so-and-so is one's father, mother, brother, sister, etc.

There are prejudices which are sanctioned politically, socially and ethically as things quite normal and necessary. These normalcies are taken by us as inseparables from our own lives, and these so-called inseparables are our real foes. Our enemies are not persons, nor are they things. They are certain ways of thinking. There are peculiar ruts of thought along which the mind moves, like a train running on rails. It cannot change its direction except on the rails, like a river that flows on its own bed which is laid out strongly. Certain aptitudes of the mind are considered by us as normal and the only right things that we can think of. These are the sentiments, our pet prejudices.

But to think in any segmented manner, isolating one aspect of life from another, rejecting one way of thinking from another way of thinking, would be the tendency of the mind to divide itself into a few sections with no proper organic relation among the parts. Meditation is not an activity like the other works we perform in the world. The first thing that we have to remember is that work tires us, fatigues us, exhausts us and we wish to take rest after work. There is a depletion of energy in every kind of work. Some part of the total quantum of energy in the system gets diverted for the performance of the world. Energy is lost in work. If it is true that energy is lost in meditation also, we are likely to say, "Yes, we feel exhausted; we cannot go on meditating for hours together. It is a tedious job."

Meditation becomes a job rather than anything that is spontaneously acceptable to the mind; it becomes a discipline and imposition when it is something somebody asks us to do, rather than what we have accepted of our own accord. A tiring work is that which someone wants us to do. A work that we take upon our own selves, deliberately, cannot tire us so much, because, then, the mind gets identified with the work. The dissociation of work from the organic structure of the psyche is the cause of fatigue. Now, one may wonder, "What is meditation? Is it a work?"

Every activity is a process of becoming. It is a tendency of the subject to move towards an object. Here, by *object,* we need not necessarily mean any concrete, solid substance. Anything that is conceivable in space-and-time is an object; and if our thought moves towards any such thing outside, in the direction of the object, it requires a flow of energy from the whole system. Perception, cognition, or any decided act of consciousness requires an amount of energy to flow from the subject to the object. The sage Patanjali mentions psychological functions, or *Vrittis,* spoken of as *"Klishta Vrittis"* and *"Aklishta Vrittis",* etc., meaning thereby the psychosis of the mind operating in the processes of perception, cognition and feeling, all which he regards as obstacles in Yoga.

The perception of an object is considered an obstacle in Yoga. Now, if we perceive a tree, what is the difficulty about it? "I am enjoying the perception of a tree, or the rise of the sun or the moon, or a beautiful flower. How do you call it an obstacle?" We can know why this is an obstacle only when we go deep into the structure of the mind itself, in its relation to reality as a whole. What we call meditation in the spiritual sense, strictly, is not a work that is performed by the mind in respect of an object outside. It is not a tendency to *becoming,* but rather it is a tendency to *being.* These are significant terms, whose meaning should be clear to us. What is becoming? What is being? And what is the difference between the two?

Becoming is an active process of transformation of conditions or events in the direction of a goal that is yet to be reached externally in space and time. Everything changes into something else, transforms itself from one condition to another. And this tendency of things, to transformation into a different state, is indicative of restlessness characterising the condition in which they already are. There is this restlessness because it is dissatisfying to be in that condition for a protracted period.

It is dissatisfying because it does not indicate what one requires. What is required is outside oneself, and, so, there is a spatial movement, a temporal activity, outside oneself, in the direction of some conceivable goal. Thus, *becoming* is an objective movement of consciousness. Meditation is not any movement towards an object outside it, though in certain types of meditation, it may appear that we are meditating on some object. Even here, the movement is only an appearance and is not really an activity in the sense of an alienation towards objects. We shall come to this point again a little later.

Being is different from *becoming*. The difference should be ostensible. While *becoming* has a tendency to transformation in the direction of something outside itself, *being* is a tendency to its own self; it is a self-withdrawal into the core of one's own being and not an isolation of oneself into something other than what oneself is. "What is an object, and what is a subject?" is a question, again, before us. What do we mean by an object? Anything that we cannot regard as identical with ourselves, anything which is, from our point of view, totally disconnected from what we regard ourselves to be - that is an object, a "This-is-not-me."

And anything with which we are vitally connected in an inseparable manner, in whose context we affirm a self-identity - that is a subject. When we speak of subjects and objects, we naturally refer to consciousness which plays an important role in all experience. It is the consciousness of some particular circumstance that brings about the distinction between subjectivity and objectivity. The consciousness of a thing dissociates itself from that thing and assumes the presence of some spatial distance or, at least, a spatial difference logically conceived between itself and the object. But when no such spatial distinction can be conceived between the object and consciousness, then, there is no object; it is only subject.

Consciousness alone can be the subject; everything else is object.

Anything that is separable from consciousness is an object of consciousness. Now, this separability may be merely notional; it may not be factual. Whether it is an imaginary concept of difference or a factual distinction that is there, as long as the mind or consciousness cannot accept its unity with that particular context or thing, it remains as an object. In meditation, the consciousness is enabled not by exertion of any force from outside, but by an education introduced into it from within to effloresce into a wider comprehension of facts wherein its notion of objects gets changed and transformed.

It is not that things actually change in meditation, but our idea of objects changes. To give a common example, we have the phenomenon of the difference that we make between dream objects and waking experience. The objects in dream are totally disconnected from the perceiving subject. We are the dreamers and we do not know that we are such, while we are actually dreaming. The question of dream does not arise when we are actually in that condition. It is as good an experience as anything else. The things that we see in dream are disconnected from us and, therefore, we have pleasures and pains in dream, also.

There are all kinds of things in dream as we have in waking life. There are hills and dales, persons and things, experiences that are pleasurable and miserable. All these objects of the dream world causing pleasures or pains are disconnected from that particular degree of consciousness which experiences them; and that is the reason why there is pleasure or pain. Pleasures and pains are caused by reactions set up between the subjective consciousness and its relation to the object concerned. When we wake up from dream, what happens? The objects which we saw in dream, which were the causes of our pleasures and pains, have vanished altogether. Since they have vanished, the pleasures and pains connected with the objects also have gone. Where have these objects gone? Where have they vanished into?

The objects in dream, which caused us pleasures and pains, were notionally distinguishable from the experiencing consciousness, but factually not. This is known by us when we wake up from dream. The tiger that pounced upon us in dream was not really outside us. It was a particular modification of our own mind which concocted a spatial and temporal difference between itself and the content called the tiger, or whatever it is, and the pleasures and pains were due to the space and time difference between the experiencing consciousness and the object. If the dream-space or dream-time were not to be there, we could have no pleasures and pains there.

The cessation of pleasures and pains in waking, after the dream, is entirely due to the cessation of the space and time which operated in dream. When the dream-space-time has gone, the dream-objects also have gone. Earlier, we have noted that space-time and objects go together. We also observed the hint from the discoveries of modern physics wherein science has come to the conclusion that objects in the world are indistinguishable from what we call space and time. They are rather configurations of space-time themselves. There are no objects. There is only space-time.

By the dream analogy, we come to the awareness that objects may appear to be outside us and cause us pleasures and pains even though they are really not so. We may have a large fortune in dream and we may feel very happy. We may earn a million dollars in dream by lottery. We may fall from a tree in a dream and break our legs and feel pain. But what are these experiences? They are nothing but the effects of space and time in which we are involved. Our dream-consciousness has got involved in the notion of the difference between itself and the space-time in which it is perceiving the objects.

When we wake up, what happens? The space, time and objects of dream get absorbed into our own minds. A so-called objective world of dream gets assimilated into the mind which is now awake, which contains within itself all the factors that went to constitute the dream experiencer as well as the dream objects. This analogy will give us an idea of what is going to take place in meditation. If we are consciously to wake up from dream, *i.e.*, if we are aware of the very process of getting up from dream into the world of waking experience, if we are going to be aware of the involvement as well as the disentanglement, that would be the series of processes through which we have to pass in Yoga meditation.

Instead of getting suddenly stirred up into waking by some phenomenon of which we have no knowledge, as it happens usually, if we are to be aware of every step and every stage of the working of the psyche by which it wakes up from dream, that would be a sort of analogy which can explain the process of meditation. And the comparison is this much: when we wake up, the objects of dream get absorbed into our minds and that is why they do not cause us pleasure and pain and they do not bother us afterwards. Because, they do not exist at all. They are 'we'. The objects of dream, and the space and time of dream have become what we are.

The object has become the subject. Hence, there is no pleasure, no pain in connection with the things that we saw in dream. Now, this so-called 'we', which has absorbed into itself the whole of the dream phenomena, should be regarded as inclusive of both the subject and the object of dream; we had reduced ourselves into the dream-experiencer and separated a part of ourselves into the objects in the dream-space-time. And when we wake up, they get withdrawn. This process of withdrawal is like the process of Yoga. In Yoga, the process is a conscious and deliberate one. It is not an unconscious occurrence or a sudden kick that we receive from somewhere. We are enabling the mind to educate itself into the true situation of things. The world outside us is connected with us in the same way as the objects of dream are connected with the dream-experiencer. The buildings that we see outside, in which we are seated, are all connected with us, even as the dream-room or the dream-buildings are connected with the dream-experience. These analogies can explain themselves.

The connection in dream was inseparable because the things were not really outside. This reference will also explain why meditation should not be considered as an activity or a business that we perform. It is not a job that we are hunting after, so that we may get tired of it. Meditation should become a source of satisfaction and relief from tension rather than a source of exhaustion and fatigue. The more we become ourselves, the more are we free from tension. A tension is an alienation of oneself into something other than oneself. There is an unnatural distinction drawn within the function of our own psyche, a pressure exerted upon it by conditions over which it has no control and which it somehow regards as outside itself.

The withdrawal that we speak of in Yoga practice is not a painful activity. It is not to be considered an activity at all. It is the regaining of the health of consciousness from the diseased state in which it is in its individualised state. If we can consider dream as an unfortunate nightmare and not a healthy state of the mind, then this objective world-experience can also not be regarded as a spiritually healthy state. That is why the sage Patanjali regards all perceptions as unnecessary activities of the mind in respect of things with which it should not concern itself. They are *Vrittis*, obstacles to be overcome. In the subjugation of the *vritti,* or *vrittis-Nirodha,* in Yoga, every notion of objects gets transformed into a higher subjectivity. Here we have to underline the word *higher subjectivity.* It is not the empirical subjectivity we know.

The consciousness of waking is a subjectivity which is higher in dimension than the subjectivity of dream. That is why we are more free in waking than in dream. Otherwise, we would be sorry that we have woken up from sleep. We do not so feel, but are rather relieved that the nightmare has gone, the bugbear is no more, because the waking consciousness is a larger dimension of comprehension than the one in which we were as dream experiencers. So, to withdraw ourselves from objective consciousness into the subjectivity we are speaking of here does not mean an introversion in the sense of the Freudian or the Jungian psychology and psychoanalysis. We hear of extroverts and introverts, a distinction drawn by Jung in his analytical psychology. We are not talking of this kind of introversion.

Many times, people consider Yogis as introverts. It is a bad name like the one we give to the dog in order to hang it. The Yogis are not introverts in the psychological sense. We may call them introverts in the same sense as we have become introverts now after waking up from dream. It is a metaphysical inwardisation of being. We introvert in this particular sense as the objects of the dream-world go into our subjectivity in waking. But, then, we do not say that we are in a morbid state when we are awake. The psychological introversion is a partial expression of the mind towards itself, bifurcating itself from extrovert activities. Jung advocates a blend of the extrovert and the introvert. Any kind of overemphasis on one side is supposed to bring a psycho-pathological condition. Yoga is far removed from it.

We have great psycho-analytic teachers like Patanjali, but their teaching is quite different. While it is true that meditation in its higher reaches is an attempt at self-withdrawal, it is not a withdrawal into this cocoon of our individual personality. Yoga is a healthy remedy that is prescribed for the illness in which the mind finds itself by alienating itself into the false notion of an outsideness of objects, which is not really there. The *pratyahara* spoken of in the Yoga system, the withdrawal of the senses from the objects, does not mean a cutting oneself off from the realities of things. If this wrong idea persists in the mind, one has to be unhappy in meditation. The mind will say, "When will this meditation be over? I shall get up and go for a walk." This, because we feel that going for a walk will be an entry into the reality of things from which we have withdrawn ourselves unnaturally in meditation.

The mind has a notion that, after all, the reality is outside. "I have forcefully severed myself from reality in the meditation hall, so I want to get up from this place as early as possible." This is a sorry state of affairs. Meditation is not a withdrawal from reality, even as waking from dream is not a waking from reality into some unreality. One knows very well that waking is a greater reality than dream, and the subjectivity into which the objective consciousness withdraws itself in meditation is not the individual subject of a Mr. or a Mrs., a Tom, Dick, or Harry. Here what is considered is a larger subject which includes our present idea of a subject in ourselves and the objects outside, in the same way as the dream-subject and the dream-objects get both subsumed in the waking subject. Even when we listen to it and hear that this is going to be the true achievement in meditation, the mind will jump into it as if it is going to enter into a river of nectar. "Oh! It is this! I am going to become a larger being in meditation than what I am today, just now! I will be more vitally connected with all things than I know now!" If the mind is convinced by an educational process, in the Yoga sense of the term, it will not open its mouth afterwards.

You will forget your breakfast and lunch and dinner, you will be weeping, "When will I enter into this state?" rather than feel, "When will this meditation cease?" People have a wrong notion about meditation, about Yoga, and about God Himself, an erroneous idea about themselves and their relationship with things. Before we enter into any serious attempt at meditation we have to clear our minds of all the cobwebs and the dirt and the rubbish of sentiments and prejudices which have been thrust into us by the social conditions into which we are born and remake ourselves for the purpose of the practice.

The Conflict and the Aims of Life

The whole of life is permeated with various conflicts and irreconcilabilities varying in nature from person to person. The aim of Yoga is to resolve all such conflicts and make us perfectly normal in the absolute sense of the term. Whenever there is an inward feeling of irreconcilability in a family, there is a conflict, and when it gets deepened, it can become a malady, a disease by itself.

We have a rough idea of what these conflicts are, and they are the common difficulties that we face in our day-to-day life. We cannot bear too much heat or too much cold, we cannot bear hunger and thirst, we cannot tolerate the presence of certain persons, and so on; of an unending nature are our pin-pricks. But all these diversified conflicts of life can be boiled down to four conflicts finally, in the philosophy of Yoga, or, we may say, the philosophy of the Vedanta. All problems are reduced to four fundamental conflicts.

The lowest or the immediately cognisable conflict is the social one, where people cannot get on with one another for one reason or the other, *i.e.*, the immediately visible external conflicts. We are unable to face situations created by people outside; and others, too, cannot strike a reconcilability with our own conducts and activities. There is a mutual difficulty, one hanging on the other, each one attributing its cause to the other, thus making life a scene of sorrow. Everyone is unhappy, saying that the cause is somebody else.

Now, apart from this ostensible external conflict of a social character, we have internal conflicts in our own selves. We are not aligned in the layers of our own personality. We have the physical body, we have the pranas, we have the sense-organs, we have the mind with all its various functions, we have our reasoning capacity; we have so many things in us, which we study in psychology. These facts or aspects or layers of our personality are not in harmony, so there is an internal conflict apart from the outer social conflict. There is a psychological conflict in addition to social frictions.

There is a third type of conflict which is of a more serious nature. We cannot get on with the world itself. There is something seriously wrong with the very structure of things, and nothing does attract us. We cannot see any perfection or beauty in this creation of the physical Nature. The seasons, even the five elements, appear to be very defective to us. We are not happy somehow, and we have a feeling that we are harassed by the very make-up of Nature. The elements create a torturous irreconcilability with ourselves; we are grief-stricken.

And, finally, as the last but not the least, we have a tension with God Himself. There is no harmony between us and the Ultimate Reality. The truth seems to be made of characters which do not appear to be the characters which we exhibit in our life. We are at loggerheads with God, Nature and human society.

These four conflicts can be called the social, personal, natural and spiritual irreconcilabilities. In India we have a great scripture called the Bhagavad-Gita which has devoted itself entirely to the resolution of these conflicts.

While the Bhagavad-Gita is openly dedicated to the resolution of these problems, every other text on Yoga also is devoted to the very same subject, including the Sutras of Patanjali, the Upanishads, or the scriptures of any nation, for the matter of that.

Before we go into the details of these peculiar conflicts which are to be resolved in Yoga, so that we may become universally healthy and perfect, we have to consider another aspect which we observe in our life, *viz.*, the aims and objectives that we are pursuing - the intention behind activities, which has something to do with the joys and the sorrows that we pass through in our life. We are here for some purposes and these may be called our desires, broadly speaking. We have certain basic desires, longings, and if they are not fulfilled, they create problems in our own selves.

Ancient adepts have classified these desires also in the same way as they have categorised the conflicts. The aims of existence, or the aims of human life with which we are concerned now, appear to be manifold on the surface, even as conflicts. Just as conflicts appear to be a hundredfold, or a thousandfold, but really they are only fourfold, likewise, our aims, too, are fourfold. They are not many as they appear on the surface. It is not that we have some millions of desires. We have four desires, to which every desire can be reduced finally.

The first one is the physical or the economic need of our personality. We have hunger and thirst, and we require clothing and shelter. To fulfil these requirements we have today what we call money or wealth. In ancient times, this money idea was not there. There was only the barter system. If you have some commodity which I need, I take it from you in return for some other commodity which I have but which you need. But as it was a very inconvenient system, we have created a new policy of currency, which is very helpful because we cannot carry commodities from place to place for purpose of exchange. This is the principle of wealth or the economic system of life. But wealth has only an instrumental value. Money is a means to the fulfilment of our needs which are primary. We do not require money as such. Nobody wants money only. It is a tool to the fulfilment of our desires. So, when we ask for economic fulfilment, what we actually ask for is the fulfilment of the bodily or physical needs, with all their social relations. However, it is not actually currency note, or money; that is not the requirement. Money is an instrument which is utilised as a necessary means to the fulfilment of the longings of man. All the material requirements of human life come under this particular category. This is one desire.

Then we have certain other stronger desires, at least as strong as the urges for material requirements. And they are our vital urges. These are the emotional needs of the human personality. It is not that we require only bread and jam and a house to live in and clothes to put on. We have also emotional necessities. With all the material needs we can be unhappy if our emotions are not satisfied. So this is another aspect of human longing or desire - the loves, the affections, the aesthetic promptings of human nature.

Now, in Sanskrit, there are certain technical names given to these desires. The whole of economic or material requirement comes under what is called *Artha*. Anything that is material or economic comes under this head. In short, it means all material values. And the vital longings come under what is known as *Kama* (not *karma). Kama* as a desire of an emotional or instinctive type is different from the grosser ones that are material.

But there is a need for another regulative principle to assist in the fulfilment of these longings which are material and vital. These desires, when they arise from within an individual, come with a tremendous vehemence. They have a power of their own. They insist on satisfaction, and everyone has this urge from within. The peculiarity of these desires is that they are never satiable. They have an endless requirement. However much we may feed them, they do not appear to be satisfied, and this for certain other reasons which we shall not touch upon just now. It is well known that a person cannot be satisfied with any amount of material property. One wants more and more of everything. Similar is the case with the desire for emotional satisfactions.

One requires more and more, and as much as possible, and this strange devilish implication behind these desires bordering upon an endlessness of their longings affects the similar longings of other people. If each one wants things endlessly, what will happen to human society and life as a whole? One cannot have endlessness everywhere. If one wants endless things and another also wants endless things - and two endless things cannot exist - there would be a clash of desires and personalities. There would be battles and wars.

It is not possible to give a long rope, in an indefinite sense, to the desires of people. There should be a restriction, not in the manner of a pressure or subjugation by force, but a rational acceptance of the presence of similar needs in all people, everywhere. If I am hungry and I want food, a fact that has to be accepted, it is also to be accepted that another will also be equally hungry and he needs food. It does not mean that I am the only person who requires food.

But the selfishness of a person can go to an inordinate extent and can violate the rationality of the presence of similar needs in others. Selfishness is a devil. If there is a Satan, here is he, violating law and asserting isolation. Such an impetuousness of the will conflicts with everybody else, because it wants everything for itself. And if each one is to project a similar attitude, there will be a complete chaos and an imminent destruction of human existence itself. Each one will fly at the throat of the other and no life will be there in a few days. This is not a happy state of affairs, and human beings who are selfish are also intelligent.

Intelligence is used even to fulfil the demands of selfishness, and when selfishness realises that its own purposes are going to be defeated by an excessive asking or an overdosed projection of itself, it accepts the necessity to collaborate itself with the similar needs of other people. This is the social side of the law or *Dharma* that people generally speak of. We should be righteous. We must be virtuous. Righteousness, goodness, justice, rationality are essentials. These are only various terminologies indicating the need on the part of every individual to accept similar needs in other persons also. Only then, there can be social peace and human solidarity. We cannot get on in life, or even exist in this world, if we insist on an infinite satisfaction for our own selves, individually, personally. The law of mutual respect and cooperation is called *Dharma*, or the righteousness of the law.

And our *Artha* and *Kama* are not going to succeed if *Dharma* is not to be there. Their very purposes may be defeated without it. They defeat themselves by a wrong notion of their own good. *Dharma* has many other implications, but we are here concerned with the basic notion of it - namely that the longing of the human personality, material, vital, or psychological, cannot succeed unless there is a collaboration and cooperation with the vast creation called humanity. *Dharma* may extend even beyond humanity to other regions also, with which we have a secret connection. *Dharma* is the regulative principle of life which conditions or puts a limit upon the extent of satisfaction that one can have without detriment to the similar requirements of other persons.

This attitude of charity and regard is called goodness. If I can accept that you are in as much need of things as I am, I can be called a good person. "Yes, he is good, he knows my difficulties," say people. But if I refuse to accept your difficulties and insist on my own, then I would be called a selfish person. Thus, *Dharma* is there as inviolable, inexorable insistent law, which is to be accepted on the very nature of things. Human rules, political laws, social customs, etc., are based on this natural law of the necessity for mutual collaboration and cooperation in life.

But what are all those for? Why should we fulfil all these desires? We have to observe the principles of *Dharma* because our longings can receive a logical listening only if *Dharma* is followed. Our material needs and our vital longings can have justifiable satisfaction only on the basis of *Dharma*. Yes, *Dharma*, *Artha* and *Kama* are the three absolute, categorical imperatives of life, without which we cannot live. But what are we living for? Why should we live at all? Let nobody live. What is the harm? Why should there be a law? Why should there be regulation and system? Why should we eat and drink? Why should we fulfil our emotional needs and have satisfactions? What is the matter? What is the point in all these? What is this great drama of life? Why stress? Why run about? Why work? These are more difficult questions to answer than anything else. We may with some acumen of our learning and education be in a position to answer the lower questions of immediate existence. But these latter poses take us beyond the human and even the natural realm of things. Here is a metaphysical question, if you would like to call it so. It is to enter the realm of philosophy. It is a bordering upon spiritual life, to put it in another way.

These questions concerning the very existence of a person go beyond the ordinary understanding of the intellect. I have to live, but why should I live? There is no answér to this question. It is an answer to its own self. It answers without raising a question. It is taken for granted that one should exist, one should live. Why should we live? "Do not put such a question," says the conscience. It is a foolish question and one would laugh at this very point itself. Why should I exist? Because, that is the base of everything else. One cannot put a question about the basis itself. But what is the base? The base is the love for existence, love for life, love for one's own self, for as long a period as possible, a struggle for existence, or a survival of the fittest, as our present-day men put it.

These doctrines arise from a fundamental trait of the human personality, which is present in everything, and not merely in the human being. It exists in a measure which can be as large as possible. We do not wish to merely exist like a tree or a stone. Accepting the fact that our final aim is existence, what sort of existence is it that we are longing for? We qualify this existence with certain characteristics. We do not like to exist merely, like a nobody, just vegetating. This is not our intention. We wish to enhance this existence by a qualitative improvement of understanding and satisfaction.

The characteristic of existence in its desire to enhance itself is intelligence and joy. We wish to know more and more, become wiser and wiser, have greater and greater intelligence for the purpose of greater and greater satisfaction. Why should not we exist like a tree or a stone? We feel there is no sense; there is no joy in it. If a human being is happier than a tree or a stone, we can imagine that an animal is not happier than a human being. Even if you are a beggar, you are happier than a pig because of the increase in the intensity of knowledge in the human being. The capacity to appreciate is more in man than in swine or an ass. We seek an existence which is to be qualified with higher knowledge and which goes simultaneously with greater joy.

So, what is the kind of existence that we long for through *Artha, Kama, Dharma?* It is an existence which is to be coupled with intelligence, consciousness of an intensified type. "How much intelligence?" may be another question. "Endless" is the answer. And if we are asked how much knowledge we want, we will not say, "It is one kilogram or two quintals." We want to know everything. We desire to know all things, as much as possible, in as intense a manner as possible. The largest amount of knowledge in the greatest intensity and quality is what we would like to have. People are never satisfied with knowledge and learning and education. Man wants to know the whole universe.

Our asking for knowledge is a kind of infinite asking. It is not that we want only a limited knowledge and want to remain ignorant of something else. We would never like ignorance; one dislikes the very word 'ignorance'. "I do not want to be unaware of certain things; I want to know that also." There is a curiosity to know everything. It can be said to be a desire for omniscience itself. We wish to be all-knowing. Our existence has to be qualified with all-knowingness; otherwise, it is an inadequate existence. Why do we want all-knowingness? Because it gives us infinite joy.

We want to exist, and towards this end it is that we want to fulfil all our longings. And this existence is not merely a stony existence, but an existence with knowledge, which is again inseparable from infinite satisfaction and joy. These three features - existence, consciousness, and joy - are known as *Sat-Chit-Ananda*. We must have heard this term repeated so many times at so many places in various scriptures and Satsangas.

People speak of *Sat-Chit-Ananda*. It is the name of God. Well, it is the name of the ultimate perfection. We call it God, the Absolute.

This is what we want, and we eat our breakfast only for this purpose. We do not know what connection things have with the ultimate aim of ours. Even if we take a cup of tea, it is for this supreme reason. It is not merely a joke that we are making when we take our meals. Wonderful! We will be surprised that our aim is something much vaster and grander even in the littlest acts of our life. This realisation of the infinitude of our existence and the infinitude of our knowledge and happiness is called *'Moksha'*, or the liberation of the spirit. Thus, the aim of life is fourfold: *Artha, Kama, Dharma, Moksha.*

All the aims of the so-called diversified human life are boiled down to these four types of aim. One can put these in any order, according to convenience. The foundation behind the practice of Yoga, or meditation proper, is the resolution of conflicts and fulfilment of all longings to the utmost extent until one reaches infinity itself. What a grand thing is Yoga! Now we realise! We will be surprised that our very life is there only for that goal. Now we will be able to appreciate that Yoga is not a religion. It is not Hinduism. It is not Buddhism. It is not Christian mysticism. It is not anything of that sort.

Yoga is the science of life. It does not belong to the East or the West. It is not even a prerogative of the human being. It is the great process through which all creation has to pass, right from the lowest electron till the solar system and the whole astronomical universe. The evolution of the cosmos is the greatest Yoga, and our participation in it, consciously, is properly called Yoga.

All these things, the resolution of the conflicts and the purpose of our life, imply a kind of adjustment of ourselves with the existing nature of things, and it roots out selfishness totally. Selfishness is a misnomer under the law that operates in the cosmos; it has no sense and is an utter stupidity. It is a meaningless apparition—what is called selfishness. A person who is selfish knows nothing of the law of Nature. He cannot succeed because selfishness is contrary to the existing law of the universe. And what is the existing law? It is a gradual ascent of all things from the lowest stage of mutual cooperation to the highest peak of attainment where things merge into one another, ultimately. There they do not merely cooperate. They all exist as one being.

In the beginning our aim looks like the coveted one-humanity. Why do we have a United Nations Organisation and all the enterprises for commonwealth? All this is because there is an urge within man to recognise a basic universality which is at the root of humanity. Otherwise, why are these efforts at organisations and institutions, etc.? What is the intention behind? But this is not the end of it. Our goal is still higher. It is greater than 'The United Nations.' It consists in the desire to comprehend the whole cosmos within one grasp, if it could be possible, and it is not merely a grasp in the physical sense; rather it is a union, until the state is reached where that which one loves is inseparable from oneself.

The object of our loves, affections and desires becomes inseparable from our being. The world becomes ourselves and our reason communes with the Universal Intelligence. We become united with the All-Being. Towards this purpose is the practice of Yoga, whose culmination is meditation - *Dhyana.* Now, this is a very important introduction to the actual practice. Unless we have clear thoughts before us, we cannot sit for meditation. We would be bored with meditation itself if the ideas are not clear and our emotions not happy. We must be relieved even when we think of meditation. Meditation is such a glorious thing. It is so wonderful.

It is our bread and life. We cannot exist for a minute without it. We are here only for that. Anyone would jump into it when the love for the practice of Yoga spontaneously rises within on account of the understanding which one has developed of the nature of all life. Yoga comes of its own accord even without our asking for it. We would be perpetually in a mood to meditate. We would not be resenting it, we would not be unhappy about it, we would not take it as an imposition of external discipline. Our life itself is a Yoga. We would become aware of this great truth.

To prepare ourselves for the gradual stages of the ascent to the largest dimensions of *Moksha*, we have to practise certain techniques. We require a certain atmosphere which is conducive to the practice. That is why people go to Ashramas and monasteries, to the Himalayas, and so on. In the beginning, one has to be a little away from the din and bustle of life and from too much distraction, whether social or personal. One craves for some isolation.

Now, this isolation cannot be taken in any extreme sense, in the earlier stages. We must know where we stand, first of all. One may be a student. One may be a teacher. One may be a professor. One may be a householder. One may be a businessman. One may be anything. But, from the point of view of the occupation or the performance of one's life, one must rise gradually. If you are a shopkeeper, what would be the Yoga that you are to practise? What would be one's Yoga in the circumstance of any vocation?

The whole of Yoga is a graduated practice. It is a systematized attempt at self-transcendence, not rejection of things. We have heard of religious renunciation. The spirit of renunciation is inculcated in all the religions of the world. But many a time renunciation is misconstrued as rejection of objects, the throwing away of homestead and chattel, a cutting of connections with family and relations and segregating oneself, somewhere, far off physically, geographically. This is the usually accepted austere sense of renunciation to which people betake themselves. But this attitude does not always succeed, because one cannot wrench oneself from the atmosphere in which one is placed, unless one has outgrown that atmosphere by experience. Yoga is a growth and not a plucking of the bud before it blossoms.

We have to educate ourselves in a systematic manner. There is a need first of all to appreciate the principle to dissociate ourselves from entanglements and attachments. If the mind is not accepting the principle of detachment, our cutting away of physical connection with family, etc., will be of no avail. If the mind accepts it, if it feels that it is prepared for it, that it has had enough of all things, it has seen things to the core, had a surfeit of everything, then, detachment follows naturally like the dawn of the day.

Renunciation, detachment, the spirit of sequestration or isolation, should be an educational career and not an austerity that we thrust into ourselves by the power of the will without the understanding backing it up. Understanding is the soul behind the force called will or volition. If the soul is absent, the practice becomes a corpse. The student should not be too anxious to become a Yogi unless he is emotionally prepared and the basic longings are fulfilled, at least to an appreciable extent. You have seen the world and therefore you have no desire for the world. Why is it that you have no desire? Not because you hate things, but because you have seen through everything. You know what the world is made of, and your understanding is the reason for your non-attachment to things.

One does not drink poison, not because of a special religious renunciation of poison, but because it is known very well that poison is detrimental to life, and one renounces a thing because it is harmful, a fact accepted by the power of intelligence or understanding. You do not renounce venom because somebody told you to do so. But, normally it is not possible to reject anything unless one understands its nature. Things we cannot understand are a source of fear. When we do not know what a thing is made up of, we are very insecure about it. When we have understood threadbare the structure of a thing, we, automatically, feel a detachment for it. Knowledge removes desire.

The detachment comes because we cannot desire the thing any more. We cannot desire it any more because we know that it cannot fulfil our longing. We have a wrong notion of things and then cling to them. When the notion gets clarified about things, there is a spontaneous rising from the level of attachment to them. We rise up rather than cut ourselves from that particular circumstance. There is a wholesome overcoming of attachment by an emotional and intelligent preparation of oneself. This is the basic spirit of Patanjali's admonition on what he calls *Yamas* and *Niyamas,* the canons of self-discipline in Yoga.

We have firstly to be friendly with society. We cannot be inimical to it. This friendliness is not a makeshift, and we are not to convert ourselves into hypocrites by appearing to be friendly with people. The basic requirements of natural law demand a spirit of friendliness with all things, and friendliness is a part of the fulfilment of the law. Any kind of resentment would border upon selfishness. It is the selfish centre that resents things. The more we become unselfish the more are we able to love and appreciate, and friendliness is nothing but a spirit of cordial recognition of human life and life in general. We cannot have enemies in the world and then be friendly with God, because that would be an unholy attitude repugnant to the wholeness of life.

The friendliness that we establish in creation, again, is a practice stage by stage. From the level in which we are, we rise to a higher stage of friendliness. The whole of Yoga is an attitude of friendliness at different levels of being. Friendliness is a system of harmonisation of oneself with the existing system of things. The more are we friendly, the more also are we in harmony, the more is the spirit of appreciation and the feeling of oneness with things. Friendliness is an attitude developed by consciousness in the direction of union with creation. The intention of friendliness is atonement with reality. The eight stages of Yoga propounded by Patanjali are the different degrees of harmony and unity realised in one's life, from the down-most form of social amity and love to the highest absorption in All-Being.

Meditational Self-analysis

To recall our memories to the subject of meditation, we noticed that there are principally three approaches to the technique of meditation. There is the subjective method, the objective method and the transcendent method. There are also ways of approach which synthesise all these envisagements. The system of Yoga propounded by Patanjali, particularly, touches upon all these aspects, and so we shall reserve this subject to a later time, because it is the most popular system, and it has also the special advantage of being a blend of all these avenues of approach to Truth. The objective method borders finally upon the universal method, and this, again, is a subject we have to set aside for a later consideration, as it entails an entry into advanced techniques.

We shall touch upon a system of thinking in meditation which is peculiar to the philosophies and religions in India, particularly. It is not so much in vogue in other countries, though a suggestiveness of this type can be found also in the mystical doctrines of the Western saints and sages. But it is predominant in the Indian systems, not only in Hinduism, but also in Buddhism and Jainism. It is a special feature because it comprehends within its perspective the essential relationship of the individual with the whole of creation. The central emphasis laid by almost all the philosophies in India is the coordination of the individual with the universal. Whether it is a metaphysical system or a psychological one, every system of thought has, as the ultimate objective of all its approaches, the bringing together of the apparently diversified facets of the individual and the cosmos. For this purpose an analytical technique is being adopted.

The individual, the *Jiva*, as it is usually called, the person, 'You' and 'I' is a complex structure of body, mind and spirit. The spirit which is the deepest essence in the individual ramifies itself as a controlling power through the various functions of the individual or the personality.

If we could bring to our memories certain interesting points, which we noted earlier, we would recollect that we observed by analysis that there is a permanent relationship of an inextricable nature between the individual and the universe. We need not repeat the theme here because we have already touched upon it. But what is this relationship that involves a threefold linkage by which the individual is connected to the universal or the cosmic, in the process of knowing? In the process of knowing there is an undercurrent of activity going on without our being conscious of what is happening.

Let us take a gross example, of looking at a tree and becoming conscious of its existence. This simple, commonplace cognition of the presence of an object outside is not so simple as it appears on the surface. It is a very complex activity that manifests itself as the end result, *viz.*, knowledge of the object, the tree, for instance. For the simple act of even standing on our legs, about 450 muscles are supposed to work simultaneously, a fact of which we are not always aware. When we throw into our mouth even a little piece of raisin, the whole body is set into activity, like a dynamo working in a factory. It is not a simple act of a little stuff being put on the tongue. The entire alimentary canal and the respiratory system, the bloodstream and every cell of the body is set into motion because of the entry of a particular object, which is there for the purpose of absorption into the system.

Likewise is the perception of things, knowledge of objects, awareness of anything. We become aware of the objects by the interaction of three facets of reality - the subjective side, which is known as the "Seer", the objective side which is the object "Seen", and a third element which is absolutely essential for establishing a conscious connection between the "Seer" and the "Seen". In Indian theological systems or epistemological analysis, it has been discovered that the very consciousness of an object, even if it be the simple consciousness of an insignificant thing in the world, is a universal phenomenon. There is no such thing as an individual function, anywhere.

The whole world is active when even a single event takes place at any point in space, just as the whole body is active even if a little thorn is to prick the sole of the foot. It is not a local effect merely; it is the entire body-organism getting energised into the requisite action. The whole world becomes aware of even the wisp of a wind, the fall of a leaf or even the movement of a bird, and this is not merely a gospel that you hear in the New Testament, the sermon of the Buddha, or the Upanishad; it is a scientific fact. This is a great revelation which came to Seers of such profundity as the Upanishads, for instance, where we are awakened to the fact of a cosmic interconnection of things, which sets itself into motion at the time of the occurrence of any event, perception, or whatever it is. This takes us deep down into its further implications, which have direct relevance to our practical life.

We are not really independent individuals. We are not isolated persons with no connection among ourselves. We are participants in a government which operates as the central system of the universe. When we become the citizens of a particular nationality or country, we automatically get transformed into a vital relationship with that organism of administration called the government, whether or not we are always conscious of this circumstance. Likewise, the revelation of these great sages brought before their eyes a mysterious circumstance of the inter-relationship of things, so that everything that we are, let alone what we have, belongs to the whole cosmos. We have no personal property; we may call it a universal communism or socialism, wonderful even to contemplate! We have no personal belongings. We cannot say that even the body is our own property. Everything belongs to the All, at once.

The physical body of ours is constituted of the five elements, and how do we say it is our property? Just as all the walls of a building are made up of bricks, mortar, etc., our body is made up of earth, water, fire, air and ether. We cannot say it is 'our' body. The very substance of the body belongs to the structure of things, and the body can be resolved back into the cause from which it has come and out of which it is manufactured. Now we are discussing a very important subject in meditation. The very first step that we take in the direction of the assessment of the circumstances of our physical body will take us to a point of concentration, where we will lose the sense of individuality.

Let us just imagine, as persons endowed with a little commonsense, a situation where the cells of the body and everything that our body is made of - the flesh, bones and marrow - all belong to the world outside. What does remain to belong to us afterwards? We will be stunned even to imagine this situation. We cannot breathe for a moment. It appears that we have borrowed all things from others, to whom they belong, and we have unnecessarily appropriated them and got introduced into that false apprehension of a sense of consciousness which is called egoism, an unwarranted assessment of proprietorship. When we assert our consciousness in the direction of a false proprietorship, we are supposed to be egoistic persons or, can we say, thieves?

So, our awareness or consciousness or mind or reason or intellect, whatever we call it, somehow wrongly reconciles itself to the appropriation of things which do not really belong to it, and then we find ourselves in hot waters in a second. We have dragged into our own personal cocoons of individual life things which belong to somebody else. The five elements are the owners of this body, and they are everywhere. Everyone's body belongs to them, so that none of us has an independent physical existence. We have lost our physical personality in a moment. This is one step in meditation, even without our going further into the greater implications of this system of self-analysis. We will be surprised even to realise this initial fact of the dissolution of our physical existence into the cosmic elements. Our breath will cease because of the shock that has been injected into our minds by the realisation of this tremendous, unexpected revelation.

Apart from the body that we are endowed with, we have the sense-organs. The cosmology of the Vedanta philosophy, the Samkhya, and even the Yoga system of Patanjali accepts that there are subtle layers of our personality. Apart from the physical body is the subtle body, the astral system in which the mind is located and through whose operation the sense organs begin to work in the direction of objects. Different from the physical body constituted of the five elements, we have the subtle body inside, in which there is the *Prana* with its fivefold activity, there are the senses of perception, and also the mind and the intellect. All these are present here as one organisation. In fact, what we call the subtle body is only a name that we give to the total of all these internal functions - psychic, sensory and vital.

These may appear to be 'ourselves' just as the body appears to be 'ourselves'. But in the same way as we falsely imagine that the body is ours, we also falsely imagine that the mind is ours, the senses are ours - for even these do not belong to us. We may be further surprised here and may not be able to stomach all these things. We now realise that the body has gone, and the mind even seems to go, and then what remains? The cosmological deduction in the systems of thought tells us that the sense-organs are controlled by certain deities and they are the owners of the sense-organs, even as the five elements are the owners of our body.

The theology and the cosmology mention that the solar system centralised in the Sun is the divinity or the deity presiding over the eyes. There is a subtle system of connection between the eyes and the Sun. We cannot physically observe what this connection is. Something about this mystery we learn from the Upanishads.

So is the case with the ears - by ears we do not mean the fleshy eardrum but the particular capacity of hearing within, which operates through the eardrum and enables us to hear sound. So are the other sense-perceptions: smelling, tasting, touching. They have all their central governing systems behind them and these so-called perceptional organs are only instruments operated by powers that are cosmically set up in various directions - powers known as deities, the angels that govern and guard us.

This is just to indicate the principle behind the recognition of a relationship between the individual and the cosmic even in the subtle body, and not merely the physical body. The eyes have gone to the Sun, the ears have gone to some other divinity; the smell and the taste and the other senses, even the powers of grasping and locomotion, all go to the presiding principles which are internal to the physical universe. Even as there are layers of the individual personality, internal to the physical system of ours, there are planes of the cosmos.

The planes are the levels of existence; we call them *Lokas,* the different densities of the manifestation of the cosmos, internal to the physical, and functioning as the vital, the mental and the intellectual realms. These cosmic vital, mental and intellectual planes are internal to and transcending the physical cosmos which we see with the physical eyes.

So, the whole physical universe is the owner of our physical body, and the whole astral or the causal or the subtle universe is the owner of our subtle body. We have technical terms for these cosmic principles, as we find them in the Vedanta philosophy. The whole physical cosmos animated by a coordinated function is called 'Virat'. The internal subtle universal coordinating principle is called 'Hiranyagarbha'.

The individual layers of personality are inseparable, not merely in spirit but even literally, from the existing system of the universe. The physical body having gone to the five elements, the senses going to their divinities, the mind to the moon and the intellect to Brahma, and so on, we will find that there is practically nothing remaining in us, to call our own. We have not only become beggars with nothing belonging to us, but it appears as if our very existence is getting threatened. We cannot exist, even. This seems to be the point towards which we are slowly heading, a most uncomfortable thing for every one of us. We are not going to get even the least recognition of even being an existent entity, let alone as a person with property and individual status. What can be worse for the ego than this?

When all the property has gone a person would at least want to live, but even that we are not going to be conceded. We cannot even live. What does one say to this? The universe wants to swallow us completely even to the utmost extent, and meditation is nothing but a conscious awakening of ourselves to this great truth of our reality belonging to a different order of things and not suddenly getting perplexed or surprised at the revelation of this fact thrust into us by force, by the process of universal history.

All the processes of events we call history, even the processes of birth and death, are only the forceful introductions into ourselves of the law that operates in the universe. If we would not abide by the law - we are not prepared to abide by the law voluntarily and honourably - we are perforce brought into its acceptance by the sufferings through which we pass in life, the sorrows we call our fate, and the penalty of reincarnation.

It is nothing but the urge of the individual to unite itself with the universe that manifests itself as all these events, visible or otherwise. Now we revert to the point with which we started in the beginning. This system of meditation has a cosmological suggestiveness, whereby we may be seated in a calm and sober posture and rouse ourselves to this consciousness of our belonging to all things. We belong to everybody. Literally, we are a property of all things. We are not supposed to have any personal property, because we are a property of all. Nothing belongs to us, but we belong to everybody.

What a change of affairs! Earlier I thought I am the owner; now I realise I am owned by somebody else, and by everyone everywhere. This is the deathblow dealt by knowledge to the ego's complacence. The ego cannot tolerate these things any more. It resents vehemently even a talk about these possibilities. It will hush you up and say "talk not", and then the vehemence of the affirmation of the personality will get stirred up so intensely that, if we are not careful enough to go stage by stage without being in a hurry, there is likely to be a revolt from the ego, a revolt from everything that we are, because we have been accustomed to think in terms of personality and self-affirmation, and today there is none to do it reverence. Our parents teach us false values: "This is your friend, this is your enemy." We are told this from the very childhood. "This is your land, this is not yours, this is your uncle's property, that is your enemy's business." We are told this, and it is told so many times that we get totally brainwashed early. We are taught these very same things in our schools and colleges, so that we become embodiments of stupidity and we know nothing of the true nature of things.

We can imagine what an effort is necessary to counteract this erroneous notion that has become an incrustation on our personalities, a part of our false being. What effort is necessary! Do you think a few minutes of sitting with closed eyes will be of any avail? We have taken many births. In all the births that we have undergone, down to this incarnation, we have been thinking wrongly, and a mountain of errors has grown over our personalities; and now, today, since a few years, or months, or a few days, we have been trying to rectify these errors. If we do not recognise any tangible progress in our practice, we should not be disappointed. We should be able to understand our position. After all, since how long have we been trying to think rightly? For ages and ages we have been thinking wrongly and now since five years or so we have been trying to think at least rightly.

Well, it is a good attempt, and praiseworthy, and we must be happy about it that we are blessed with a proper thought. But we should not be in a mood of melancholy, or disappointedness that no success has come. How can there be visible success when the effort has started only a few years back and there is a huge ocean-like atmosphere which has to be encountered in our meditation? We have to be, however, confident that we are on the right path. Part of the success is in the confidence that we have in our minds. "Yes, now I have understood what the matter is."

This satisfaction of certainty and confidence in our minds is a large percentage of our success, and we will gradually realise that things are not so bad as they appear on the surface. If our heart is really given to this practice with a sincerity that arises on account of a hundred-percent conviction of our going to achieve success, this truth will triumph, and under the law we are bound to succeed. It may be that we may take years to realise tangible results, or it can be that we may achieve results more quickly by the ardour and intensity of the practice. What is conducive to the success is not merely a study of books or listening to discourses but the welling up of feelings, the stirring of the spirit and the ardent longing that we evince in ourselves for the realisation of this truth, which alone is, and nothing else can be.

This ardour of consciousness is the principal prerequisite for success in Yoga, and, in fact, no other qualification is necessary. There is no need for a great academic qualification or a learning in the manner of a library. Nothing of the kind is the essential in Yoga. It is a concentratedness of the whole spirit due to the realisation of this great fact and awakening that matters finally, and in reality.

We have already observed that there must be regularity in practice. There should not be a slip-shod approach to the things of the spirit. Habit strengthens the practice. Anything that is continued daily becomes strong, by the very continuance of it in a systematic manner. What do we think every day? Among the many methods of meditation that may be there, we are to choose only a few, because there is no use burdening our heads with hundreds of techniques. A few essentials will do, from which each individual can select what is suitable to one's own predilection and make-up of the psychic personality.

This, then, is the peculiar technique adopted in Indian systems, by which the various components of the individual personality are recognised to be part and parcel of the different orders of things altogether. To recapitulate, the earth-element in the body goes to the earth; the water-element goes to water, the fire element goes to fire, the air-element goes to air, and what remains is space, which is everywhere.

We have heard chemists and physicists telling us that if one is pumped out of all the space that is within, one's whole material body would be compressed into a cubic centimetre of substance. You are not six feet tall, as you are imagining. There is the space inside, and so you look bulky. If you remove all the space and compress yourself, you will be so little, less than the pigmy of Lilliput. We are not really so important as we appear to be. There is nothing in us, ultimately. We are unnecessarily imagining ourselves and pompously parading our false show in this world of vanity. We would, on analysis, turn out to be empty shells, vainglorious individuals, patting ourselves on the back for nothing, while there is the danger of our being threatened out of our wits by the law that operates.

It is up to us to realise the presence of this universal law, transfer this body to the five elements, and transfer the senses, mind and intellect to the deities. Let the sun take the eyes, the ears go to their divinities, the mind end in the moon, the intellect go to Brahma, the ego merge in Rudra, and the conscience go to Narayana. All things that we are have gone to their causes. 'Pure Being' remains, and there is only an awareness of Being, not the awareness of being so-and-so or such-and-such, but an impersonal characterless continuity of Being as such. This is the point we noted earlier also, the fact of Existence-consciousness-bliss, *Sat-chit-Ananda,* which is our essential nature. We are God-Being in essence.

We are not the body, not the senses, not the mind, not the intellect, not anything of the kind. These are all expressions of the higher order of the universe. What remains in us is not a property or a substance or an object but that basic residuum of truth, which is commensurate with the truth of All-Being. When we go deep down into the base of any wave in the ocean, we will find that we are touching something which is everywhere, that which is at the root of all the waves. When we go down into the barest minimum of our personalities, at the root, we touch that which is within everything also, at the same time, and we, then, need not have any difficulty in universal communication. When this end is achieved, one is supposed to become cosmic-conscious, like the wave becoming ocean-conscious because of the entry of itself into the very substance of it.

At present, we are individually conscious, 'I'-conscious, 'You'-conscious, 'This'-conscious, 'That'-conscious. It is like a this-wave-consciousness, to the exclusion of that wave, but when the wave subsides into the very base of them all, it touches that root, which is the root of all other waves, all individualities. Try to meditate like this. Let the whole wave of your individuality subside into the ocean of Pure Being, and then you become, not merely your being or somebody's being, but All-Being, and this is what is called God-Consciousness. This is what they call *Samadhi,* in technical Yoga terms. This is *Moksha* or liberation. There is no rebirth afterwards, because the causative factor of rebirth, which is the clinging to personality, has gone altogether; it has been dissolved in meditation.

Why should you be reborn into phenomena? Who will force you when you have become the very cause of the entire manifestation of things? This is freedom in the real sense of the term. Until this is achieved, you cannot be regarded as a free person. You are always under the thumb of the universal law that compels you to abide by its requirements. Our so-called political independence or social freedom is no true freedom. We cannot be regarded as really free until we are absolutely independent. And that independence is called *Kaivalya,* Aloneness, with no counterpart of other's aloneness, in which every other aloneness gets subsumed and included. This is the Supreme Goal to which meditation directs us.

The Object of Meditation

The object of meditation is the degree of reality aligned to our state of being. This is a sentence which may appear like an aphorism. We have to meditate only on that which is the exact counterpart of our present level of knowledge and comprehension. There should not be any mistake in the choice of the object. If the object is properly chosen, the mind will spontaneously come under control. The restlessness and the resentment of the mind is due to a wrong choice that is made in the beginning. Often we are too enthusiastic and try to go above our own heads. The mind is not prepared to accept such a sudden revolution which is beyond not only its comprehension but also its present needs or necessities.

There may be many good things in the world, but they may not all be necessary for us. It should not mean that merely because something is grand and great, it should be the proper thing for us all. A thing may be, on the other hand, small and insignificant, but it may be just the thing that we need, and we should not be under the impression that it is a small, petty thing. Often we are happy over petty things, and they cease to be petty when they become our needs, and then they assume an importance. There should be an exercise of proper discrimination; the true rationality of ours has to take possession of us and free us from unnecessary emotions and sentimental exuberances of any kind.

Spiritual seekers are certainly after God. This is very well known. But we must know who is our God. God is the fulfilling counterpart of the present state of our evolution. Anything that is capable of making us complete is our God. Anything that allows us to remain partial is not going to satisfy us. That which completes our personality in any manner, in any degree of its expression, is to be considered as our necessity, and teachers like Patanjali, who were great psychologists, have taken note of this important suggestion to be imparted to students.

We are not asked to jump at once to the great theological doctrines of the creator of the cosmos. That would go above our minds. The teachings remain merely as theories and gospels in books. We have internal necessities of a peculiar nature. We have psychological hungers and thirsts which project themselves from our feelings, apart from the hunger and thirst of the physiological system. The mind, too, hungers and thirsts. Emotions also hunger and thirst. Sentiments hunger and thirst, and whatever we are made of has its own hunger and thirst. We cannot regard these as devils that have to be exorcised and thrown out. Such a mistake is not to be committed in the scientific approach called Yoga meditation. The more are we cautious, the greater is the chance of our success. The more are we emotional and miss the point, the greater is the chance of reversion and retrogression and a feeling of failure.

Our problems are our desires, and they have to be tackled in a very careful way. Some of them may have to be fulfilled immediately. One may be having a very strong urge from within to have a cup of tea, for instance, and then one should not be stupid enough to say "I am a spiritual seeker, I am not going to take this cup of tea", even when the impulse is annoying. So is the case with medicines, when one is ill. Some of the desires are simple, harmless, physiological and have to be fulfilled in a systematic manner - not with the intention of indulging in them but with the higher purpose of subduing them. Sublimation of desires is to be distinguished from a suppression or repression of them, because the latter is harmful to one's wholesome growth.

There are other desires which are either meaningless or impossible of attainment, and they have to be sublimated with the strength of understanding. They have no sense, practically, and are just crotchets of the head of a person. But these are more difficult things to understand than the ordinary, simple desires. These idiosyncrasies, as we may call them, are harder things to tackle because they are more internal than these external appearances of the normal desires. They are part of our sentiments, emotions, or ego and here we require an expert guidance from a master, a teacher, who has to act not only as a physician but as a psychotherapist in the above circumstances.

The more internal we go, the greater is the need we will feel for guidance outwardly. One may look all right and not feel the need for any kind of assistance from others. But the internal forces are more difficult to subdue and handle. They are impetuous, uncontrollable. The desires which are of this character have to be sublimated with a great analytical understanding by the study of scriptures, resort to holy company, isolation and self-investigation, and methods of this nature. Thus, and in these similar ways, we have to check up the strings which connect us with the world. They cannot be snapped suddenly; they can only be thinned out so that they break later on due to the feebleness of these threads.

One cannot cut off a strong bond, just as one cannot sever a limb of one's body, or peel one's own skin. The desires are so much part of oneself that they can only be compared to the limbs of one's body and to remove them at one stroke with violence would be something unimaginable. Desires which are forcefully cast out like devils can work havoc afterwards, because they are actually driven down to the unconscious. They are not cast outside in space, as one imagines. They are pushed inside, which is still worse. Unfulfilled desires are not going to keep quiet and live in the space outside. They go inside and remain in a seed form and may manifest themselves when there is suitable rainfall, and then they sprout and germinate into living creepers once again; and even after years and years, nay, even after births, they can demand satisfaction.

Desires are like creditors, who cannot simply be shunted off with a 'no'. They are to be paid their dues, either by an actual disbursement of their parts, or by a reconciliation with them in some intelligent manner. The object of meditation is not necessarily the highest God of the universe, at once, in the beginning itself, though we may call our object of meditation as our God, for the time being. This concept of the degrees of reality or the necessity to consider the object of meditation as a deity in itself under every degree of manifestation has led to the notion of the many gods of religion. Often we say that some religions are polytheistic since so many gods are there. There are, in fact, not many gods. They are only the necessary acceptances on the part of the individual of degrees in the concept of reality. They are not many gods, but the many stages of acceptance. It does not, however, mean that the one God has many degrees. There are no partitions in the existence of the Absolute. But there appear to be partitions distinguishable one from the other in the degrees of concept because of the distinguishing layers existing in our own psychic personality. The degrees are in us and not in the reality.

There are not, actually, degrees of reality, as it is sometimes thought. There are degrees in the consciousness of reality, degrees of the perception of reality, degrees of our capacity to understand the nature of reality. So, the gods come into existence and our God can be anything that attracts us as an absolutely essential item under the conditions in which we are placed. When one is seriously ill, a particular medicine may be required, though that medicine has nothing to do with one's spiritual life, apparently. But it is not true. Anything that sustains one and enables one to live a wholesome life is God revealed in one degree.

One cannot say easily what is spiritual and what is unspiritual, if one only goes deep into things. All is a question of understanding the relevance that a particular thing has with our mind, our consciousness, our being as a whole. In the Sutras connected with the subject, Patanjali gives suggestions for varying types of concentration on the requirements of the seeker under different conditions.

When one is in these stages of the choice of the object of meditation, one requires guidance from someone who is competent, who has trodden the path, who knows the pitfalls, who has seen the difficulties and known the remedies for the problems. The seeker is treading an unknown path, a path whose future is completely out of sight; he cannot know what is ahead of him, and therefore, the need for guidance and timely instruction and assistance of a personal nature, from a Guru.

A Guru is not a professor or a schoolmaster. He is intimately related to the disciple's very existence. People have many Gurus these days, but that is not what we mean by a real Guru. One who has spiritually taken charge of the soul of the disciple is the Guru, and not merely one who gives an intellectual instruction and goes away. Tradition considers the relation between the Guru and the disciple to be a perpetual one until the salvation of the soul is reached. The Guru helps, not merely in this life, but even in the future life, because the relationship is not social. It is not even merely psychological; it is spiritual.

The choice of the object of meditation, to come to the point again, is an important aspect of the very beginning of spiritual life. This choice is the initiation that the disciple receives from the teacher. What is called initiation in the mysteries of the practice of Yoga is nothing but the initiation of one's spiritual being into the technique of tuning oneself to that particular deity, the form of God, or the object which is going to be one's target at the present moment. This is a secret by itself and the teacher will teach it to the disciple. The object of meditation should satisfy the student; that is why it is called 'Ishta Devata' (loved deity). The 'Ishta' is that which is desirable, beautiful, attractive, required, that which attracts one's love and one's whole being. One pours one's self into it. One likes it so much that one cannot like anything else as much as that. 'Ishta' is the beloved. 'Devata' is deity. It is a deity because it is one's God. It is that thing which one really requires, so that without it one cannot exist.

That which causes a cessation of one's restlessness, satisfies one's whole being and not merely one's sentiment, is one's Devata or deity. And it is most lovable: obviously one cannot have love for anything else under the circumstances. An Ishta-Devata is a chosen Deity over which one pours one's emotion and love and affection. Now, what connection has this Ishta-Devata with God, the Creator, the Almighty?

Everything has a connection with everything else. There is nothing which is not internally related to the Almighty, the

Supreme Being. Every atom is so related, and every atom can be a teacher under given conditions. We can touch God through every speck of space, because there is no such thing as a universe outside God. God is in everything that is experienced here as the world, or the universe, pervading and permeating all things, so that one cannot touch anything without touching God in some way. There should not be any misconception that the deities, even the images, the so-called idols that the people worship, are all just nonsense or insignificant nothings; these are necessary prescriptions for the illness of the spirit in the stages of its evolution.

We see people changing their aims constantly. They cannot stick to any particular scripture, ideal or teacher. They cannot stick to a Mantra, cannot stick to a method, cannot stick to a place, cannot stick to anything. There is a perfunctory external touch with the ideal of life and not a going deep into it. The choice of the object of meditation is a final act and once we make this choice, we have to adhere to it, and there should be no misgivings. There should be no doubt in the mind if a wrong choice has been made. The choice is to be considered as correct when it has been made by a teacher. Secondly, any object can take one to anything, because of the connection it has with all things. What is required is deep concentration. We can dig the earth at any place and we will find water, provided we go deep enough. We have to go to the oceanic level at the bottom.

Thus a concentration on the chosen ideal or the given object, wholeheartedly, continuously and regularly for a lifetime, is essential. It would be a wonder to hear stories of great saints and sages who are supposed to have spoken even to idols, to inanimate matter, a bronze idol, or a stone image. How can matter speak? It speaks because of its getting charged with the spirit of the consciousness of concentration. Nothing non-material exists in the world, finally. Matter is sleeping consciousness. What we call the inanimate is the slumbering Absolute, and it can be awakened by a deep concentration of consciousness. The awakening takes place when the consciousness gets communed, but the object appears as a material thing as long as it is outside consciousness in space and time. So one should not be too much fidgeting about the propriety in the choice of the object of meditation.

Once the choice has been made, it has to be adhered to, and the student will succeed. The object has to be such as would satisfy the emotions. It should satisfy even the intellect and reason. There should not be a resentment from any side of our nature. Sometimes it may so happen that the emotions may like the choice but the intellect does not agree, and when the intellect agrees the emotions do not. It is necessary that there must be a blend of these aspects of our inner being; the emotion and the reason should accept the propriety of one's having made this choice. "Yes, this is the thing meant for me, and for such and such a reason." The intellect always seeks a rational justification, a confirming logic.

The head and the heart have to be in unison. Then there is a coming together of the understanding and the feelings, and meditation is nothing but this union of the understanding and the feelings in respect of the object that is chosen as the finale of one's life. Mere intellectual deliberation is not meditation. Thinking of some object intellectually cannot be called meditation. In meditation there is a total atonement of the whole of being with the object that is chosen as the great aim. Whatever we are made of or constituted of has to take part in this concentrated effort. There should be a wholesale conscription, as it were, of all the parts of the personality, and every part is involved in this universal cause.

There should be no reluctance on the side of any part of our being in this act of concentration. There should be no difficulty felt in this whole-souled attention on the object. The reluctance arises on account of a mistaken choice, when some part of the personality has felt the need for the object and the others have not felt that it is so essential. We have to bring our forces round, by some method which is apt under the circumstances.

We know how one has to work in order to reconcile people. There are variegated types of personalities in this world. How will one reconcile them? One person does not agree with the other, but if one has to live a peaceful existence in this world of human societies, some sort of arrangement for reconciliation of opposites has to be made, and it has to be done in an intelligent manner, for the good of all. This technique of a reconciliation of differences among the aspects of a thing has to be adopted. If we take time to do this, there is no harm. It does not mean that, today itself, everything has to be done. We may take one month to come to a conclusion as to what that suitable object is.

But once the object is chosen properly, the mind will certainly rush towards it, because it is the thing it needs. Sometimes, it may be difficult to find one single object which can satisfy every part of our nature, even as we cannot have only one article of diet which can satisfy hunger, thirst and every requirement of the body. In the earlier stages, it may be necessary to resort to different kinds of concentration with the intention of reconciling them and bringing them together. The programme of our daily Sadhana may have to be spread out to some extent in some manner which will fulfil the various needs of the self.

One may have many other requirements of this nature, such as a desire for study and learning, a desire to go on pilgrimage to holy places or to see a great saint or a sage. Now, all these urges have to be fulfilled in an organised manner. They become essentials on account of their pressing nature. They have to be paid their dues. Thus, in the beginning, it need not necessarily be a single object, literally, but there can be a group of various aspects - we need not call them various objects - which are really aspects of a single intention that is behind the mind, all which may commingle later on into a single object. It is necessary, in the earlier stages, to go slowly and have three, four or five items for the purpose of practice, such as Japa, or chanting of a Mantra, a formula, which has been given by the Guru, or which occurs in a scripture.

Japa can be of a single word, or a group of words or letters, which is called a Mantra or a formula. This practice is necessary because it is difficult to keep the mind elevated always in a high vision of thought. It often comes down to lower levels. To stir it up to a consciousness of the higher levels of being, one requires constant instruction and habituation to one thought. If one does not have a personal Guru to instruct constantly, one has to resort to the secondary method of studying. One takes to a concentrated study of scriptures which will inspire the mind at once. This will prepare the attention for Japa, or recitation of the sacred formula or Mantra.

Swadhyaya is sacred study. This does not mean study of books from libraries. One generally sees the catalogue and whatever appeals to the sentiments is picked up and one starts reading a novel or an encyclopaedia. But Swadhyaya is a religious, dedicated study. It is not just a gathering of information from several tomes. It is not a historical survey that we are making of doctrines, religions and philosophies. It is rather a meditation by itself. Only it is a little spread-out type of meditation, not so much concentrated as the purely technical absorption.

These spread-out types are more diversified forms of meditation, and they are the studies that we make. In a book that we so study, there are various ideas which entertain the mind and do not bore it with one thought on a monotony. The vastly spread ideas which are expressed in the scriptures are meant to tend towards one point, in the end.

Though many things are told us in the scriptures, they are told for a single purpose. The mind gradually converges upon a single point of attention. When we read the Bhagavadgita, for instance, with all the details throughout the chapters, we will find there one ringing note into which we are introduced finally, at the end. But the crucial point cannot be revealed immediately, because we want variety. So, people take to Bhajans, Kirtans, singing, etc., in the methods of Bhakti-Yoga especially. While these provide us with an entertainment by way of a diversity, they have a very pious and spiritual motive behind, of allowing the mind to concentrate on a single object. The Japa of the formula or a Mantra, the study of a scripture, sequestration and holy company, attending Satsangas of great souls wherever it is possible, are all to be regarded as parts of our meditation, because they are needed by certain aspects of our personality.

Our personality is very complex. It is constituted of different items of creation and they all ask for satisfaction of one type or the other. We have to move gradually, stage by stage, to transcend ourselves. The practice should not be any sudden assertive renunciation in the form of rejection of values, but it should be a growth of the personality into a wholeness which has overcome the lower, not rejected the lower. This is important to remember. We do not reject things but overcome them by understanding, by fulfilment and an increase of comprehension. Spiritual life is not a rejection of values but a fulfilment of values, a fulfilment for the purpose of the transcendence of values. This is a healthy method, and most positive, to which we have to resort as an aid to meditation.

The Abstraction of the Senses

The most renowned technique of meditation is, of course, that which is propounded in the system of sage Patanjali, because this system of practice takes into consideration almost all the aspects of human nature. The well-known stages, *viz.*, Asana, Pranayama, Pratyahara, Dharana, Dhyana and Samadhi, are gradational attunements of the individual with the cosmos.

We usually do Asanas, practise Pranayama, and sit for meditation with a wrong notion at the very back, namely, that we are human beings, persons unconnected with other people and absolutely not related to the world at all, so that when one does Pranayama, it is his nostrils and lungs that operate; it is his business, and it has nothing to do with others. This is not the attitude intended by sage Patanjali when he asked us to do Yoga, because the rationale behind it will quickly get missed if one thinks that it is merely a personal physical exercise, like football and games of other sorts.

Why, even the physical exercises, even the Asanas, which are apparently connected with the body, are not a bodily exercise merely, particularly so in the case of that group of Asanas which have connection with meditation. The Asanas that are spoken of in the system of Patanjali are directly related to meditation, because the aim of Yoga is meditation. Anything that we do is finally towards that end. It does not mean that meditation will start after some time, a few years later, and today we will do Asanas for the flexibility of the body and the training of the muscles and nerves. No, the Asanas have to sow the seed, even in the very beginning, of the essential spirit of the end of all Yoga.

There is a basic spiritual impulse injected into the very root of the practice. The body, the mind, the senses and the intellect are the things that are trained properly in Asanas, Pranayama, Pratyahara, Dharana and Dhyana. We have to know what these processes actually mean. They are, in essence, methods of harmonisation of the different layers of the personality, the body, the Prana, the senses, the mind and the intellect, and finally, the Spirit in which last step one takes a plunge into the Absolute.

The Asana that is connected with meditation is the art of the stabilisation of the physical body, because meditation is a stabilising process, a gradually ascending movement of increased intensity and expansiveness. But every stage is a stage of stabilisation of that particular level of experience in which one is at a given moment.

We have already seen that we are in a human society. We are not just in the body alone, locked up, as if in a prison. We are social units, a subject with which we have dealt earlier, and which is the theme of the practice of the Yamas and Niyamas. Our relationship with human society and the behaviour of our own body are the concerns of the practices known as Yama and Niyama.

The Asana is a higher degree of practice. It is not the beginning of Yoga, for it is the third step of the ascent. From this, we can imagine what an importance is there attributed to this system of practice known as Asana, though it appears to be concerned with the body alone. The Asana that is connected with meditation is the culmination of the practice of all other Asanas such as Sirshasana, Sarvangasana, Matsyasana, etc. They all, finally, tend towards a complete stabilisation of the individual frame. It is for this purpose that the other Asanas are advised to be practised. They are not ends in themselves but act as means to another end, the capacity to totally fix oneself in that particular seated posture which is requisite for meditation. Otherwise, when one is seated, the body may become fidgety, and there can be aches and distractions of the muscular system.

Even at the very outset, Patanjali gives instructions which have a spiritual connotation. When he speaks of Asana, the principle of contemplation is somehow tacked on even there. One cannot be seated in a physical posture for a long time unless the mind is agreeable to this procedure. If the mind is dissenting, we cannot sit in one posture, as emotional disturbance or mental occupation, anxiety, or worry is likely to act as an obstacle even to a seated posture. We know very well what an important role the mind plays in relation to the body. There is no need to comment on this matter. If the mind is disturbed for any reason, can one sit in a stable posture? One would then get up and go for a walk, rather than sit quietly.

The mind has to collaborate with the intention of the body, and vice versa. That is why Patanjali mentions in one aphorism that the mind has to think of infinitude even when one tries to sit in a posture. The idea of infinitude has a great influence upon the way of the stabilisation of the body. Distractions, whatever be their nature, are caused by the presence of objects. The directing of the mind towards things outside is the distraction. Whether the mind is forced by the presence of the objects to move in the direction of the objects or the mind deliberately moves because of its desires - whatever be the reason - the presence of the objects, or rather the consciousness of the presence of the objects, is the reason behind the distraction.

The thought of infinity (Ananta-Samapatti), as the term used in the relevant Sutra of Patanjali suggests, is the secret. The contemplation on the infinite, conceptually of course, is what is to be understood here. We cannot actually grasp the infinite as it is in itself, but we can entertain an idea of the conceptual infinite, which will stabilise the mind automatically, which means to say that the mind attempts to feel its presence in the atmosphere around and also to feel the harmony of the atmosphere with its own self. And, thus, a rapprochement is established between the mind and the world.

You will be surprised that when the mind is completely contented, it is satisfied thoroughly, and there is an automatic stabilization of the mind. The mind affects the body to such an extent that the vibrations produced in the mind on account of its activity, passing through the nervous system and the muscles, can change the very conduct of the body. Even when we are seated in the posture here when I talk of the posture, I am referring to the posture concerning meditation and not the other exercises—the mind gets stirred in some way. When we are seated in the meditating posture, the mind has to realise that it is preparing itself for meditation, and it cannot be prepared for meditation unless its pre-requisites are fulfilled. These requisites are well-known things.

A satisfaction which frees the mind from anxiety and insecurity is the foremost essential. For, a dissatisfied mind, in any way whatsoever, is unfit for meditation. We cannot sit merely with the hope that meditation will bring the needed result. It is true that meditation brings satisfaction but the mind will not go for meditation at all because of the basic distractions which pull it down to the level of the earth. So Patanjali does not ask us to jump to the highest peak of contemplation, or what is called *Samapatti,* or *Samadhi*. He advises the practice of lower techniques and the simple methods of harmony so that every stage of Yoga becomes a stage of satisfaction.

It is no more painful to us, and we need not be frightened. This process is not a struggle but a gradual flow with the natural atmosphere of meditation. Whenever one feels uneasiness on the thought of meditation or when one is attempting at the practice, one has to realise that there is a frustrated background of the mind. The mind is not so eager to go to meditation, because it has other interests. Concentration is the consequence of interest and right appreciation. The Yamas and Niyamas are not to be regarded as insignificant stages. They are the very foundations of the entire edifice of further practice. We know the importance of the foundation of a building. It is on the rock-bottom of correct perspective that the structure of all Yoga is raised.

It is advisable to go slowly, with caution, in regard to the various strings that connect us with the objects of sense, and to deal with these connections in a rational manner, and never act in haste. "Haste makes waste", is an old adage. There is a necessity to be judicious and scientific, gradual and slow and cautious, because the more are we systematic and careful in our approach, the greater is the chance of our moving further and the lesser the chance of retrogression or a fall back. Else there can be a sudden reversal to the level which has been turned a deaf ear to on account of over-enthusiasm or an emotional adventure.

There is an internal mechanism which pulls us outside in the direction of objects, and it has to be set in tune with the higher atmosphere, and not the external one. The mechanism is constituted of the senses, the mind and the intellect which work through the Prana directly connected with the body. The body which is formed of muscles, nerves, etc., is set into motion by the Prana, as electricity moves the vehicle through which it passes. We may compare Prana with electric energy to some extent.

It is subtler than electrical energy, but for the time being we can regard it as something like that. And when the body is charged with Prana-Shakti, it assumes life. When we say that the body is alive, what we mean is that the Prana is entirely present in every part of the body. When we say the wire is live, we mean to say that the live-wire is charged with electricity. So is this body. Without the Prana, the body is a corpse. If the Prana is not functioning in a particular limb of the body, there is numbness and a paralytic stroke affecting that particular part; there is lifelessness and one will not even know that it is there.

The Prana, therefore, is the liaison between the inner structure of the psyche and the vehicle that we are carrying, lumbering with the load that we are having with us. The body is like a cart. It is simply a vehicle driven with an engine inside, the Prana, but the Prana works in a peculiar manner. Even as the movement of the wheels of a vehicle is dependent on the way in which the steering is moved, the Prana is directed by the mind. The Prana acts as a kind of instrument, in the same way as the body acts as an instrument.

The Prana is the energy that impinges upon the particular thing which is the intention of the mind and the senses. When I think of you and look at you, my Prana is supposed to have an impact on you. When you look at an object, it is not an impersonal activity that is going on. You are affecting it in some manner. If your gazing is deliberate, concentrated and purposive, there is a telepathic action taking place then, and the Prana shakti is driven from your personality to that particular thing, the object, which you are gazing at intentionally.

Thus, the Prana, though it is working within the body, is also distracted in the direction of the things towards which the senses compel it to move. While the Prana is internal to the body, the senses are internal to the Prana. You may be wondering, what are these senses? You must have heard that there are the eyes, ears, etc. The eyes and ears that we speak of are not merely fleshy organs, like the eyeballs, eardrums, etc. The senses that we are referring to here have the power to control the working of the Prana, and are, again, impulsions from inside.

The senses are ramifications of thought itself. They are the powers injected by the mind through the apertures of these organs, the eyeballs, eardrums, and the like. These organs are only external locations through which the energy of the mind is charged out and the senses are only names we give to the various rays of the mind which have action upon the Prana, which, again, in turn, has its action on the body, and on society outside.

In the practice of the Asanas and Pranayama, therefore, the body and the mind are taken into consideration simultaneously. But, while doing this, we cannot forget the psychic pattern inside, and it is important that the mind has to be satisfied even at the time of the practice of the Asana for meditation, and it is also true in the case of Pranayama, with greater effect.

The more we go inside, the greater is the caution that we have to exercise. While there is difficulty in seating oneself in a fixed posture when the mind is disturbed, there will be a greater difficulty in practising Pranayama if the mind is distracted. Not only will there be difficulty, but there can be even danger. There can be a resentment of the Prana to such an extent that it may ruin the health of the person. And if the Pranayama is coupled with retention, so much the worse for it, because it will be like forcing a river to go back, against its current and flow. Hence, in the earlier stages, no retention should be practised during Pranayama, *i.e.*, only deep inhalation and deep exhalation should be resorted to, because no one can say that everything is perfectly all right with one's emotions or that one is perfectly desireless. For some months one may practise only deep inhalation and deep exhalation. This is good for health, and it will somehow assist in the retention of the breath finally, though gradually.

We might be surprised that the system of Patanjali does not lay much stress on Asana and Pranayama as the Hathayoga-Pradipika, etc., do. This is so because Patanjali is more concerned with the basic factor of meditation, the mind. The whole of the system of Patanjali is primarily psychological. It aims at the higher objects more than the lesser ones in the scale of evolution. For, it is perfectly acceptable to reason that when the higher layers are satisfied, the lower ones automatically get controlled. But if the higher ones are ignored, the lower levels go amuck. So a direct attack upon the mind is the real intention of Patanjali's system, though he accepts that the lower stages are important enough in their own way, and allows the student a graduated passage from the level of social involvement onwards through the levels of the personality.

The disconnection of the senses from their objects is called *Pratyahara*. It is not merely a forceful withdrawal but a kind of sublimation that is effected through the very cessation of desire for objects. In the commentary on the Sutras of Patanjali certain hints are given regarding the withdrawal of the senses. There is a gross form of it, a subtle form, and a spiritual form. The gross form of withdrawal is the wilful intention to "think not" the object but think something else, instead. You compel the mind not to think of the object, first of all, by physically dissociating it from the atmosphere in which the objects are located. This is why people go to solitary places for internal peace. They want to be physically away from things and environments which are distracting. That is a force which one applies upon the mind. It is not that one has no desire for the objects but here one wants to physically disconnect oneself from even the perception of the objects, as an initial and tentative measure of sense-abstraction. This is the grossest form of *Pratyahara*.

But the subtler aspect of it is to educate the mind into a knowledge of the mistake that it is committing when it entertains the notion that some advantage accrues by contact with objects. Why does the mind go towards the objects? Why does it order the senses to come in contact with things outside? There is a benefit accruing from coming in contact with desirable things. Every business in life is based on some idea of profit. If nothing comes, who will do anything? The mind rather feels that something that is good will come out by a contact of the objects through senses. However, there is a mistake in this way of thinking. It is not true that some advantage accrues, really speaking, by any amount of contact in space and time.

It appears that there is a satisfaction. But it is only an appearance and not a reality. This is an education that we have to impart to the mind. It will not accept these arguments easily. If you tell the mind, "No, you are making a mistake, do not go on blundering thus," it will not understand what you are speaking. Even a child will not accept the advice, "Do not go to the fire, do not touch the flames," for it does not know what is fire and what are flames. It has to get burnt in order to learn the lesson.

But by deep study, *Svadhyaya*, by true education one can rationally convince oneself of the futility of this so-called craving of the mind for gaining advantage from contact with objects. And what is the advantage? A surge of joy is what anyone seeks, in the end. And it is sought in things of sense. But is it true that there is joy? That is what we have to ponder over. Or, are we under a delusion? Usually, the mind will not accept that it is under the spell of an illusion. What, then, is the causative factor that has worked in the rousing of a fog of satisfaction in the mind when one apparently comes in contact with things? Here is a psychology with which the mind is not acquainted.

There is an obvious error in imagining that objects bring satisfaction. And, finally, there is a metaphysical error and a spiritual blunder involved in the notion of deriving happiness from things. The psychological mistake is patent. What happens to people who run after things in the world? They are perpetually in a state of anxiety. In the case of people who run after money, for instance, there is always an anxiety, a restlessness and an agitation in the mind. There is an anxiety as to how the object could be obtained. The world does not belong to you, and it is not anyone's property. Yet everybody claims it as his property. There is a tussle among people for proprietorship of things. This is why there is a social conflict everywhere. Everyone wants everything. Now, it is not possible that everybody can get everything on the very face of it. Thus, apart from social conflict, there is also a psychological background of sorrow.

The great anxiety preceding the attempted acquisition of an object cannot be regarded as a state of happiness. Man is anxious how he can find ways and means to grab the objects of his desire. That anxiety is not equivalent to satisfaction, for it is unhappiness unadulterated. When the object is acquired, there is, again, an anxiety, which is of a different nature, because one knows that one cannot possess anything for a long time. Things are made in such a way that they can be taken away from us by natural causes or other factors of life. There is a possibility of deprivation of possession even after one's having it with so much of worry and strain.

There is another anxiety: how to keep things intact. There is a preceding anxiety and also a succeeding anxiety. But there is something more serious involved in this, a third factor. Even that temporary satisfaction of possession is a false one. An illusion or mirage has been counted for a reality. Yes, there has resulted a fiasco in all this.

What happens is one thing and what we are thinking is another thing. What is it that is really happening, when there is a joy emanating from within one's self at the time of the contact of itself with a desired object? Something mysterious is taking place, which the mind is not able to understand. Let us not go into the psychology of this situation just now, but think of the outer aspect of it. Take for one moment the example of a particular thing which you like immensely and which you regard as the source of your joy. If this satisfaction is really the characteristic of the object, it should attract everyone, naturally. Everyone would jump on that object instantly. But it is not true that what is apparently the intended object behind one's mind is the object expected by other people also. On the other hand, the reverse may be the case. That which you like may be hated by someone else.

It can be the object of aversion in the case of other people, whereas in your case it is an object of intense like. Not only that; even in your own case, it is not true that you like only one thing. Why is it that you change your mind? Do you desire the same thing today which you liked twenty years ago? And do you think that after a few years you will be for the thing which you are hankering for today? Why is the mind changing thus, if the object has the inherent characteristic of satisfying it? The object, therefore, is to be considered not as the true source of satisfaction, but only an instrument that stirs up certain functions in the mind, and the so-called satisfaction is not an emanation from the object, but a reaction that is set up mutually between the structure and location of the object and the condition of the mind at that particular moment of time.

While the presence of the object may be necessary for evoking a feeling of joy in the mind, it is the evocation of the feeling that is more important than just the presence of the object. The finale to which we are driven in this analysis is that happiness comes from within; it does not come from without.

How, then, is it possible that when I eat a sweet mango I feel a satisfaction? How can I say that the happiness comes from inside, when it is clear that it has come from the mango? Does not the mind know this? Yes, but it is also true that it does not come entirely from the mango. The fruit has acted only as a kind of spade to dig out the treasure that is inside. A suitable instrument has been applied and the suitability of the instrument cannot be equated with the presence of pleasure in it.

What has happened is really something different. The mind has been contemplating the object for a reason which is beyond the field of psychology. It is, in fact, a metaphysical event. At the time of the contemplation of the object, the consciousness was turned away from its own source. The selfhood of consciousness was converted into an object-hood for the time being. The subject became the object for a short time, and the moment one loses consciousness of oneself and becomes conscious of something else, one is anxious and is in sorrow. Grief is loss of consciousness of self.

The more one loses oneself, loses contact with one's own source, the more is one grief-stricken. The greater the intensity of the desire, the greater is the sorrow attending upon it, because the intensity of the desire implies an equal extent of turning away of consciousness from its own source. If the desire for an object is one hundred percent intense, one has lost oneself totally. One is a complete loser of oneself, and that is a veritable hell. But if the attraction is of some lower percentage, the sorrow, too, is, then, equally of that percentage.

The possession of the object tentatively makes the mind feel that there is no further need to move away from the source in the direction of the object. The complete possession of an object immediately puts an end to the movement of the mind in the direction of the object. When the mind ceases to think of the object, the consciousness that was driven towards the object returns to its source. Then one is possessed of one's own self. The example generally given in texts to illustrate this point is the instance of a dog licking a bone piece which is having thorns in it, and the dog's tongue getting torn because of the pricking bone, blood oozing out from its own tongue, the dog imagining that the blood comes from the flesh sticking to the bone and so licking still more.

The beast licks the blood that comes out of its own tongue, but the idiot does not know that it is its own blood coming out, and it is licking itself alone. But the dog is so foolish that it thinks it comes from the bone, and licks more on the thorny piece. All happiness comes from within, but we are under the impression that it is rising from the object, and so run after the thing further more, like the dog that goes to the bone. The cessation of the desire, tentatively brought about on account of the notion in the mind that the object is possessed, is the cause of happiness, not the object.

For all these reasons, and many others, the mind should be told that there is a mistake in the contemplation of objects and consciously nobody would fall into a pit. The mind jumps into the pit unconsciously under the impression that it is all velvet, but under this cover there is a well dug for its own ruin. The mind has to be enlightened about this fact. This is the psychological secret that is unearthed to help us in the practice of *Pratyahara*, the withdrawal of the mind from objects, a little more useful and advanced method than the forceful turning away from things, physically.

But the highest kind of *Pratyahara* is the non-awareness of the presence of things themselves. You are not even aware that things exist. There is no necessity to withdraw the mind here. The non-awareness of externality arises on account of the positive consciousness of a larger universality. You have not deliberately withdrawn the mind. The mind has not felt the need for contemplating things. You do not think of anything in the world, though the things are there. Do you know how many things exist in this world? Are you all thinking of them? No, because you are not concerned with them. You are thinking only of those things with which you are related. And, if your concern is a larger reality, with a greater comprehensiveness and profundity, the necessity to think of externalities drops off automatically. Hence, this inward rising of the consciousness to the higher level of apprehension is the true *Pratyahara*. The lesser the force that is exerted upon the mind in *Pratyahara*, the greater is the success, and the quality of it. It should be a spontaneous process of acceptance, deliberately with delight. It should not be an imposition upon the mind by social dogmas or religious mandates.

So is the case with *Dharana* or concentration. *Dharana* is concentration, and *Dhyana* is meditation. In all this, there is always a positivity of approach. It is not that you deliberately give pain to the mind, severing its relationship with things, whether in concentration or meditation. You give joy to it, rather. Instead of telling the mind, "I am not going to give you this", you may better say, "I am going to give you this". There are people who admonish, "You should not do that. Don't touch, don't look", and so on. The mind does not like these instructions. Negativity is abhorred. Many of our religious doctrines are "do's and don'ts". Religions have become too much social and ethical and have lost the spiritual meaning behind them. So there is an agitation in the mind.

It is not happy. Therefore, it is necessary to introduce positivity into the practice, spirituality into the very concept of meditation. And as you go further you will realise that the whole teaching of Patanjali in the art of meditation is an entire positivity everywhere. There is nothing of the negative in it. In the later stages known as *Samapatti* or *Samadhi*, which form the real Yoga, there is a fullness of experience and bliss. The stages we are discussing now are the earlier preparations for gaining entry into the higher training in the form of the union that has to be established later. In an advanced stage you do not dissociate yourself from anything. On the other hand, you associate yourself with everything. So, Yoga, although it is a process of dissociation apparently in the earlier stages, is really a union of all the components of the personality with everything in creation.

Towards Absorption

We have been moving along the lines of Patanjali's system of Yoga, to culminate in meditation. In the same way as the other systems of Yoga have their own techniques, Patanjali has a novel method. He has prescribed various psychological techniques of controlling the mind, all which are supposed to tend finally to a cosmic type of meditation. The true Yoga of Patanjali commences with what he calls *Samyama, Samapatti,* or *Samadhi.* We are likely to be surprised that Yoga should start with Samadhi, rather than end with it.

The reason behind this definition that "Yoga is Samadhi" is that Yoga is essentially a method as well as the attainment of union with reality. The great revolution spiritually takes place when *Samyama* starts. Until that time one is just a novice in Yoga. The terms *Samyama, Samapatti* and *Samadhi* are not identical in their literal meanings or even in their particular connotations. They signify different shades of implication in the process of self-absorption.

Only an expert who has mastered the entire technique can take to Samyama or total concentration. The word "Samyama" has a specific intention and it is used in the system of Patanjali to designate a whole and thorough concentration of self on the given object. There are two difficulties in the practice of Samyama, *viz.*, the procedure to be adopted in collecting oneself into an integration or wholeness of being, and the art by which to conceive the object of meditation itself. Both these are problems enough.

While in ordinary types of concentration, a faculty may be utilised for the purpose on hand, in Samyama it is not merely one of the psychic faculties that is employed, but the whole of one's being. To prepare yourself for this total concentration called Samyama, you are asked to train yourself in the lesser types of concentration which go by the name of Dharana and Dhyana, the art of fixing your attention on any given thing, for the matter of that, to the exclusion on any other thought.

A distinction has got be drawn between the stages of Dharana, Dhyana and Samadhi - concentration, meditation and absorption or union. The stages gradually intensify themselves as they go higher and higher. But they are not basically different in their qualitative essence. In the art of concentration, in the technique of fixing the attention, Dharana, there are only four aspects, and the four become three, finally converging into a single continuity of experience, wherein even the duality is not experienced. In Dharana, or mere attention or concentration, there are four simultaneous practices involved.

The exclusion of all extraneous thoughts is the first thing to be done in Dharana. Thoughts which are irrelevant to the task on hand, ideas which have no vital connection with the idea that you are expected to entertain, feelings which have no real connection and which are not going to be helpful in any way, are to be regarded as extraneous and are to be shut out. This shutting out of extraneous thoughts is the first step in concentration.

The next stage is to gather together those ideas which are positively necessary for the purpose of concentration. Even among the ideas that are necessary there may be a diversity. It does not mean that you have only one thought always, for there may be many thoughts in the mind. Suppose you are going to concentrate on a tree. You know very well that it is not only one thought that is there in the mind at this moment. There are various thoughts meeting at a total of the thought of the tree. When you look at a painted picture or any other object, you have various ideas connected with that object.

These are the positive ideas as different from the negative ones which are the extraneous features to be shut out, yet maintaining a variegatedness requiring to be brought together into a focus. When you think of a tree, you may have the thought of the seed from which it has arisen, the way in which it has grown, the nature of the trunk, the branches, the foliage, etc. All these varieties of thoughts concerning the tree, which is the object on hand, have an internal relationship among themselves though they appear to be diversified on account of the variety of structure in name and form. The emphasis on this internal relation is the second step.

The third aspect is the concentration on the structure of the object itself. The objective side is as important as the subjective. You bring together all the thoughts that are necessary, positively, to fix the attention on the object, and then try to visualise the object in an impersonal manner, *i.e.*, as the object is in its own status and not as it appears to your mind. Everything has its own status. You will see that there is a difference between the way in which I think of you and the way in which you think of yourself, or rather, to put it more precisely, the status of your own individuality. The subjective ideas of the object are to be set in harmony with the objective nature of the object.

Herein is involved the connection between yourself and the object. This is the subject of Epistemology, the process of sensation, perception, cognition, etc. All these take place simultaneously as it were in Dharana, or concentration, though they are capable of being distinguished one from the other, theoretically, or logically. But, in practice, they appear to suddenly arise as events in the mind. But when you go further, when concentration deepens, when attention becomes meditation, when Dharana becomes Dhyana, the four aspects boil down only to three. There is no necessity to worry about the extraneous thoughts now. They have been shut out completely and now you are wholly absorbed in the idea of the object. There is only the contemplator, the contemplated and the process of contemplation; the seer, the seen and the seeing process; the knower, the known and knowledge.

In Dhyana, or meditation, these three processes take place automatically and simultaneously. The culmination of Dhyana is what true Yoga is. As you might have heard, Yoga is union - that is, when the union is established, you are in a real state of Yoga. You cannot be said to be in a real state of Yoga or in union with anything if the harmony between yourself and the object is not wholly established and you somehow retain an individuality of your own. The requirement is something like two friends who have one soul and one way of thinking, though they have two different bodies. Such friends do not really exist, for it is not easy to see one consciousness uniformly functioning in two forms. However, the subject and the object unite in some such way, only to lose their separatist identities in the union.

There is the rising of Dharana and Dhyana into Samapatti or Samadhi, where an equilibrium is established in consciousness. There is a harmonious flow of awareness, on account of whose emergence the distinction between the seer and the seen gets diminished and is reduced to the minimum. The gulf between the subject and the object is narrowed down almost to a point of identity, or oneness. In Dhyana, this union does not take place, but there is a tendency to this union. In Samadhi, there is absolute union. This is the fourth state of the effort in Yoga.

Now we come to the *forte*, or the main point, which Patanjali makes out in his Sutras, as his final message in Yoga, towards which all other teachings move as preparatory stages. If you read the Sutras of Patanjali directly, you would not be able to understand as to what you are expected to concentrate upon. You will be in a mess even after you read all the Sutras, because he does not specifically mention that you have to develop any concept of God in a theological sense. Though there is a mention of *Ishvara* or God in some place, it is stated as a method of concentration, one among the many ways, and not necessarily the only method, or as the goal of Yoga. The point that Patanjali makes out in his Sutras as the final plunge is difficult to understand, because he is precise and concise in his expressions, and does not dilate upon the theme.

Before we touch upon this magnificent point that is going to be unravelled, we may consider one of the Sutras which has an intimate connection with Samapatti, or Samadhi. In the state of absorption, the modifications of the mind are thinned out. They are not robust as during contemplation of objects externalised. A psychosis of the mind in respect of an object is called a Vritti. The more the intensity of the idea of the existence of an external object, the stouter is the Vritti, and the stronger is the ego attached to it. A Vritti, or a psychosis, is supposed to become thin when the idea of the externality of the object is worn out, gradually, in deep concentration.

An object, philosophically, is nothing but the externality attached to being. A thing goes by the name of an object, because of the externality, the spatio-temporality, the isolatedness, the distinction, which is foisted on that thing. Anything that is totally outside you, external to your consciousness, is an object and the form, the shape or the modification which the mind undergoes in respect of this externality of a thing is called the Vritti. This is what is called a psychosis. And it gets thinned out in deep concentration, when it moves towards the ideal or the goal of the abolition of the distinction between the subject and the object. It gets thinned out because the idea of externality gets diminished in intensity during concentration. The object comes nearer and nearer to you as it were, or, the other way round, you go nearer to it. To such an extent does this phenomenon manifest itself that at an advanced stage, the subject gets reflected in the object, and the object gets reflected in the subject, in a mutual coalescence of characters, wherein the specific identities of the two are overcome in an essential uniformity, not only of function but even of being itself.

You see yourself in me, and I see myself in you, as if we both are mirrors reflecting one in the other. We do not remain as things cut off one from the other with no apparent connection between ourselves. This is the example of two mirrors facing each other. One is reflected in the other; one is seen in the other; one is the other. When a pure crystal reflects an object, you will find the two commingling, one being seen in the other, so that you cannot know which is the object and which is the crystal. A red flower, a lotus, or a rose that is brought into the proximity of a crystal gets so much reflected in the crystal that the crystal assumes wholly the colour of that object. It appears as if it has become the object itself. *Grahitr, Grahana, Grahya*: These three terms used in the Sutra refer to the perceiver, the perception and the perceived; the seer, the seeing and the seen; consciousness, the process of the movement of consciousness, and the object itself.

These three, the grasper which is the subject, the grasping which is the process, and the grasped or the object, reflect one in the other. This is a highly advanced stage of meditation. A student in the earlier stages will not have this experience. When you begin to feel a throbbing sensation of the presence of the object in your own self, and it looks as if you have become the object or the object has become you, you do not know which is the side that can be called the Subject or the Object. Great mystics, saints and sages who are in this condition are supposed to have lost the consciousness of even the environment around them and do not distinguish between themselves and the things that they see as the objects around them. They remain in a kind of inundated condition; a flood overtakes them.

Samapatti is the attainment which is characterised by the whole-souled absorption of the subject into the object, and, vice versa, a total immersion of the object into the subject. These things are very important to remember. You become completed in your being and do not remain as a partial personality as you are now, when you are conscious of an external object in respect of which the mind forms a judgement of its own, positively or negatively in the form of love or hatred, and the like.

But here you raise yourself to the status of spiritual apprehension in an atmosphere of totality of experience, and you are not conscious of an object. You are conscious of a completeness, and it is the completeness that is the joy. It is all happiness, all satisfaction, all pleasure. Even the temporal pleasures of this world are an outcome finally of a filledness or a completeness that takes possession of you at the time of that experience. A loss of the distinction between you and the object possessed is the reason behind your feeling of satisfaction. While in ordinary contacts with objects of sense it takes place artificially and it leads you to suffering later on, in this union, the joy takes place spiritually.

And, now, what is this Samapatti, and what is this attainment, and what are you expected to concentrate, meditate upon? The Yoga system of Patanjali is based on the system of the Samkhya, as its metaphysics. The Samkhya philosophy, in its cosmological enunciations, gives us a gradation of the categories or evolutes; and the objects of meditation in the system of Patanjali are nothing but the categories of the Samkhya. And what are these categories?

The highest reality is the *Purusha,* which is pure consciousness, infinite in its nature. The Purusha does not mean a man or a male, as you will read it in its dictionary meaning. It is a metaphysical principle and not a personality or an individual. The Samkhya considers the Purusha as the Ultimate Reality, and the attainment of its consciousness is the goal of all life. The highest meditation, therefore, is absorption in the Purusha. Next, in importance, comes *Prakriti,* which is the matrix of all phenomena we call creation.

By Prakriti what the Samkhya means is the barest minimum of objectivity, while the Purusha cannot be an object in any sense of the term. The Purusha is infinite subjectivity; Prakriti is all objectivity. Creation is impossible unless there is a tendency to externalisation, which is what Prakriti does at all times. Prakriti is defined as a blend of three properties, or Gunas, known as Sattva, Rajas and Tamas, usually translated as Equilibrium, Distraction, and Inertia.

These three constitute the condition of Prakriti and are the very substance of Prakriti, not merely attributes external to or inhering in it. We may say in a sense that the Prakriti is a condition, rather than a substance or thing in itself. It is a state of affairs, and this is a point very important to remember. This Prakriti which is constituted of the three properties is the cause of this whole creation, the phenomena, this universe.

The Samkhya tells us that the reflection of the Purusha in Prakriti in a cosmical sense is the seed of creation. This is the first function of Prakriti, to reflect the Purusha in cosmic Sattva or the equilibrated condition of itself. The Samkhya has its own technical terms for all these stages.

The first stage of this universal reflection is called *Mahat.* We may call it the Cosmic Intellect, or, the Universal Intelligence. This Intelligence is the bare, impersonal, featureless transparency of awareness at the root of and precedent to all objectivity.

This Mahat which is cosmic awareness further concretises itself, in a cosmic manner of course, and becomes Self-conscious in a cosmic connotation, again, of Self-consciousness. When it attains this state, it is called *Ahamkara.* This is not the ego that we are speaking of in ordinary sense, but a metaphysical principle, cosmical in its nature, the universe becoming aware that it is.

There are variations in the description of what takes place further on. The mostly accepted form of the Samkhya proceeds along the following line. After the manifestation of Ahamkara, there is a split, as it were, in a tripartite manner, or in a dualistic way, or, we may say, into the objective universe, and the subjective individualities. The Tamasika Ahamkara becomes the cause of the five subtle principles, known as *Tanmatras* - Sabda, Sparsa, Rupa, Rasa, and Gandha - meaning respectively the objects of hearing, touching, seeing, tasting and smelling. It is these that, by a process of permutation and combination, become the five gross elements: Earth, Water, Fire, Air and Ether. This is the physical world that we see with our eyes. On the other side there is the subject: myself, yourself, everybody, all individuals. All beings and all levels, right from plants onwards up to the angels, are the individuals forming the subjective side of Prakriti.

Now, all this detail is intended only to give us an idea as to what Patanjali expects us to think in our minds when we move towards Samyama or Samapatti, the highest kind of meditation. These Samapattis, or Samadhis, as they are sometimes called, are practised and experienced by stages. One does not suddenly get identified with the highest reality. Patanjali is highly systematic and scientific in his processes. He takes us, psychologically, gradually, from one stage to the other.

The Samapattis are the Samadhis technically known. You must have heard of the names: *Savitarka, Nirvitarka, Savichara, Nirvichara, Sananda, Sasmita, and Nirbija.* These are the stages of Samapatti, or Samadhi, or union, which is effected, stage by stage, by profound attention of consciousness on these categories of the Samkhya, enumerated above. The process aims, finally, at Universal Self-consciousness, the establishment of consciousness in its own Self. Consciousness becoming Being, *Chit* becoming *Sat,* as they say, is the goal of the Yoga's Samapatti, Samadhi or Samyama. These are all affiliated terms, fraternal in their nature, and commingle at the point of a total dissociation of Self from the universe at every level, ultimately from Prakriti, the very principle of objectivity.

The Entry into Universality

We shall be considering what should be regarded as the highlight in the system of Patanjali's Yoga, at which all his teachings converge in the end. These great feats are known as the *Samyamas,* or the absorptions by way of a whole-souled concentration of one's being. We may call them also *Samapattis,* in his own language. They are equivalent also, in some way, to what are usually known as the *Samadhis*. These are the highly technical sides of his teachings and very meagrely understood even by students of this system. But that is the strong point of his gospel. Everything that Patanjali says anywhere in his work has an ultimate reference to this achievement, *i.e.*, the final plunge that the seeker takes into the supreme objective, the goal of life.

As it was noticed, different terms are used in this case, almost all meaning the same thing, practically. The word *Samyama* is very important. It actually means a restraint of an all-comprehensive nature. One musters in all the forces of one's personality and concentrates it as a totality. The entirety of one's being is focussed. This graduated identification of the seeking spirit with the objective of meditation is what is called Samapatti in its various stages. Even this process of self-identification and absorption takes place by stages. Thus, what is called *Samapatti* is not a sudden jump into the depths of the ocean. It is a gradual going in. Even when one enters the bottom of the ocean, one goes by degrees of descent. One touches the surface first, then goes deeper and deeper, stage by stage, until the bottom of the ocean is reached. Something like that is the gradual ascent and entry through the Samyamas, Samapattis, and Samadhis.

Samyama, or concentration of this nature, can be practised, according to Patanjali, on any object. You can absorb yourself in anything and everything-it may be even a pencil or a wrist-watch. Whatever can be conceived in the mind can also become the object of Samyama. But in its spiritual connotation and with its relevance to the ultimate liberation of the spirit, Samyama means the practice of an organised attention on the categories of the Samkhya as was observed earlier. The stages of Samyama on other things are experiments. They are trainings given to the mind. We are told sometimes, when we begin to concentrate, that we may start with a dot on the wall, a rose flower, a beautiful imagery, sunrise or sunset, and the like. These instruments are familiar to people who take to the art of meditation. But these are only processes of disciplining the mind, and are not the end and aim, or the finale of Yoga proper.

When Patanjali takes us seriously to the point he is driving at, he refers to Samyama on the categories or the evolutes according to the Samkhya. These categories may be regarded, for all practical purposes, as the conceivable stages of the manifestation of the universe in the process of what we may call creation. The lowest category is taken as the first object of meditation. The immediately visible phenomenon is the object that is concentrated upon first. The minor types of Samyamas, the concentrations which are purely of a preparatory nature, are not our concern in these courses of studies, and hence we go straight to the concentrations properly so called. The lowest categories, or the immediately visible evolutes in the cosmological scheme, are the five gross elements: Earth, Water, Fire, Air and Ether.

Whatever we see in this world is constituted of the five elements. There is nothing anywhere except these objects of experience. The material of the structure of all objects consists of these five elements and these are also the bodies of all individuals whether organic or inorganic. Now you have to listen to me with attention, because there are certain important technical points involved in this Samyama. This method of meditation is not intended for everybody, and it cannot be prescribed as a wholesale remedy or recipe for all seekers, indiscriminately. It is meant only for a selected few who are fit for this type of thinking, and, so, caution has to be exercised in its implementation, under the guidance of a teacher.

The world is constituted of these five elements in the region of name, form and substance. These elements have three aspects. There is firstly, a substance in them, a materiality. The earth has substance. It is made up of something; it 'is' something. We cannot say it is 'nothing'. We may not be able to say, immediately, what it is made of, but it is clear that it is something substantial. It is not an emptiness or an airy void, and it has a characteristic which is definable.

This characteristic is the name-form complex. We call it earth, for instance, and that is a name, a nomenclature. A definition is a name, whatever be the form of it. The characterisation of anything may be called its name. Generally, in India particularly, the name given to a particular person or a thing describes that person or thing. It is not just anything that one imagines by a crotchet. If your name is such-and-such, that name connotes what you are made of in your characteristics, psychologically.

So, the name is the definition of the object, and this definition has reference to the form of the object. If the form had been different, the definition would have also been different. And behind the name and form, there is the essentiality of the object. Now, this essentiality cannot be visualised immediately. We cannot see what the earth is made of. We see only the outer form of it, that is, as it appears to our sensation and perception. The appearance of this object is the point on which we have to practise Samyama, initially. Naturally, one cannot do anything else. One cannot even imagine in one's mind what is behind the appearance of this wall. We have to concern ourselves, at present, only with the so-called appearance of these five elements.

The elements have a gross form of their own *(Sthula)*. They have a characteristic, or a property *(Svarupa)*. They are constituted of certain inner components *(Sukshma)*. Firstly, they have a "name-form complex". Secondly, they have a "specific characteristic". Thirdly, they have an "inner component". Fourthly, they are "reducible to certain ultimate properties which go to constitute every element" *(Anvaya)*. And, finally, fifthly, "they have a reference to the universal determining Will" *(Arthavattva)*. We may call this final power the Will of the Absolute. We may call it the "Supreme Idea" of Plato. We may call it the "Substance" of Spinoza. We may say it is the Force of the Purusha, or the God of the religions. There is something that determines everything in the universe, above all.

Now, therefore, these elements are the initial objects of Samyama. Though we are now concerned with the Earth, obviously, the rule applies to the other elements also. These five stages of description of any particular element, or all the elements, are the points of concentration. We may take the entire physical universe constituted of the five elements. It will be difficult to envisage this, the totality of all things. The mind will refuse to think in this manner, because it is not accustomed to visualise things in a collective way. We are only used to think particular objects.

The totality of physical phenomena cannot become the object of thought, for ordinary persons. However, here is a great subject, very interesting and worth considering. The Earth is solid, Water is liquid, Fire and Air are not only gaseous but also have their own specific distinguishing properties. Ether has its own comprehensive characteristic, for it contains everything.

Everyone knows what these elements are, because they are sensed by everyone, every day. We can understand, in outline, grossly, what these distinctions are among one element and the other. The solidity, etc., mentioned, are the differentia of the elements. The outer shape is their nature. When we look at the Earth, it appears to be something. When we look at Water, it appears to be another thing. When we see Fire, Air, or Ether, they are quite other things. They are all definable by way of their characteristics, solidity, liquidity, gaseousness, etc. These are the properties. Anything that is solid can be regarded as having the Earth element in it. Anything that is liquid can be said to have the Water element, and so on, with the other elements.

The first stage of Samyama is concerned with the five gross elements, in which their essential substantiality (Artha) is mixed up inseparably with our notion about them, the form, or the idea (Jnana) as well as the name associated with them (Sabda). This first attainment is known as *Savitarka-Samapatti*. In the second stage the name and the form are dropped and the gross elements in their essentiality become the objects of Samyama. This is *Nirvitarka-Samapatti.*

The third stage of the ascent concerns the point of the inner subtleties of the elements. We are told today that behind the solid bodies of things there are the molecules, behind the molecules there are the atoms, and behind the atoms there are forces, electrical energies, electro-magnetic phenomena. Something like this is the way in which we have to conceive and contemplate the inner constituents of the elements. These inner components of the elements are called *Tanmatras. Tanmatras* actually mean the specific substance out of which the gross elements are essentially made, and from which anything can be deduced by an increase in the density of these components through a mixing by way of proportionate combination.

The Sanskrit words for the five Tanmatras are Sabda, Sparsa, Rupa, Rasa and Gandha, *i.e.*, the principle of sound connected with Ether, the principle of touch connected with Air, the principle of sight or colour connected with Fire, the principle of taste connected with Water, and the principle of smell connected with Earth. These in their universal significance are the Tanmatras, the essential subtle ingredients behind the five gross elements.

When Samyama is practised on the Tanmatras of the elements, together with the notion of their spatiality, temporality and causality in the scheme of the evolution of the universe, it is called *Savichara-Samapatti.* When Samyama is done on the Tanmatras in their essential form, free from these associated notions of space, time and cause, it is called *Nirvichara-Samapatti.*

All these five subtle ingredients are reducible further to certain final cosmic properties and that is a more advanced step in the analysis of the five elements. The Samkhya or Yoga calls these final properties as Gunas. These Gunas are Sattva, Rajas and Tamas, reference to which has already been made. Sattva, Rajas and Tamas are the ultimate substances out of which the Tanmatras and the elements are formed. The Gunas are not qualities in the sense of abstract definitions. When we say that the rose is red, we know that redness is the property or quality of the flower, but we do not speak of property here in this sense, because we feel at once that the rose is not the same as redness. There is something which is the rose other than the quality called redness. But, here, this is not the case. The Gunas, as properties, are the very essentialities, the substances, the very existence of Prakriti and its evolutes, the Tanmatras, etc.

The example usually given is of the rope that is made up of three strands. We can twist three strands to form a rope, and we do not say that the strands are qualities or properties of the rope. The rope is made up of the strands, and they form its substance. Just as threads constitute the cloth - we cannot say that the threads are only a quality of the cloth for they are the constituents of the cloth—they are the cloth itself. The Gunas make up all things. These Gunas are Sattva, Rajas and Tamas, the conditions of all things in the ultimate analysis. The universe is a 'condition' and not a 'thing'.

The final stroke is the most magnificent step. What are these three Gunas? How are they bifurcated? And why should they mix themselves up in certain proportions to constitute the Tanmatras, and so on? Why should anything at all happen in the world? Everything happens in the way it does on account of the original permutation and combination of these three properties. If they are mixed up in some other proportion, the universe would be something else. This world would not have been what it is now.

There is a supreme determining power immanent in and transcending the whole universe of experience. What it actually is, no one can speak about. There is something indescribable and unintelligible at the foundation of all things. We may compare it with the Archetypal Ideas of the Supreme Good of Plato. The Vedanta calls it the "Absolute", or "Brahman". The Samkhya calls it the "Purusha". Here we need not go deep into the mysterious base of things, for all this will go above the heads of everybody. However, suffice it to observe that there is some deciding principle, which wills in a manner the structure of all creation, and determines its functioning. This Great Idea of the cosmos is the reason why the three properties are mixed up in certain proportions at a particular time, and everything then follows as the patterns of universes.

When we conceive of anything, see anything, or try to define anything, three aspects of knowledge are involved: we have a name or characterisation given to the object; say, it is a stone, it is a tree, it is a person, and so on. Everything has a name. The associated name is called 'Sabda', in the terminology of the Sutra. Sabda actually means a sound; and the name is nothing but a sound, which is connected with an idea thereof. The idea going hand in hand with the name or definitive limitation is called 'Jnana'. We have an idea of an object as invested with a name defining it such as Mr. John. John is the name, and in connection with this name of the person, we form an idea of the person.

This idea of the person, or any other thing, is another aspect. But the person as such or the thing as such, independent of the idea and independent also of the definition or name, is a third something altogether. Do we not think that we are different from the name that we have and the idea people have about us? Who has told that this particular tall thing is to be called a tree? Everybody has agreed that it should be called that way; that is all. Well, if the dictionary changes and the whole of humanity agrees that what is known as a tree should be called a stone, it is a stone from that day. The name can change.

So, the name is not an essential element in the object. The name is only a convenient descriptive definition of a particular something for purpose of practical dealings. However, the more difficult and more important factor is the idea that we have about it. The least aspect of the object is the name. The more important aspect which determines it in an intensive manner is the idea. Everything is conditioned by the idea that goes with it. Our dealings with things in the world are conditioned, determined by the ideas that we have about them.

But our ideas are not necessarily a correct representation of the object. We may be mistaken and we are often mistaken. According to Patanjali, our ideas about things are always a set of errors and we never know the truth of things. No one can have a true concept of the essentiality of anything in this world. Everything is known only as conditioned by the idea and the name. So, when we do Samyama on anything with the admixture of name, idea and the substantiality of the object, then this kind of achievement, called Savitarka-Samapatti, is the lowest stage of absorption. We can conceive or even gaze at the object that we have chosen for the purpose of Samyama as constituted of this blend of three aspects. The thing as such, of course, we cannot conceive immediately. But at least we do believe that there is such a thing called tree, in its own essentiality, transcending the idea or the definition that we have associated with it.

But the difficulty increases as we go further, so that, at a point, we may find that it is a hopeless affair and we cannot go ahead any more. This is because we are asked to drop the aspects of name and idea and try to be attuned to the thing as it is in itself. This struggle is almost an impossible one for ordinary persons. How can you think of another as he is in himself apart from the idea that you have about him and the name that is associated with him? But this is precisely the true Samapatti, or attainment.

The practice requires a little effort, and some sweating is necessary here. An easy-go-lucky life is not the life of Yoga. We have to be serious in this matter, if we really want freedom in the ultimate sense. But how, on earth, is it possible to do Samyama on the thing, as it is in itself, independent of the idea that I have about it, and dissociated from the name that is connected with it? Yes, it is not easy. It is not possible in the initial stages and the Teacher of Yoga does not want to tell you what the second stage is, when you are still in the first stage, when you have, perhaps, not yet stepped even into the first stage.

These steps of Yoga are not academic definitions. They are not theories. They are not something to be told to you, now itself, wholesale. They are, on the other hand, stages of experience and not admonition or teaching. You cannot ask, "What shall I do after attaining Moksha?" These are stupid questions, not intended to be answered, because these doubts arise from utter idiocy. The attainments are experiences and you will know what the answer is, yourself. It is like a dreaming man asking, "What shall I see when I wake up?" Nobody can say what he will see. He has to wake up and see; then he will know what it is about.

The stages of Samapatti are levels of direct realisation and experience. They are not theoretical discussions. They are not mere informations given or teachings of a logic school, academic in nature. It is absurd, therefore, to put questions as to what are these stages, 2nd, 3rd, 4th, 5th, 6th, etc., when you have not even entered the stream. But a general solacing message can be given to you to enthuse the spirit. This is what the teachers generally do. They console you and give you an inspiration that something magnificent is coming, though it cannot be described in human language. There are types of meditation which you will find described in standard works on the subject, wherein you will be asked to transpose yourself into the object on which you are practising Samyama, or total absorption.

This is not merely a spiritual technique; it is also a technique of even ordinary success in life. I am referring to pure psychology and even good social living. If you wish to be a good social individual, you must be able to transfer yourself into the society or the set-up of the society, the placement of the persons around you. You must be able to think as the people around you think; at least you should attempt to think in harmony with the way in which other people are thinking around you. You would be regarded as an anti-social person, you would be a misfit in that atmosphere, and you would be unhappy every day, if you are not versed in this human art.

The capacity of your mind to transfer itself to the position of the particular object or objects in the midst of which you are living is a great Yoga by itself, and these stalwarts are the people who are the great men of human history. This requires a little bit of a surrender of one's ego, a sacrifice of one's personality and a relinquishment of one's own ideas. Why should you think that your own ideas are the correct ones? Why should you go on sticking to your own guns? It may be that others are also right, and there is no harm in conceding some value to the thoughts of other people. Why should you think that you are always right, and others are always wrong?

So, even to succeed in life, by way of a happy social and personal existence, it is necessary, on one's part, to be able to think in terms of the existence and feelings and needs of other people also. This is a kind of concentration and adjustment done in a mild manner, though not so intensely as in Yoga. If you can think as another thinks, feel as another feels, and try to recognise another's needs and requirements as your own, become the other, for the time being, and lose yourself in the 'other', you 'are' the 'other', if this could be possible, you are in the first stage of Samyama. I do not think that this essential of a good life is so difficult as it appears, and perhaps no one can be truly happy in this world if this rule could not be successfully employed, with some effort. When this method is carried to the technical point of complete concentration and absorption, it becomes the Samapatti of the Savitarka type. This is the real *Yajna,* or sacrifice. This is real service. This is to be really humanitarian in the deepest sense.

The greatest service that one can do to others would be to think as others think. Everything else comes afterwards. When you are able to feel as others feel and be as others are, you have done the greatest service to people, and no charity can be greater than this act of goodwill. That is a real friend who has become you and exists as you. What can be a greater glory than this ideal?

The Great Attainment

We may, now, resume and sum up our studies on the profundities of Yoga-Samadhi, or Samapatti, for purpose of a better comprehension. The meditation on the categories of the Samkhya, which is known as the Samapatti, goes also by the name of Samadhi, a gradual absorption of the meditating principle in the object of meditation. We have seen the four earlier stages which go by the name of the Savitarka, Nirvitarka, Savichara and Nirvichara attainments. The object associated with name and idea and the object as such in its own status unqualified by the idea of the percipient and by the name associated with it, both in its gross and subtle forms, is the content of these stages. When the contemplation is practised on gross forms, it is Savitarka or Nirvitarka when associated or not associated with conditioning factors.

When the meditating consciousness so gets absorbed in the object that the idea of the object and the name of the object drop out altogether and there is a consciousness of the object alone, independently, without any kind of external associations, where one becomes the true friend of the object, not merely an observer or a judge of the object, but an organic mass of sentience in which the object is dissolved, as it were, in one's being - that is to be known as the great freedom of the self.

When you commune with the gross form of the object, you become the object itself, in essence. You occupy its own position and there is an interchange of characters. The subject enters into the object, or, you may say, the other way round, the object enters into the subject. There is an equilibrium established between the status of the subject and that of the object. This equilibrium is known as Samadhi. The object does not any more stand in the position of something which you have to describe or hold an opinion about or judge, etc. There is no necessity any more to have ideas about the object. It does not any longer exist as an object at all.

This is as regards the gross form of the object. But, it has a subtle form wherein it exists not as a tangible solid object, but as a force which is called the Tanmatra, the subtle essential principle, the power, or the constitutive element which is more general and pervasive in its character than the isolated form of the gross object. This is a stage which cannot be conceived in the mind at present. We can speak about it as if we understand it, but really it cannot enter into our heads because we do not know what this essential force is behind the physical object. We can only stretch our thought and visualise that every physical object is constituted of an electromagnetic force in its core.

We cannot see this force but only conceive in a laboured manner what this electromagnetic constitution of an object could be. These stages in Yoga are not subjects for discussion or academic description. They are stages of actual experience and we describe them for the purpose of a guidance that is given beforehand to the student as a sort of forewarning concerning what is going to come and what is to be encountered. The invariable feature of everything, whether it is gross or subtle, is its position or location in space and in time. This is an important fact which we have to bear in mind. Everything is in space; space is inseparable from time, and time is inseparable from space. These days we say it is 'space-time' and not 'space-and-time'. The two are not different things. When the one is there, the other is also there, automatically.

But, everything is in space-time, whatever be the intensity of our thought in regard to an object, gross or subtle. We will find that we cannot escape the predicament of space-time-association when we conceive of anything. Even when we think of such featureless things as electricity or the electromagnetic field, which is really not a space-time content, we have somehow to imagine that it is some power that is moving like air in space. The so-called electricity or electromagnetic power can be imagined only as a content of space-time.

It exists somewhere. Even if it exists everywhere it is in space, and it exists sometime. It is now, it was here, it will be there, etc., are unavoidable notions. These ideas cannot leave us. And, this is the last trouble that we have to face in our quest. The notion of the grossness of the object is also a difficulty which we have to overcome by an intensive self-identification by which we drop the idea of the object and the name associated with it, and 'become' it rather. But more difficult is the other problem of the 'location' of the object in space-time. We cannot get over this idea as long as we remain as human beings.

This stage of meditation is not a stage of human thinking; we are no more supposed to be persons, thinking something, because when we remain as persons, we are in space and time. The subtle form, the Tanmatra, is then taken up for consideration and it becomes the object of meditation. But it is in space-time, again. So we deeply ponder, brood over, meditate upon this subtle pervasive principle behind the element, the Tanmatra, the force that is inherent in and forms all that is gross, as conditioned by space-time, because we cannot do anything else. We have to agree that it is in space and in time, due to the very limitations of the mind which cannot think in any other way. This association of consciousness with the subtle principles behind the elements, as conditioned by space and time, is a tendency towards an absorption of a higher order.

Things as they are in themselves, the *thing-in-itself*, the reality that is independent of any association with the perceiving consciousness, the reality that is unconditioned, and not the reality as we think it, is not in space, not in time. The pervasive character of reality, the omnipresence of it, precludes any interference in the form of space-time associations, for, to be in space and time is to be located somewhere and sometime. But reality is not somewhere and sometime. It is everywhere and at all times. Now, we cannot imagine what it is to be everywhere and to be at all times, because our imagination can conceive this everywhereness only as a kind of existence inside space, though it is everywhere in space, and an existence for a lengthened period of time, an indefinite period, for, the idea of time does not leave us.

Even when we think of an indefinite, endless period of time, we are thinking of time only. But reality is timeless and not endless duration. Even if we are to conceive of an infinitude of the series of durational existences of something, we are thinking in terms of space and time, again. But the absorption becomes so intense that the ideas of space and time evaporate into pure being. The thing ceases to be a thing by itself. Neither are we somewhere, nor is the thing anywhere. The idea of 'where' and 'when' does not arise. This, again, is an unintelligible experience for the beginner. No human being ever born can imagine what this state can be, where space is not, and time is not, too. Even the idea of there being no space and time is in space and time. When you abolish the idea of space and time, you have done this feat in space and time only.

We cannot escape this difficulty however much we may try. It comes as a direct experience which each one has to pass through and know by one's own self. This is a stage where one becomes a superhuman force and not an individual any more. No more is the humanness present there. The individual is taken possession of by the powers of the universe. One becomes a part and parcel of the entire Nature in its vast expanse. Man, then, is not a national of any country; one is no more a man or a woman. One is, then, not a human being at all. Nothing on earth can be adequate to describe one's presence there. The 'I' and the 'you' are not there. The ideas of 'you' and 'I' cease. This is the penultimate state of the divine merger of the individual in the Supreme Reality.

The union has not taken place, as yet, but it is as if one has touched the ocean of Being and is enchanted by its very contact, is transformed through every fibre of one's being, and the iron that man is has become the gold, the philosopher's stone, of that great reality. The soul reveals itself in its pristine purity. The peace that passeth understanding, the joy of the soul, reveals itself here, and one is happy merely because one is. The very fact of being becomes a source of inexpressible and immeasurable satisfaction. One exists not as a person but as a Super-Person, a Super-Individual, a God-Man.

This joy itself is an object of experience. There is no object any more, in the sense of the objects we speak of. We have been referring to objects on which we have to meditate or do Samyama. Now, there is no more the object. The gross form of the object has gone; even the subtle has been transcended. The self is in possession of the infinite joy of a cosmic comprehensiveness. This joy is an experience, inasmuch as consciousness experiences this joy.

The joy itself is the object of consciousness; though for all practical purposes, joy cannot be regarded as an object in the ordinary sense, it does not remain any more outside consciousness. Yet there is a supreme Self-Consciousness of a universal character, though not the self-consciousness that we have as individuals. It is an indescribable, pure and subtle Awareness of Being which remains at the time of that experience - a joy that does not come from things and objects, because they are not any more there-a joy that is the very characteristic of the Self, the Consciousness, supervenes. This experience is super-physical and super-psychic, even. It is not the mind that experiences the joy, not even the intellect, not anything that is psychological. The spiritual root in us effloresces and reveals its own nature to its own self. The revelation is not to somebody else. It is not like sunlight falling on someone's face. It is the Sun shining on himself and becoming aware that he is shining upon himself and feeling an immense satisfaction born of the very luminosity and resplendence of his being.

There is a Universal Self-Awareness at this stage of the satisfaction that arises from consciousness in its essentiality. This joy-experience is *Sananda-Samapatti.* The Self-Consciousness which is attending upon this joy universal is *Sasmita-Samapatti.* Here the efforts of the individual do not continue. One need not have to struggle to meditate. There is no effort on the part of a person, because there is no person at all. Individuality is carried by the current of the universe, of God Himself, if we would call it so. One is possessed by a Power that is super-individual.

One is no more oneself, and therefore one has no responsibility over oneself. Hence, there is nothing that one can or need do. The very question of 'doing' ceases, as the individual is not there as a person. There is no agency in action. There is no doership. There is no individual performer of actions. There is the pure sense of Being, that which sometimes we are told about as the condition of 'I-Am-What-I-Am', or 'I-Am-That-I-Am'. Words fail here. Speech is hushed. The mind is transported into an inebriating cosmic sense.

This is the ultimate union of the soul with All-Being and this is the final stage, practically, of *Samapatti,* where the river has entered the ocean and does not any more exist as the river. One does not know in the ocean which is Ganga, which is Yamuna, which is Amazon, which is Volga. No one knows what is where. Everything is everywhere at every time in every condition. One becomes the centre of the Being of all things, the heart of everything. One becomes the Immanent Principle of the cosmos. This is God-Experience, in the language of religion. This is the realisation of the Absolute, *Brahma-*

Sakshatkara. Here the consciousness reverts to Itself and stands on Its own status. It has not become aware of something. It is aware only of Itself.

The Drashta, or the Seer, becomes himself. As one proceeds higher and higher through these Samyamas or Samapattis, one becomes more and more oneself in the true metaphysical significance of Selfhood. When the Samapattis grow intense and rise higher, one becomes less and less the object that one is, and more and more the subject that one has to become, until the Pure Subject as an all-inclusive experience is realised.

In the Sananda and Sasmita stages, consciousness becomes the Whole Subject, without even the least trace of objectivity in it. This Pure Subjectivity of experience cannot be designated even as subjectivity, because the human mind has a prejudice on account of which it regards subjectivity as something counterposed to objectivity. But this is not the logical subject that we are speaking of, but the metaphysical subject, the spiritual Being-in-Itself. It is subject, no doubt, because of the fact that it is aware; but of what is it aware? It is a subject which has no object in front of it and, so, it cannot be called even a subject as known to human thought.

There is a complete melting away of even the sense of cosmicalness of consciousness in that Being-Qua-Being. When all ideas melt into Being and the very seed of Self-consciousness ceases, the experience is called *Nirbija Samadhi*, or the seedless 'Communion'. The seed referred to here is the potentiality to revert to individuality. This seed of experience phenomenal is burnt up in this Supreme Transcendence. The tree of Samsara or world-consciousness will not grow any more from this seed which has been fried up in the fire of wisdom. There is no more bondage in the form of entanglement of any kind. This ends in *Moksha*, final liberation.

Liberation is not an attainment in the future, for to think of the future is to think of time, once again. We have already decided that the notion of time has to go. So we cannot say that this is something that will come afterwards, because the idea of 'afterwards' is the idea of time. Moksha is eternity, and we cannot *think* what eternity is. We can only utter some words, and they cannot convey any proper sense to us at present. Eternity is not endless duration, it is durationless existence, the very absence of time itself.

This is the state of the *Purusha,* according to the Samkhya, and the Yoga of Patanjali. It is the state of Brahman, according to the Vedanta philosophy. It is the state of the Absolute, as the philosophers explain. It is the liberation of the Spirit, the *Nirvana* that one hears of. This is the Goal of life, and when this stage is reached, it does not remain as a stage any more.

Moksha, known also as *Kaivalya*, or Absolute Independence, is not one of the stages of experience. It is all-experience melted into one mass of Being. All that was there earlier will also be found there. It is not that the earlier stages are forgotten and one has gone to some new thing altogether. We may wonder where are all these physical objects, these trees and mountains, these friends and relatives, this wealth and status, all these wonderful and beautiful things in the world. Where are they? Have they been left out somewhere, down below? No, not so is the truth. They have not been left behind. They have been transformed into the 'reality' that they are, and they will be seen as they *are,* and not as they *appeared* earlier. This is the great solacing message to all Doubting Thomases who imagine that they, perhaps, lose something valuable as they reach God, or attain liberation.

Friends! You do not lose anything. Rather, you gain everything, and even that which you have apparently left will be found there in its true form, as great thinkers like Plato are never tired of telling us that the 'Ideas' are the realities. The Archetypes are there, the shadows of bodies are not the realities. These things that we see here are the reflections cast by the eternal 'Ideas' or the Archetypes, which may be found there, in the cosmic realm. We ourselves are shadows. The so-called 'you' and 'me' here are the shadows cast by realities which are in that Supernal Realm, so that when we look at ourselves, we are not looking at our real selves; we see only our own shadows. Our reality is in the heavens. We are there, as angels, in our true forms. The form that we experience in dreams is not our true form.

The things that we see in the dream-world are not real things. The true things are those which we see in waking, whose shadow is cast, as it were, in dream. So is this world. It is a shadow which we are pursuing unnecessarily, under the impression that something will come out of it. It cannot be pursued with advantage. It will keep you always in tenter-hooks, because you cannot pursue the shadow. It will run ahead of you, as the horizon recedes as you move towards it. The original is somewhere and the reflection is somewhere else. We are under the wrong impression that we are located in the reflection seen in the mirror. This is what the great teacher Acharya Shankara mentioned in an image. When you see yourself in a mirror, you see yourself, of course; but do you see yourself really there?

Suppose you wish to decorate your body by looking at yourself in a mirror, do you decorate that thing which you see inside the mirror? Suppose, then, you want to put a beautiful mark on your forehead by looking at your face in the mirror, do you put it on the mirror because you are there? You want to dress yourself. Do you dress the mirror? You dress the original, rather. When the original is decorated, the reflection is automatically decorated. You need not worry about the reflection at all. You concern yourself with the original rather than the reflection. But, in this world, unfortunately, we are after the reflections, the shadows. We are trying to satisfy and please and decorate and beautify the reflections that we are, and things are, and forget the original. Here is our sorrow, the malady of all life on earth.

Man is not going to be happy with his boasted knowledge. Human enterprises in this world are a pursuing of the shadow. The reality is elsewhere. This is a message which all the great philosophers, saints and sages have given us through the ages. The original, again, is not somewhere far away. This is another misconception that has to be removed from the mind, for the original is not even as much removed from the reflections as our face is from the mirror. The two are juxtaposed, and stand self-identical. The Great Reality, the Archetype, is inseparable, spatially and temporally, from the reflection.

God is here, and not in the heavens above. The Absolute is just here, under the very nose of ours. The eternity that we are going to experience, the *Moksha* that we are to realise, is not merely an original Archetype that is removed in space. Again the idea of space comes in, and the notion of time persists in our minds. The Goal is not outside in space, and is not to be reached tomorrow as a future of time experience. All this is difficult indeed for the human intellect to understand. One becomes giddy when thinking about it. But, God loves you more than you love Him, and you are bound to achieve this glorious consummation of life.

Union with the Lord

Yoga is the spiritual science of self realization which is closely related to god realization. By realizing the true inner self, one automatically comes to know the true nature of the Lord and vice versa.

The word YOGA comes from the Sanskrit root YUJA which means to link-up or to unite. The process of linking oneself with the Supreme Lord is therefore called YOGA. The English word YOKE comes from the same sanskrit root. The yoke is used to link or to connect two bulls for ploughing fields.

In the Indian Sanskrit books yoga is defined as the process of establishing a link-up between the individual consciousness of the living entity with the Supreme consciousness of the Lord. This process of establishing a link-up with the Supreme Lord leads to God consciousness, the ultimate aim of all yoga processes.

Terms like: "Yoga for beauty, vitality and health", are perverted meanings and are definitely not the goal of yoga. They are nothing but by-products of the yoga-process and are achieved automatically. These by-products of yoga are taught by pseudo yogis or westernised gurus who do not practice any spiritual life. Pseudo-spiritualists consider these by-products more important then to establish a link-up with the Lord.

Persons who are only interested in mere gymnastic feats or mystic powers (siddhis) should know, that the aim of yoga is lost in that way. If a yogi is attracted to the by-products of yoga, he can not attain the state of perfection, which is to establish a personal relationship with the Supreme Lord.

YOGA or union with the Lord is therefore not a mere abstract idea of dissolving one self into "nothing" or "becoming God oneself" but yoga leads to a spiritual relationship of the living entities with the supreme Lord.

Pseudo-Spiritualists try to unite with the Lord my merging into him or by becoming God themselves. Those who want to merge into God and become one with him, in all respects, suffer from nothing but hallucination.

When a lover and beloved unite, they may be lost in ecstasy do to the happiness of their union but they nevertheless remain as individual entities. They do not dissolve and neither merges into each other or into the nothingness. Such is the union with the Lord.

Yoga means, that the Supreme Lord is there, the devotee is there and the activity of exchange of Love between the Lord and his Devotee is there. Therefore the individuality of two persons is present; in the Supreme Personality of the Lord and the individual Soul who tries to unite with him, otherwise there is no meaning to yoga. Yoga therefore means to unite oneself in a spiritual relationship with the Supreme Lord who is the real object of one's love.

Although there are different types of yoga, the process of spiritually uniting with the Lord can be experienced best in Bhakti-Yoga, because this process fully manifest's all the spiritual characteristics of the living entities.

Philosophy

In order to unite with the Lord one has to understand the science of God. Self-realization and God-realization, therefore, go hand in hand. By self-realization one automatically becomes god-realized or vice versa.

By knowing the science of God one also can understand his real Self in relationship to the Lord. This is real yoga-philosophy. Philosophy without religion is sentimentalism and religion without philosophy is fanatism.

The next subject of yoga-philosophy is the constitutional position of the living entities, or jivas. There is isvara, which means controller, and there are jivas, the living entities which are controlled. If a living entity says that he is not controlled but that he is free, then he is insane. The living being is controlled in every respect, at least in his conditioned life.

All living entities are engaged in activities, which is known as karma. Therefore the whole cosmic manifestation is full of actions and reactions due to the different activities of living beings. There is also prakriti [the material nature] and kala [the time factor] which regulates the duration of existence of the whole universe.

In order to properly understand the philosophy of yoga, one must learn from such vedic scriptures as Bhagavad-gita and Srimad-Bhagavatam, what God is, what the living entities are, what the activities of the living entities are, what prakriti is, what the cosmic manifestation is and how it is controlled by time.

The fife basic truth are therefore:

1. Isvara—the Supreme Lord
2. Jiva—the living entities
3. Prakriti—the material nature
4. Kala—the eternal time
5. Karma—material activities

Out of these five, the Lord, the living entities, material nature and time are eternal. However, the other factor, karma, is not eternal. The effects of karma may be very old indeed. We are suffering or enjoying the results of our activities from time immemorial, but we can change the results of our Karma, or our activity, and this change depends on the acquisition of spiritual knowledge.

Activities of the living being are different varieties of aptitudes which can entrap or liberate the living being within and without material nature. By transformation into spiritual quality, materialistic activities can be rectified and thus cease to produce material qualitative reactions.

The living entity, material nature and time are under the direction of the Supreme Lord, who is absolute and completely independent of any other control. The Supreme Lord is the Supreme Controller.

Material Nature is composed of inert matter and can not act without the help of the Supreme Lord, who is completely spiritual.

Everything that exists in this material world, is a product of spirit and matter. Spirit is the basic field of creation, and matter is created by spirit. Spirit is not created at a certain stage of material development. Rather, this material world is manifested only on the basis of spiritual energy.

The time factor, which is beyond the existence of material nature, is eternal and thus material creation is not a one time affair but a perpetual process of repeated creations and destructions.

The living entities, being part and parcels of the Supreme Lord, are originally spiritual also, but under the conditions of material nature, the living being misidentifies himself with matter and considers himself being different from the Lord.

Both the Lord and the living entity are cognizant, and both have the sense of identification, of being conscious as a living force. However, the position of isvara is that of Supreme consciousness. The living being can not be supremely conscious at any stage of his perfection and the theory, that he can be so, is a misleading theory. Conscious he may be, but he is not absolutely or supremely conscious.

The distinction between jiva and isvara is that the Lords consciousness is all-pervading. He is conscious of the psychic movement of all living entities, whereas the living beings consciousness is limited to his own particular identity only.

The original spiritual consciousness of living entities can become contaminated and perverted reflected as material consciousness, whereas the Lords consciousness remains always spiritual or transcendental to the three modes of material nature. When we are materially contaminated, we are called conditioned souls. False consciousness is exhibited under the impression that I am a product of material nature. Liberation [moksa] from this materially contaminated consciousness and establishment in pure spiritual consciousness is the aim of all yoga processes.

Who am I?—Am I this Body?

Who am I? The face I see every morning in the mirror? The eyes that scrutinize it? The heartbeats within my chest? Or the thoughts that race through my brain while I am wondering about all this? Am I the body that I have obtained from my parents? Or am I the mind or intellect by means of which I am busy making plans and breaking resolves?

According to the ancient Vedic scriptures, I am none of these things. I am an eternal soul - a jiva - a living entity, by nature spiritual, but now embodied in a material form.

Inquisitiveness into the nature of the self is the first step on the path of self-realization which leads to the entity known as 'I'. But 'who am I'? Who is the entity known as 'I'?

This 'I am' is the sense of the self called ego. When the sense of 'I am' is applied to this temporary material body it is called false ego. When the sense of self is applied to the spiritual reality, the soul, that is real ego. False ego means considering oneself to be a product of this material world and accepting this physical body as oneself. When one understands that he is not his material body and is spirit soul, that is real ego.

There are some pseudo-philosophers who say that we should give up our ego altogether, but we cannot give up our ego because ego means identity. We, of course, should give up the false identification with the physical body and realize the spiritual nature of the self called the soul. Ego is always there. False ego is condemned, but not the real ego of the spirit soul. Real identification pertains to the living entity dwelling within the physical body. Unfortunately, because of ignorance, the living entity identifies himself with the material body and therefore becomes confused when he tries to find out who he really is.

For example if we ask someone 'Who are you'? he may reply 'I am Mr. Johnson, an Englishman, 35 years old, tall and rather sunburnt', but all these designations are attributes of the gross physical body. He may regard himself as possessing a good ear for music or as being rather short-sighted, which are really comments on the sensory apparatus.

He may feel that he is clever and energetic, and is probably conscious of having a limited individuality different from other people and of being sometimes happy and at other times depressed; these are all in fact modes of the subtle mind and ego along with its emotional and psychological functions.

The changeless element within the personality, which provides the background against which all the changes in body and mind take place, is essentially unconnected with those changes. The activities of the body and mind in the waking-state, dream-state as well as deep-sleep are retainable by one's memory and witnessed by the observer of the body. Those activities take place in the light of the inner self which is transcendental to the gross physical body and subtle mind.

Self-realization

Self-realization, as the word implies, is the process of finding out one's real self as distinct from ones bodily self, called the false ego. The difference between self-realization and material illusion is to know that the temporary or illusory impositions of material energy in the shape of gross and subtle bodies are superficial coverings of the self. The coverings take place due to ignorance.

Self-realization means to reduce the material activities of the gross and subtle bodies and becoming serious about the activities of the self. The impetus for activities is generated from the self, but such activities become illusory due to ignorance of the real position of the self. By ignorance, self-interest is calculated in terms of material sense gratification, and therefore a whole set of activities is spoiled, life after life. When, however, one meets the real self by spiritual culture, the activities of the self begin.

The Srimad Bhagavatam describes the process of self-realization as follows:

"If the illusory energy subsides and the living entity becomes fully enriched with spiritual knowledge by the grace of the Lord, then he becomes at once enlightened with self-realization and thus becomes situated in his own glory."[SB 1.3.34]

"Whenever a person experiences, by self realization, that both the gross and subtle bodies have nothing to do with the pure self, at that time he can see himself as well as the Lord." This means that perfect self-realization is made possible by adoption of godly or spiritual life.

The Srimad Bhagavatam concludes with the following words: "One who is enlightened in self-realization, although living within the material body, sees himself as transcendental to the body, just as one who has arisen from a dream gives up identification with the dream body. A foolish person, however, although not identical with his material body but transcendental to it, thinks himself to be situated in the body, just as one who is dreaming sees himself situated in an imaginary dream body.

As long as the spirit soul forgets his real nature, mistakes his reflection in the buddhi [intelligence] and thinks himself to be one with the internal organs [indriyas], the intellect, the false ego and the mind, thus identifying with the products of material nature [prakriti], illusion continues and factual realization can never be attained.

To discriminate therefore between body, mind and soul, or between matter and spirit, is the basic principle of self-realization.

The Nature of the Self

The old saying "Know Thy Self" implies that man does not know his own nature completely and in truth. Just as an illusory snake is superimposed on the rope, similarly an illusory personality is superimposed on the real self. Thus a man tends to think of himself as other than he really is.

This state of misidentification is traceable to the misconceptions that the soul is identical with the physical body. The conviction that this gross physical body is myself is the cause of mistaking one thing for another. "I am this physical body which is liable to be damaged by time; I have been scolded by such and such person" these and such-like statements are applicable to the relationship of the gross and subtle physical bodies.

The real unalloyed "I" has no beginning nor end. I am neither the gross physical body, nor also the mind. I am not the emotions that change when the morning changes into noon and noon into evening. I am not the mind which is sometimes cheerful and at other times miserable. I am the self who is experiencing the physical, mental, and emotional operations of body and mind. The real self, which is the spirit soul, is obscured by the cocoon of false identification with the gross body, mind and senses, which are nothing but coverings of the real self, and so the living entity imagines himself to be a product of this material world.

Therefore to differentiate between body, mind and soul, or matter and spirit, is the first step in yoga.

Everyone can observe that his body and mind is constantly changing from infancy to boyhood, to old age and death, but that the self inside the body is always the same; it does not change. The changeless self is the observer of the changing body and therefore ever different from the physical body, which is its object. As the observer is different from that which is seen; similarly the self which is the witness of everything can never be the same as that which is witnessed. The changeless self, which is transcendental by nature, is therefore not the body, mind or intellect but the spirit soul which is encaged within this material body.

The Srimad-Bhagavatam describes the nature of the self as follows:

> *"Just as fire, which burns and illuminates, is different from firewood which is to be burned to give illumination; similarly the seer within the body, the self-enlightened spirit soul, is different from the material body, which is to be illuminated by consciousness. Thus the spirit soul and the body possesses different characteristics*

and are separate entities." [11.10.8]

"Just as fire may appear differently as dormant, manifest, weak, brilliant, and so on, according to the condition of the fuel; similarly, the spirit soul enters a material body and accepts particular bodily characteristics." [11.10.9]

Such analytical study leads to differentiation between body, mind and soul. This process of understanding is also known as self-realisation and called in the vedic scriptures 'aham-brahmasmi :I am spirit'. This means that one should understand that he is spirit soul and not this material body.

The Dream Personality—Reality and Illusion

One who understands his spiritual nature, although living within the physical body, sees himself as transcendental to the body; just as one who has arisen from a dream gives up identification with the dream body. A foolish person, however, although not identical with his material body but transcendental to it, thinks himself to be situated in the body, just as one who is dreaming sees himself to be situated in an imaginary dream body. Because of this misidentification the conditioned soul is subjected to the miseries of material life. A man may see a tiger swallowing him in a dream, and he may even cry from the experience of this nightmare. But actually there is no tiger and there is no suffering; it is simply a case of misidentification with the dream-personality.

Another man who is awake by the side of his sleeping friend sees no tiger there. The tiger is a myth for both of them, namely the person dreaming and the person awake, because in reality there is no tiger; but the man forgetful of his awakened life is fearful, whereas the man who has not forgotten his position is not at all disturbed by nightmares.

Similarly, a person who is awake to his spiritual nature is not disturbed by the temporary appearance of material happiness and distress.

One who is sleeping may also see many objects of pleasure in a dream, but such pleasurable things are merely creations of the mind and are thus ultimately useless.

Similarly, the living entity who is asleep to his spiritual identity also sees many sense objects, but these innumerable objects of temporary gratification are creations of the Lord's illusory potency and have no permanent existence. The dualities of happiness and distress experienced in this so-called awakened life are said to be dreamlike for a person who has awakened to his spiritual nature.

All miseries experienced in the hard struggle for material existence are, therefore, only due to the ignorance of our spiritual nature. The subtle and gross material bodies are created by the material modes of nature, which expand from the potency of the Supreme Lord. Material existence occurs when the living entity falsely accepts the qualities of the gross and subtle bodies as being his own factual nature. The illusory state, however, can be destroyed by real knowledge.

Reality and Illusion

In our ordinary lives we live mainly in ignorance of our spiritual nature and can be compared to dreaming people who are in illusion. To understand spiritual reality it is necessary to wake up to the process of self-realization. Briefly, it is our desire and attachment for worldly enjoyment, based on the conviction of the reality of this world, that supports the illusion in our waking life just as it is our conviction of its reality that supports the dream. In the dream our hopes of happiness and fears of destruction will never be realised because they are unreal. Through the process of yoga-meditation and self-realisation we should understand that this is true of the waking world also.

The temporary appearance of this world is not absolutely unreal. It has some reality behind it but we cannot know its true reality while we are desperately clinging to the false appearances of things. The material creations are manifested for some time as perverted reflections of the spiritual world and can be likened to cinemas which display a false reality of shadows and light. They attract people of less intelligent calibre who are attracted by such false appearances. Such foolish men have no information of the reality of spiritual life, and they take it for granted that the temporary material manifestation is the all in all.

But more intelligent men with knowledge of self-realisation understand the material manifestation to be nothing but the shadow of the Lord's spiritual abode. The Lord's external manifested energy in the form of material existence is only temporary and illusory like the mirage in the desert. In the desert mirage there is no actual water. There is only the appearance of water. Real water is somewhere else.

Similarly, the manifested cosmic creation appears as reality. But reality, of which this is but a shadow, is in the spiritual world. The Absolute Truth is in the spiritual sky, not the material world. In the material world everything is temporary and relative truth. That is to say, one truth depends on something else.

This cosmic creation results from interaction of the three modes of nature, and the temporary manifestations are so created as to present an illusion of reality to the bewildered mind of the conditioned soul, who appears in so many species of life. In actuality, there is no reality in the manifested world. There appears to be reality, however, because of the true reality which exists in the spiritual world, where the Supreme Lord Sri Krishna personally resides with all the eternally liberated souls.

Dream and Sleep

A dream, although temporary in its occurrence, is a factual experience of the dreamer and cannot be considered as false. We all have dreams and this fact cannot be denied, because dreams are a by-product of the sleeping process. But the visions that we see in dreams have nothing to do with the reality of an awakened person. They are just our mind's imaginations. If a dreaming person identifies himself with the dream body and considers the dream to be reality that is certainly an illusion.

Similarly a mirage in the desert is a factual occurrence of nature and cannot be stated as false, but to consider the mirage as reality and seeing water in a hallucination is certainly an illusion.

In the same way, this material world is also a temporary effect of nature and cannot be stated as false. But, however, to consider the temporary appearance of nature's manifestation to be the only reality and to misidentify oneself with the by-products of matter is certainly an illusion.

A dream is only real in so far as it is part of the dreamer's consciousness. But the dreamer is not only emanent in his dream creation but he also transcends it. On awakening he can distinguish between reality and the illusion of the dream world.

Just as the dream personality and the dream objects lose their appearance of reality when the dreamer wakes up, similarly this material existence, which is compared to a dream, loses its apparent reality when the heavily obscured self wakes up to his spiritual identity.

The spirit soul is actually transcendental to the modes of nature and has nothing to do with the temporary appearances of this material world.

Spirit and Matter

Every thing that exists is a product of **spirit** [purusa] and **matter** [prakriti]. Spirit is the basic field of creation, and matter is created by spirit. Spirit is not created at a certain stage of material development. Rather, this material world is manifested only on the basis of spiritual energy. This material body is developed because spirit is present within matter, a child grows gradually from infancy to boyhood to old age because of that superior energy, spirit soul, being present in the physical body.

Similarly, the entire cosmic manifestation of the gigantic universe is developed because of the presence of the Supersoul, Vishnu, the Supreme Spirit. Therefore spirit and matter, which combine together to manifest this gigantic universal form, are originally two energies of the Lord, and consequently the Lord is the original cause of everything. This material world is a temporary manifestation of one of the energies of the Lord.

In the material energy, the principle manifestations are eight as explained in Bhagavad-Gita by Lord Krishna; "earth, water, fire, air, ether, mind, intelligence and false ego - altogether these eight comprise My separated material energies. Besides this inferior nature, however, there is a superior energy of Mine, which are all living entities who are struggling with material nature and are sustaining the universe."

This verse clearly mentioned that the living entities belong to the superior nature or energy of the Supreme Lord. The inferior energy is matter in its gross and subtle form. Both forms of material nature, namely the gross (earth, water, fire, air, ether) and the subtle (mind, intelligence, ego) are products of the inferior energy. The living entities, who are exploiting these inferior energies for different purposes are the superior energy of the Supreme Lord, and it is due to this energy that the entire material world functions.

The cosmic manifestation has no power to act unless it is moved by the superior energy, the living entity. Prakriti or material energy, which is unconscious and inert by nature, cannot create or act without the touch of purusa or spirit, which is completely antimaterial and the conscious principle behind matter.

> *"Earth, water, fire, air, ether, mind, intelligence and false ego—all together these eight comprise My separated material energies." [BG 7.4]*
>
> *"Besides this inferior nature, O mighty-armed Arjuna, there is a superior energy of Mine, which are all living entities who are struggling with material nature and are sustaining the universe." [BG 7.5]*
>
> *"Of all that is material and all that is spiritual in this world, know for certain that I am both its origin and dissolution." [BG 7.6]*

Understanding the Spirit Soul

As far as the identity of the living being as spirit soul is concerned, there are a number of speculations and misgivings.

The materialist does not believe in the existence of the spirit self, and empiric philosophers believe in the impersonal feature of the whole spirit without individuality of the living beings. Ignorant of the souls real constitution, people generally concoct their own philosophies and engage in mental speculations.

To drive away such ignorance, the Lord Himself is teaching the knowledge of the soul in Bhagavad-gita for the enlightenment of all living entities all times.

Chapter two of Bhagavad-gita explains, that the symptom of the soul's presence in a physical body is perceived as individual consciousness.

Anyone can understand what is spread all over the body: it is consciousness. Everyone is conscious of the pains and pleasures of the body in part or as a whole. This spreading of consciousness is limited within one's own body. The pains and pleasures of one body are unknown to another. Therefore, each and every body is the embodiment of an individual soul, and the symptom of the soul's presence is perceived as individual consciousness.

In the Puranas as well as the Upanishads this soul is described as a spiritual atom of the size of one ten-thousandth part of the upper portion of the hair point.

> *"When the upper point of a hair is divided into one hundred parts and again each of such parts is further divided into one hundred parts, each such part is the measurement of the dimension of the spirit soul." [Svet. 5.9]*

> *"There are innumerable particles of spiritual atoms, which are measured as one ten-thousandth of the upper portion of the hair." [SB]*

Therefore, the individual particle of spirit soul is a spiritual atom smaller than the material atoms, and such atoms are innumerable. This very small spiritual spark is the basic principle of the material body, and the influence of such a spiritual spark is spread all over the body as the active principle of consciousness.

In the same way as medicine influences a person by spreading throughout the whole body although administered locally; similarly this current of the spirit soul is felt all over the body as consciousness, and that is the proof of the presence of the soul.

Any layman can understand that the material body minus consciousness is a dead body, and this consciousness cannot be revived in the body by any means of material administration. Therefore, consciousness is not due to any amount of material combination, but to the spirit soul.

In the Mundaka Upanisad the measurement of the atomic spirit soul is further explained:

> *"The soul is atomic in size and can be perceived by perfect intelligence. This atomic soul is floating in the five kinds of air [prana, apana, vyana, samana and udana], is situated within the heart, and spreads its influence all over the body of the embodied living entities. When the soul is purified from the contamination of the five kinds of material air, its spiritual influence is exhibited." (Mundaka 3.1.9)*

The hatha-yoga system is meant for controlling the five kinds of air encircling the pure soul by different kinds of sitting postures—not for any material profit, but for liberation of the minute soul from the entanglement of the material atmosphere.

So the constitution of the atomic soul is admitted in all Vedic literatures, and it is also actually felt in the practical experience of any sane man. Only the insane man can think of this atomic soul as all-pervading Vishnu-tattva.

The influence of the atomic soul can be spread all over a particular body. According to the Mundaka Upanisad, this atomic soul is situated in the heart of every living entity, and because the measurement of the atomic soul is beyond the power of appreciation of the material scientists, some of them assert foolishly that there is no soul. The individual atomic soul is definitely there in the heart along with the Supersoul, and thus all the energies of bodily movement are emanating from this part of the body. The corpuscles which carry the oxygen from the lungs gather energy from the soul. When the soul passes away from this position, activity of the blood, generating fusion, ceases. Medical science accepts the importance of the red corpuscles, but it cannot ascertain that the source of the energy is the soul. Medical science, however, does admit that the heart is the seat of all energies of the body.

Such atomic particles of the spirit whole are compared to the sunshine molecules. In the sunshine there are innumerable radiant molecules. Similarly, the fragmental parts of the Supreme Lord are atomic sparks of the rays of the Supreme Lord, called by the name prabha or superior energy. Neither Vedic knowledge nor modern science denies the existence of the spirit soul in the body, and the science of the soul is explicitly described in the Bhagavad-gita by the Personality of Godhead Himself.

Two Types of Souls (Atma)

1) jiva-atma—the individual soul, known as the living entity
2) param-atma—the Supersoul, known as the Supreme Lord, who resides in the hearts of all living entities as the witness.

Both the Supreme Lord and the living entity are known as atma. The Supreme Lord is called Paramatma, and the living entity is called the atma, the brahma or the jiva.

Both the Paramatma and the jivatma, being transcendental to the material energy, are called atma. Generally people have many wrong conceptions about both of them. The wrong conception of the jivatma is to identify the material body with the pure soul, and the wrong conception of Paramatma is to think Him on an equal level with the living entity.

In the Upanisads it is explained that there are two types of souls which are technically known as jiva-atma and param-atma. **Jiva-atma, or the individual soul**, is the living entity and **param-atma refers to the Supreme Lord** who expands Himself as the Supersoul, who enters into the hearts of all living entities as well as all atoms.

This is also confirmed in Bhagavad-gita where it is stated that besides the living entity, who tries to enjoy in his physical body, there is another, a transcendental enjoyer who is the Lord, the supreme proprietor, who exists as the overseer and guide, and who is known as the Supersoul. He is not an ordinary living entity, but the plenary expansion of the Supreme Lord. Because monist philosophers and impersonalists take the soul and supersoul to be one, they think that there is no difference between the Supersoul and the individual soul. To clarify this the Lord says that He is the representation of Paramatma in every body. He is different from the individual soul; He is parah, transcendental.

The individual soul, deluded by material energy, tries to enjoy the activities of particular types of bodies offered by material nature, but the Supersoul is present not as finite enjoyer nor as one taking part in bodily activities, but as the witness and permission giver. He is present within to sanction the individual soul's desires for material enjoyment.

The Supersoul fulfils the desire of the atomic soul as one friend fulfils the desire of another. The Upanisads compare the soul and Supersoul to two friendly birds sitting within the same tree. One of the birds (the individual atomic soul) is eating the fruit of the tree, and the other bird (the Supersoul) is simply watching His friend. Of these two birds - although they are similar in their characteristic natures - one is captivated by the fruits of the material tree, while the other, who is self satisfied, is simply witnessing the activities of His friend.

The Supreme Lord, who enters the hearts of all living entities in the form of the Supersoul, is compared to the witnessing bird. The other bird, the fruit-eater (living entity), who is enchanted by the fruits of material enjoyment, has forgotten his relationship with his friend. Forgetfulness of this relationship by the atomic soul is the cause of one's changing his position from one tree to another or from one body to another. Thus the jiva soul is struggling very hard within the tree of the material body, but as soon as he turns his attention to his friend, the Supersoul, the subordinate bird immediately becomes free from all lamentation.

The Katha-Upanisad states that although the two birds are in the same tree, the eating bird, which has to face the reactions of his activities, is fully engrossed with anxiety and moroseness as the enjoyer of the fruits of the tree, while the other bird, who is the witnessing Lord, maintains His transcendental position without being affected by the material atmosphere. If somehow the individual soul turns his face to his friend the Supersoul, the suffering living entity becomes free from all anxieties.

The fact is that individual living entities are eternally part and parcel of the Supreme Lord, and both of them are very intimately related as friends. But the living entity has the tendency to reject the sanction of the Supreme Lord and act independently in an attempt to dominate the supreme nature, and because he has this tendency, he is called the marginal energy of the Supreme Lord. The living entity can be situated either in the material energy or the spiritual energy. As long as he is conditioned by the material energy, the Supreme Lord, as his friend, the Supersoul, stays with him just to get him to return to the spiritual energy. The Lord is always eager to take him back to the spiritual energy, but due to his minute independence, the individual entity is continually rejecting the association of spiritual atmosphere.

This misuse of independence is the cause of his material strife in the conditioned nature. The Lord, therefore, is giving advice and instruction from within and from without. From without He gives instructions through such Vedic scriptures as the Bhagavad-gita, and from within He acts as the Supersoul to enlighten the conditioned soul about his spiritual nature. Thus the intelligent person, who understands the difference between the Soul and Supersoul, can advance toward a blissful eternal life of knowledge.

Clear understanding of material nature, the Supersoul, the individual soul and their interrelation makes one eligible to become liberated and turn to the spiritual atmosphere without being forced to return to this material nature. This is the result of knowledge. The purpose of knowledge is to understand distinctly that the living entity has by chance fallen into this material existence. By his personal endeavour in association with authorities, saintly persons and a spiritual master, he has to understand his position and then revert to spiritual consciousness or Krishna consciousness by understanding Bhagavad-gita as it is explained by the Personality of Godhead. Then it is certain that he will never come again into this material existence; he will be transferred into the spiritual world for a blissful eternal life of knowledge.

The Difference between Soul and Supersoul

Generally there is a great misunderstanding about the characteristics of the individual soul and Supersoul, or **jiva-atma and param-atma**.

Some transcendentalists claim that the soul and Supersoul are absolutely one and the same whereas others claim them to be different.

The truth, however, is that the individual soul and Supersoul are two different entities which are similar in their spiritual natures but distinct in their quantitative function.

Jiva-atma, or the individual soul, refers to the living entity which is embodied in a physical form, produced by material nature.

Paramatma refers to the Supreme Lord who expands Himself as the Supersoul and who enters into the hearts of all living entities as well as all the atoms. Thus param-atma is the localized aspect of the supreme, situated in everyone's heart as the transcendental witness.

This is also confirmed in Bhagavad-Gita where Lord Krishna says "I am seated in everyone's heart as the all pervading Supersoul and from Me comes remembrance, knowledge and forgetfulness."

The entrance of the Supreme Lord into everyone's heart as param-atma sometimes bewilders the impersonalists, who think in terms of the equality of the living entities with the Supreme. They think that because the Supreme Lord enters into different bodies along with the individual soul, there is no distinction between the Lord and the individual entities. According to them, both the Supersoul and the individual soul are on the same level; they are one, without any difference between them.

However, according to the Vedanta-philosophy there is a difference between the Supersoul and the individual soul, and this is explained in Bhagavad-Gita, where the Lord says that although He is situated with the living entity in the same body, He is superior due to His transcendental situation. He is directing the living entity by giving knowledge and intelligence from within.

Mayavadi philosophers, or impersonalists, mistake the living entity for the param-atma, who in actuality is sitting side by side with the living entity. The Supersoul acts as the neutral observer, witness, adviser, guide and friend of the individual soul. Because the param-atma, the localised aspect of the Supreme Personality of Godhead, and the individual living entity are both within the body, a misunderstanding sometimes takes place that there is no difference between the two. But there is a definite difference between the individual soul and the Supersoul, and this is also explained in the Mundaka-Upanisad by the following example.

The individual soul and Supersoul are compared to two birds which reside in the same tree. One of them (jiva-atma) is eating the fruits of the tree, while the other (param-atma) is just witnessing the activities of his friend. The witness is the Lord, and the fruit-eater is the living entity. The fruit-eater (living entity) which is overcome by the reaction of his enjoyment, has forgotten his real identity and is overwhelmed in the fruitive activities of the material conditions, but the Lord (param-atma), who is always transcendentally situated, is not affected by the material atmosphere. That is the difference between the Supersoul and the conditioned soul. One should not think that the Supreme Lord becomes conditioned when He incarnates on earth or expands Himself as the Supersoul.

Equality between God and Living Entities

The Vedic scriptures explain that the living entities and the Supreme Lord, or God, are essentially **one and the same in their qualitative characteristics**, namely: God is spiritual and the living entity, in his pure state, is spiritual also. As spiritual beings both of them are certainly one in quality of character, but nevertheless, there is still a big **difference in their quantitative function**.

God is absolute and unlimited whereas living entities, who are part and parcels of the Supreme, are insignificantly small compared to the Lord. The Supreme Lord is infinite and the living entity is infinitesimal. The Supreme Lord is the creator and controller whereas living entities are the created and controlled. That is the difference.

The jiva-souls, or the living entities, who are emanations of the Lord's marginal energy, have been accepted by the Lord as His separated part and parcels. A particle of gold is gold also, a drop of water from the ocean is also salty. The quality of the part with the whole are the same, but in quantity the part remains ever different from the whole.

A drop of water is infinitesimal small compared to the power of the big ocean, and a particle of gold is never the same in quantity with the gold mine. Similarly, we, the living entities, being part and parcels of the Supreme Lord, have all the qualities of God, but in minute quantity because we are minute parts only. The parts are always subordinate to the whole.

In Bhagavad-Gita the Supreme Lord is called **param-isvara** or the **Supreme controller**. Since we are parts of the supreme controller we also have a nature to control and therefore we try to imitate Him by lording it over material nature, to control her. This tendency to control is there because it is in God. But although we have a tendency to control and lord it over material nature, we should know that we are not the Supreme controller. We may be compared to little minute isvaras, or subordinate imitation controllers, but we can never become param-isvara, or the Supreme controller.

As the creation always remains under the control of the creator, similarly all created beings are also subjected to the control of their creator. If a living entity says that he is not controlled but that he is free, than he is insane.

The living being is controlled in every respect, at least in his conditioned life. Living entities, who are controlled by either the external or internal energy of the Lord, can therefore never become the Supreme. If a transcendentalist thinks that he can become God, or isvara, by an artificial process of mystic yoga performance or by merging into the impersonal brahmajyoti, then he suffers from nothing but hallucinations. The soul can never become the Supersoul and living entities can never become God.

God always remains God and the living entity always remains an infinitesimal small part of God. Living entities are therefore described in vedic literatures as "amsa" or fragmental parts of the Supreme. The fundamental principle of fragmentation of a piece from the whole is that the quantitative dimension is changed. The part and parcels can never become the whole. The quantitative function of a part is to serve the whole.

Although one in quality with God a living entity, as a part and parcel of the Supreme, is therefore ever distinct in his quantitative function as the servant of the Lord.

The Eternity and Individuality of the Soul

As far as the identity of the living being as spirit soul is concerned, there are a number of speculations and misgivings. The materialist does not believe in the existence of the spirit self, and empiric philosophers believe in the impersonal feature of the whole spirit without individuality of the living beings.

Some transcendentalists teach the philosophy of becoming one with the Supreme by annihilating one's individuality. **Impersonalists (mayavadis), who are frustrated by the struggle of material existence, generally try to kill their identity by merging into the existence of impersonal Brahman**. There are many other theories and concoctions, but all these different speculations can be cleared off by accepting the knowledge of Bhagavad-gita or Srimad Bhagavatam.

The impersonal approach of understanding the identity of the living being is condemned in Bhagavad-gita [2.12] where the Supreme Lord says: "**Never was there a time when I did not exist, nor you, nor all these other living entities nor in the future shall any of us cease to be**." This verse very clearly establishes the eternal existence of the individual soul. The mayavadi theory that after liberation the individual soul, separated by the covering of maya, or illusion, will merge into the impersonal Brahman and lose its individual existence is not supported by this verse.

Neither is the theory supported that individuality refers to the conditioned state only. Krishna clearly says, in this verse, that in the future also the individuality of the Lord and others, will continue eternally. This is also confirmed in the Upanisads which state that the Supreme Lord as well as the conditioned souls are eternally individual beings both in their conditioned as well as in their liberated situations.

The Supreme Lord is the supreme individual person and all other living entities are individual part and parcels of that supreme individual person. All individual persons, including the Lord Himself, are eternally individuals. It is not that they did not exist as individuals in the past, and it is not that they will not remain eternal persons. Their individuality existed in the past, and their individuality will also continue in the future without interruption.

The Bhagavad-gita further states: "For the soul there is never birth nor death. Nor, having once been, does he ever cease to be. He is unborn, eternal, ever-existing, undying and primeval. He is not slain when the body is slain." [2.20]

Although the physical body changes continually from boyhood to youth to old age yet the individual self within the changing body remains always the same. We simply change our bodily dress in different manners. But, actually, we always keep the individuality of our innermost self. Therefore **even after liberation from the bondage of material dress, that individuality will continue because of all of us are individual souls eternally**.

All ling beings, beginning from the first created being, Brahma, down to the smallest ant, are individual living beings. And above Brahma, there are even other living beings with individual capacities, and the personality of Godhead is also a similar living being. And He is an individual as are the other living beings. But the Supreme Lord, or the supreme living being, has the greatest intelligence, and He possesses supermost inconceivable energies of different varieties. He is the creator and maintainer of all. No one is equal too or greater than Him.

Two Types of Consciousness

(1) pure spiritual consciousness [caitanya]

(2) materially contaminated consciousness [citta]

When a pure drop of rain falls from the sky and comes in contact with the ground it takes up the nature of the ground and becomes muddy. By association with matter the pure raindrop becomes conditioned and gets mixed up with matter, thus losing its original purity.

Similarly when a living entity comes in contact with material nature his original spiritual consciousness becomes covered up by matter and thus becomes perverted reflected as material consciousness.

The pure spirit soul, when coming in contact with material nature, becomes conditioned by it and his pure consciousness becomes perverted reflected. Material consciousness is therefore nothing but a covering or perverted reflection of the original pure consciousness of the spirit soul.

But what is this consciousness? Consciousness means to be conscious of something. I am conscious of my self. I know that I exist. This consciousness is 'I am'. Then what am I? In material consciousness one is conscious of one's physical body in relationship to the interaction with the material environment. In this contaminated consciousness 'I am' means I am a product of this material world and I am the enjoyer and Lord of all I survey. The world revolves because every living being thinks that he is the Lord and creator of the material environment.

Material consciousness has two psychic divisions. One is that I am the creator, and the other is that I am the enjoyer. But actually the Supreme Lord is both the creator and enjoyer, and the living entity, being part and parcel of the Supreme Lord, is neither the creator nor the enjoyer, but cooperator. He is the created and the enjoyed. When we refuse to cooperate with the Lord and try to artificially enjoy the material resources, by lording it over material nature, we become forgetful of our spiritual nature and our pure consciousness gets contaminated.

When we are materially contaminated we are called conditioned. False consciousness is exhibited under the impression that I am a product of this material world. This is called false ego. One who is absorbed in the thought of bodily conceptions cannot understand his real self which is spiritual and not a product of this world. One must become free from the bodily conception of life; that is the preliminary activity for the transcendentalist. One who wants to become free, who wants to become liberated, must first of all learn that he is not his material body.

Mukti or liberation means freedom from material consciousness. In the Bhagavad Gita we are advised to purify our contaminated consciousness in order to be situated in pure consciousness.

Purified consciousness establishes one in his own spiritual nature. In pure consciousness one is conscious of one's spiritual identity in relationship with the Supreme Lord. In this purified consciousness 'I am' means I am the spirit soul, part and parcel of the supreme soul and I am meant to serve the Lord. This is the original constitutional position of the living entities and the whole sum and substance of purified consciousness.

Consciousness is already there because we are part and parcels of the Lord who is the supreme consciousness but for us there is the affinity of being affected by material consciousness due to being infinitesimal small parts only. But the consciousness of the Lord, being the Supreme, is never affected by matter and remains always transcendental or spiritual.

The Supreme consciousness isvara is similar to the living entity in this way: both the consciousness of the Lord and that of the living entity is transcendental or spiritual. It is not that consciousness is generated by association of matter. That is a mistaken idea. Pure consciousness is the symptom of the living entity and manifested by the spirit soul. The foolish theory that consciousness develops under certain circumstances of material combination is not accepted in Vedic scriptures.

Consciousness may be pervertedly reflected by the covering of material circumstances, just as light reflected through coloured glass may appear to be a certain colour, but the consciousness of the Lord is not materially affected. Lord Krishna says in Bhagavad-Gita 'mayadhyaksena prakritih'. When He descends into the material universe, His consciousness is not materially affected. If He were so affected, He would be unfit to speak on transcendental matters as He does in Bhagavad-Gita. One cannot say anything about the transcendental world without being free from materially contaminated consciousness. Since the Supreme Lord is the creator He is not affected by His creation. So the Lord is not materially contaminated but remains always transcendental. We, the individual souls, who have been created by the creator, are endowed with a mixed aptitude. Our consciousness possesses a twofold potentiality. It takes cognisance of material categories and it is also open to the influence of spiritual categories which are distinguished from the mundane world.

Our consciousness at the present moment, however, is materially contaminated. The Bhagavad-Gita teaches that we have to purify this materially contaminated consciousness. Pure unadulterated consciousness is the original quality of the individual soul in his liberated state. Material consciousness is the perverted reflection of spiritual consciousness exhibited by the individual soul in his bounded state, which is due to his misidentification with matter.

Through the process of Bhakti yoga one can purify one's whole existence and thus regain his original pure consciousness.

The Five Basic Truths

The subject of the Bhagavad-gita entails the comprehension of five basic truths. First of all, the science of God is explained and then the constitutional position of the living entities, jivas.

There is isvara, which means controller, and there are jivas, the living entities which are controlled. If a living entity says that he is not controlled but that he is free, then he is insane. The living being is controlled in every respect, at least in his conditioned life. So in the Bhagavad-gita the subject matter deals with the isvara, the supreme controller, and the jivas, the controlled living entities. Prakrti (material nature) and time (the duration of existence of the whole universe or the manifestation of material nature) and karma (activity) are also discussed. The cosmic manifestation is full of different activities. All living entities are engaged in different activities. From Bhagavad-gita we must learn what God is, what the living entities are, what prakrti is, what the cosmic manifestation is and how it is controlled by time, and what the activities of the living entities are.

Out of these five basic subject matters in Bhabavad-gita it is established that the Supreme Godhead, or *Krishna*, or Brahman, or supreme controller, or Paramatma - you may use whatever name you like - is the greatest of all. The living beings are in quality like the supreme controller. For instance, the Lord has control over the universal affairs, over material nature, etc., as will be explained in the later chapters of Bhagavad-gita. Material nature is not independent. She is acting under the directions of the Supreme Lord. As Lord *Krishna* says, "Prakrti is working under My direction." When we see wonderful things happening in the cosmic nature, we should know that behind this cosmic manifestation there is a controller.

Nothing could be manifested without being controlled. It is childish not to consider the controller. For instance, a child may think that an automobile is quite wonderful to be able to run without a horse or other animal pulling it, but a sane man knows the nature of the automobile's engineering arrangement. He always knows that behind the machinery there is a man, a driver. Similarly, the Supreme Lord is a driver under whose direction everything is working.

Now the jivas, or the living entities, have been accepted by the Lord, as we will note in the later chapters, as His parts and parcels. A particle of gold is also gold, a drop of water from the ocean is also salty, and similarly, we the living entities, being part and parcel of the supreme controller, isvara, or Bhagavan, Lord Sri *Krishna*, have all the qualities of the ordinate isvaras. We are trying to control space or planets, and this tendency to control is there because it is in *Krishna*. But although we have a tendency to lord it over nature, we should know that we are not the supreme controller. This is explained in the Bhagavad-gita.

What is material nature? This is also explained in Gita as inferior prakrti, inferior nature. The living entity is explained as the superior prakrti. Prakrti is always under control, whether inferior or superior prakrti is female, and she is controlled by the Lord just as the activities of a wife are controlled by the husband. Prakrti is always subordinate, predominated by the Lord, who is the predominator.

The living entities and material nature are both predominated, controlled by the Supreme Lord. According to the Gita, the living entities, although parts and parcels of the Supreme Lord, are to be considered prakrti. This is clearly mentioned in the Seventh Chapter, fifth verse of Bhagavad-gita: "Apareyam itas tv anyam." "This prakrti is My lower nature." "Prakrtim viddhi me param jiva-bhutam maha-baho yayedam dharyate jagat." And beyond this there is another prakrti: jiva-bhutam, the living entity.

Prakrti itself is constituted by three qualities: the mode of goodness, the mode of passion and the mode of ignorance. Above these modes there is eternal time, and by a combination of these modes of nature and under the control and purview of eternal time there are activities which are called karma. These activities are being carried out from time immemorial, and we are suffering or enjoying the fruits of our activities. For instance, suppose I am a businessman and have worked very hard with intelligence and have amassed a great bank balance. Then I am an enjoyer. But then say I have lost all my money in business; then I am a sufferer. Similarly, in every field of life we enjoy the results of our work, or we suffer the results. This is called karma.

Isvara (the Supreme Lord), jiva (the living entity), prakrti (nature), eternal time and karma (activity) are all explained in the Bhagavad-gita. Out of these five, the Lord, the living entities, material nature and time are eternal. The manifestation of prakrti may be temporary, but is not false. Some philosophers say that the manifestation of material nature is false, but according to the philosophy of Bhagavad-gita or according to the philosophy of the Vaisnavas, this is not so. The manifestation of the world is not accepted as false; it is accepted as real, but temporary. It is likened unto a cloud which moves across the sky, or the coming of the rainy season which nourishes grains.

As soon as the rainy season is over and as soon as the cloud goes away, all the crops which were nourished by the rain dry up. Similarly, this material manifestation takes place at a certain interval, stays for a while and then disappears. Such are the workings of prakrti. But this cycle is working eternally. Therefore prakrti is eternal; it is not false. The Lord refers to this as "My prakrti." This material nature is the separated energy of the Supreme Lord, and similarly the living entities are also the energy of the Supreme Lord, but they are not separated. They are eternally related.

So the Lord, the living entity, material nature and time are all interrelated and are all eternal. However, the other item, karma, is not eternal. The effects of karma may be very old indeed. We are suffering or enjoying the results of our activities from time immemorial, but we can change the results of our karma, or our activity, and this change depends on the perfection of our knowledge. We are engaged in various activities. Undoubtedly we do not know what sort of activities we should adopt to gain relief from the actions and reaction of all these activities, but this is also explained in the Bhagavad-gita.

The position of isvara is that of supreme consciousness. The jivas, or the living entities, being parts and parcels of the Supreme Lord, are also conscious. Both the living entity and material nature are explained as prakrti, the energy of the Supreme Lord, but one of the two, the jiva, is conscious. The other prakrti is not conscious. That is the difference. Therefore the jiva-prakrti is called superior because the jiva has consciousness which is similar to the Lord's. The Lord's is supreme consciousness, however, and one should not claim that the jiva, the living entity, is also supremely conscious. The living being cannot be supremely conscious at any stage of his perfection, and the theory that he can be so is a misleading theory. Conscious he may be, but he is not perfectly or supremely conscious.

The distinction between the jiva and the isvara will be explained in the Thirteenth Chapter of Bhagavad-gita. The Lord is ksetra-jnah, conscious, as is the living being is conscious of his particular body, whereas the Lord is conscious of all bodies. Because He lives in the heart of every living being, He is conscious of the psychic movements of the particular jiva. We should not forget this. It is also explained that the Paramatma, the Supreme Personality of Godhead, is living in everyone's heart as isvara, as the controller, and that He is giving directions for the living entity to act as he desires.

The living entity forgets what to do. First entangled in the acts and reaction of his own karma. After giving up one type of body, he enters another type of body, as we put on and take off old clothes. As the soul thus migrates, he suffers the actions and reactions of his past activities. These activities can be changed when the living being is in the mode of goodness, in sanity, and understands what sort of activities he should adopt. If he does so, then all the actions and reactions of his past activities can be changed. Consequently, karma is not eternal. Therefore we stated that of the five items (isvara, jiva, prakrti, time and karma) four are eternal, whereas karma is not eternal.

The supreme conscious isvara is similar to the living entity in this way: both the consciousness of the Lord and that of the living entity are transcendental. It is not that consciousness is generated by the association of matter. That is a mistaken idea. The theory that consciousness develops under certain circumstances of material combination is not accepted in the Bhagavad-gita. Consciousness may be pervertedly reflected by the covering of material circumstances, just as light reflected through coloured glass may appear to be a certain colour, but the consciousness of the Lord is not materially affected.

Lord *Krishna* says, "mayadhyaksena prakrti." When He descends into the material universe, His consciousness is not materially affected. If He were so affected, He would be unfit to speak on transcendental matters as He does in the Bhagavad-gita. One cannot say anything about the transcendental world without being free from materially contaminated. Our consciousness, at the present moment, however, is materially contaminated. The Bhagavad-gita teaches that we have to purify this materially contaminated consciousness. In pure consciousness, our actions will be dovetailed to the will of isvara, and that will make us happy.

It is not that we have to cease all activities. Rather, our activities are to be purifies, and purified activities are called bhakti. Activities in bhakti appear to be like ordinary activities, but they are not contaminated. An ignorant person may see that a devotee is acting or working like an ordinary man, but such a person with a poor fund of knowledge does not know that the activities of the devotee or of the Lord are not contaminated by impure consciousness or matter. They are transcendental to the three modes of nature. We should know, however, that at this point our consciousness is contaminated.

When we are materially contaminated, we are called conditioned. False consciousness is exhibited under the impression that I am a product of material nature. This is called false ego. One who is absorbed in the thought of bodily conceptions cannot understand his situation. Bhagavad-gita was spoken to liberate one from the bodily conception of life, and Arjuna put himself in this position in order to receive this information from the Lord.

One must become free from the bodily conception of life; that is the preliminary activity for the transcendentalist. One who wants to become free, who wants to become liberated, must first of all learn that he is not this material body. Mukti or liberation means freedom from material consciousness. In the Srimad-Bhagavatam also the definition of liberation is given: Mukti means liberation from the contaminated consciousness of this material world and situation in pure consciousness.

All the instructions of Bhagavad-gita are intended to awaken this pure consciousness, and therefore we find at the last stage of the Gita's instructions that *Krishna* is asking Arjuna whether he is now in purified consciousness. Purified consciousness means acting in accordance with the instructions of the Lord.

This is the whole sum and substance of purified consciousness. Consciousness is already there because we are part and parcel of the Lord, but for us there is the affinity of being affected by the inferior modes. But the Lord, being the Supreme, is never affected. That is the difference between the Supreme Lord and the conditioned souls.

What is this consciousness? This consciousness is "I am." Then what am I? In contaminated consciousness "I am" means "I am the lord of all I survey. I am the enjoyer." The world revolves because every living being thinks that he is the lord and creator of the material world. Material consciousness has two psychic divisions. One is that I am the creator, and other is that I am the enjoyer. But actually the Supreme Lord is both the creator and the enjoyer, and the living entity, being part and parcel of the Supreme Lord, is neither the creator nor the enjoyer, but a cooperator. He is the created and the enjoyed. For instance, a part of a machine cooperates with the whole machine; a part of the body cooperates with the whole body.

The hands, feet, eyes, legs and so on are all parts of the body, but they are not actually the enjoyers. The stomach is the enjoyer. The legs move, the hands supply food, the teeth chew and all parts of the body are engaged in satisfying the stomach because the stomach is the principal factor that nourishes the body's organization. Therefore everything is given to the stomach. One nourishes the tree by watering its root, and one nourishes the body by feeding the stomach, for if the body is to be kept in a healthy state, then the parts of the body must cooperate to feed the stomach. Similarly, the Supreme Lord is the enjoyer and the creator, and we, as subordinate living beings, are meant to cooperate to satisfy Him.

This cooperation will actually help us, just as food taken by the stomach will help all other parts of the body. If the fingers of the hand think that they should take the food themselves instead of giving it to the stomach, then they will be frustrated. The central figure of creation and of enjoyment is the Supreme Lord, and the living entities are cooperators. By cooperation they enjoy. The relation is also like that of the master and the servant. If the master is fully satisfied, then the servant is satisfied. Similarly, the creator and the tendency to enjoy the material world are there also in the living entities because these tendencies are there in the Supreme Lord who has created the manifested cosmic world.

We shall find, therefore, in this Bhagavad-gita that the complete whole is comprised of the supreme controller, the controlled living entities, the cosmic manifestation, eternal time and karma, or activities, and all of these are explained in this text. All of these taken completely form the complete whole, and the complete whole is called the Supreme Absolute Truth. The complete whole and the complete Absolute Truth are the complete Personality of Godhead, Sri *Krishna*. All manifestations are due to His different energies. He is the complete whole.

2

The Systems of Yoga

The Ten Oriental Yogas

Three is great interest in the Western world at the present time on the subject of Oriental Occultism, and very rightly so, for the time has come for it to be blended in with the practical material civilization which has been so wonderfully developed in the modern world. There will be two benefits in this blending—more success in the outer world and more peace in the inner life.

The time has gone for any of us—East or West—to think of Occultism as an escape from material reality and responsibility into some vague inner condition in which one retreats from all that material life stands for. Rather it is concerned in the purpose voiced by Emerson when he wrote: "To make in matter home for mind." To make of this world a place where consciousness can enjoy to the full all the powers of its own mind and at the same time discover that there is more to the mind than is commonly known—that is practical Occultism.

To know how the mind works we cannot do better than turn to the ancient writers on what is called yoga—looking at *all* the principal ancient schools of yoga, not only one or two of them. Of these there are seven well-known surviving schools in India today, and in addition to these our survey of Oriental Occultism would be incomplete without allusion to three others—the Persian Sufis, the Buddhist "Noble Way," and the Chinese and Japanese Zen. This makes ten in all.

Many are the modern teachers of practical occultism or yoga, but all of them can be classed as especially devoted to the methods of one or other of these modes of practice.

Why have we at the outset associated the word yoga with occultism? Because yoga is the practice of occult powers—or rather the discovery and use of those powers residing unseen in the depths of the human mind. The practice could begin with the formula, "We are only part alive," and from that standpoint proceed to investigate the Introspectional Psychology of the ancients, which they said united them—yoga means union—with the latent possibilities and unseen actualities of and beyond the mind. The Introspectional Psychology, all the ancient teachers asserted, is justified by its results; it works.

That it should have been developed in elder times, in very peaceful times, in the Orient, was very natural. In those very settled days there were whole classes of society who had leisure to give to these matters. There were not only solitary and silent hermit-investigators, but also teachers with small schools, and travelling lecturers, and occasional conferences of teachers organized by the ancient rulers. But nowadays we have a phase of material activity, most fully developed in America and now invading the Orient itself, which leaves people with little energy or time to carry on the studies in Introspectional Psychology in which many people formerly immersed themselves—in which they were often at fault when they made the delights of the mind a substitute for the valuable experience of the whole estate of man. This modern activity is such that very often people have nervous breakdowns of various kinds. Many must be the material achievements left unfulfilled because of the collapse of those who could originate them but could not bear the strain of carrying them to their completion.

It is into this field of sorrow, lit up only occasionally by success, that the Oriental occultism can be brought for the discovery and use of the inner resources of the mind, increasing the power and improving the machinery of thought, emotion and the will. That peace and power are two aspects of one principle is one of the chief discoveries of the Oriental occultist—a discovery within the reach of all reasonable persons.

It is not to be thought, however, that the ancient teachers alluded to are proposing some sort of magic as a substitute for our present method of doing things through the mechanism of a healthy body. That the magic exists is true, and there is a long list of "psychic powers" which manifest themselves in various degrees quite naturally as the process of yoga goes on, but the teachers mostly refer to these as not of great value, and advise against making the mind a "playground" for them.

In India there are many who can exhibit varieties of hallucinatory or hypnotic effects, and also telepathy, psychometry, clairvoyance, clairaudience, levitation, astral travelling, transportation and apport, and similar occult or magical arts. Indeed, some people with very little education in other respects have been specially trained in one or more of these faculties and powers, so that they are able to astonish the tourist and earn a living by exhibiting these feats. But the real yogis are not interested in these. They are interested in mastering environment and finding the ethical and spiritual forces and experiences which are not only immature but positively infantile in most people.

It will be asked: "Why do not these more perfect men use both the higher powers and the magics?" The answer is, "They do. They use these constantly, but they do not display them, for they know that very many persons would be tempted out of the regular course of their evolution by the glamour of these faculties and powers. And many would use them as only another additional means for exploiting their fellow men."

As to such matters as applying a healing influence for body and mind—these can be as well used in silence as with any display. I remember that one very respected Hindu occultist, when questioned on this point said that if highly successful and convincing demonstrations of the occult powers were given, most people would be overcome by modesty and would want to lean upon the demonstrator, others would be frightened, others would call it the work of the devil, and some who had not seen for themselves would call it all a fraud—but on the other hand those who sincerely practice the yoga will invariably have before long some convincing experiences of their own, useful for their own private encouragement and essential benefit.

In my book *The Occult Training of the Hindus*, published some years ago in Madras, and recently reprinted there, I presented a brief survey of this subject, resulting from my long residence in India, during which I was chiefly interested in studying these matters. In that book I have told of my acquaintance and friendship with many of these exponents of yoga, and how I thus learned that all over the country there are tens of thousands of people who give part of their day to the pursuit of the methods of the ancient occult teachers, although they are engaged in modern occupations. There is in India, I would say, a vein of practicality in these matters which most Western persons just do not understand.

In the present small volume, intended to bring these matters more to the attention of the West, I am making use again of much of the material in that book, without feeling it necessary to employ quotation marks. This has been done considerably in Chapters 2 to 6. Chapters 7 to 9 are entirely newly written.

Let us begin then with the statement that the seven well-known varieties of yoga practice among the Hindus can be listed as follows:

1. The Raja Yoga of Patanjali.
2. The Karma and Buddhi Yoga of Shri Krishna.
3. The Gnyana Yoga of Shri Shankaracharya.
4. Hatha Yoga.
5. Laya Yoga.
6. Bhakti Yoga.
7. Mantra Yoga.

These seven can be classified in two groups—the first three being called varieties of *raja-yoga* and the last four varieties of *hatha-yoga*. The adjective *raja* means "kingly" because the man becomes king or master of his own faculties. The last four emphasize the importance of material aids, by working largely on the outside or on the "terrestrial man," which is composed of the body along with its bundle of habitual emotions and memories and knowledge.

The *raja-yogi* maintains that the inner powers of the mind can never be enhanced by any external means, but only by their own exercise.

Here the law of growth from within is paramount. By the use of thought, thought grows. This is true also of love and the will. There is no other way in which these growths can be obtained. A realization of this fact sets the novice on his own feet, and cures him at the outset of any tendency to lean or depend upon others, even upon experts and teachers he may admire.

Still, this exercise can be hindered or at least made very difficult by any bad condition of the body in such matters as nervous disorders, irregular breathing, bad balance, and undue tension. The *hatha-yogis* of the more intellectual kind accede to the proposition that all higher growth is from within, but still say "No *raja* without *hatha*" because they find that bodies generally require some preparation. The thoroughgoing *raja-yogis* however, generally reply that there is *raja* without *hatha*, and in fact that *raja-yoga* if properly done will itself put the body in order, for the mind influences the body even if the body cannot influence the mind. Still there is no harm, they often add, in just a little *hatha-yoga* as well, provided that the aspirant does not fall into a state of dependence on anything or any person, and does not seek merely the comforts of the body, emotions and knowledge, or make his purpose the increase of his power with a view to gain in these three fields.

The term *hatha-yoga*, when used strictly, refers specifically only to the fourth school on our list, for it is specially devoted to breathing practices, dealing with the incoming and outgoing—or *ha* and *tha* breaths. But the term is quite elastic and portions of the remaining three groups of teachings are generally included, to supplement the breathing exercises of the *hatha-yoga* schools. Inasmuch as all the four schools operate by external means they are all classable as in the general field of *hatha-yoga*, as they all work on the body and environment.

One of the great gains of modern yoga is that the "hair shirt" has been entirely given up. The new race is not afraid of the world. It does not regard it as evil or of the devil. Modern man can trust himself amidst all the lures. He can handle them and be their master. He knows his own powers and can very well judge the results of his use of them. He can envisage a metaphysical goal and also be aware of the metaphysical in the physical as he goes along. He feels that whatever he may gain by any exercise or experience in his will, his goodwill and his intelligence is all to the good, quite apart from any so-called material gain, and there is no objection to that in addition.

If he is caught up in any interests, enthusiasms or excitements—as he is—he knows not to go too far, and that he will come out of them richer in character, even if a bit scarred. He knows that time will heal all the wounds and ripen the character. So in the field of yoga today he is not in fear of missing anything, nor dependent upon a particular guide, but will choose his exercises with all the natural confidence with which he can choose a good cigar. He asks for information, not gifts, nor orders, and here the Orient spreads it out before him for his choice. According to individual temperament each will choose, and then travel in the way that suits him best.

Patanjali's Raja Yoga

Foremost among the Yoga teachings of India comes that of Patanjali dating back, according to popular tradition, to at least 300 B.C. His *Yoga Sutras* give definitions and instructions which are accepted by all teachers, even when they also make additions in minor matters. He begins with a description of yoga as "*Chitta vritti nirodha.*" *Chitta* is the mind, the instrument that stands between the man and the world. As a gardener uses a spade for digging, so a man uses the mind for dealing with the world. Acted upon by the things of the outer world through the senses, it presents to the man within a picture of those things, as on the plate of a camera.

Acted upon by the will of the man within, it transmits into action in the body the thought-power that is its positive characteristic. It thus has two functions—one receptive or negative, the other active or positive. It transmits from the world to the man within, and also from the man within to the outer world.

Vritti means literally a whirlpool, and *nirodha* signifies restraint or control. Thus yoga practice is control of the whirlpools or changes of the mind or, in simple terms, voluntary direction of what is commonly called thought, or control of the ideas which are in the mind.

The mind of the average man is far from being an instrument within his control. It is being impressed at all times, even during sleep to some extent, with the pictures of a thousand objects clamoring for his attention, through ears, skin, eyes, nose and mouth, and by telepathic impressions from others. In addition to all that, it is in a state of agitation on its own account, bubbling in a hundred places with disturbing visions, excited by uncontrolled emotion or worrying thoughts. Let him achieve control of all this, says Patanjali, and his reward will be that he shall stand in his own state.

That a man should be in his own true state has two meanings: first, that in his repose he will be utterly himself, not troubled with the whirlpools, which, however slight, are in the eyes of the yogi nothing but worry, and secondly, that in his activity as a man, using the mind, he will be a positive thinker, not merely a receptacle for impressions from outside and ideas which he has collected in the course of time.

Ideas in the mind should be material for thought, not merely ideas, just as the muscles are useful means of action, not mere lumps of flesh. To be a positive thinker, lover and willer, master in one's own house, is to be oneself, in one's own true state; all the rest is slavery or bondage, willing or unwilling. To its master, the man, the *vrittis* of *chitta* are always only objects of knowledge, because of his not being involved in them, say Aphorisms iv 18-20. These *vrittis* are ideas or items in the mind.

The final aim of Patanjali's yoga is to cease this slavery and achieve freedom. The technical name for this great achievement is *kaivalya*, independence. That is really only another name for divinity, for material things are in bondage, unable to move of themselves, and always moved by forces from the outside; but the divine is by definition free, able to move of itself. Every man feels in himself some spark of that divine freedom, which he then calls the will, and that is the power with which he can control his mind.

In Patanjali's yoga the aspirant uses his will in self-control. Thought governs things, we know; so much so that every voluntary movement of the body follows a mental picture; therefore all work done by us, even with the hands, is done by thought-power. But will controls thought, concentrates it, expands it, causes its flow—directs, in fact, its three operations of concentration, meditation, and contemplation. The perfection of these three is the aim of the Patanjali yoga exercises.

Before proceeding with the systematic description of the practices of yoga, which begins in his Book ii, Patanjali mentions two things which are necessary for success in controlling the *vrittis* or thoughts, namely *abhyasa* and *vairagya*. *Abhyasa* means constant practice in the effort to secure steadiness of mind. *Vairagya* is that condition of the feelings in which they are not coloured by outside things, but are directed only by our own best judgment.

This detachment of the emotions may be "lower" or "higher" according as it is born from dislike of external conditions, or from a vision of the glorious joy of the pure free life. The higher uncolouredness leads to the highest contemplation, and therefore to freedom, the goal of this yoga. Patanjali's systematic instruction for practical training is given in two portions. The first part, called *Kriya Yoga*, is often translated as preliminary yoga because a person who has not first practised it is not likely to succeed in the main portion, the *ashtanga*, or "eight limbs" of yoga practice. But it is much more than preliminary.

It is the yoga of action, the yoga which must be practised all the time in daily life. Without it, meditation would be useless, for yoga involves not retirement or retreat but a change in attitude towards the world. It is in the midst of life's activities that our freedom must be realized, for to desire to slip away into some untroubled sphere would be mere escape, a perpetuation of the dream of the best we have so far learned to know, a denial of the possibility of our real freedom. A man must become master of himself, whatever other people and beings, whose activities constitute the major portion of his world, may do.

The object of the preliminary yoga or yoga of action is to weaken what are called the five *kleshas*. A *klesha* is literally an affliction, just as one would speak of a crooked spine or blindness as an affliction. The five afflictions are *avidya*, *asmita*, *raga*, *dwesha* and *abhinivesha*, which may be translated ignorance, egotism, liking and disliking, and possessiveness. One leading ancient commentator on the Aphorisms, named Vyasa, states that these, when active, bring one under the authority of Nature, and produce instability, a stream of causes and effects in the world, and dependence upon others. They are faults of the man himself, not outside causes of trouble; the world can never hurt us, except through our own faults, and these five reduce us to pitiful slavery. Having submitted to these, a man is constantly moved from outside, governed too much by circumstances.

"Ignorance" describes all those activities of the mind which do not take into account the fact that man is in himself eternal, pure and painless. The man who does not accept his own true nature as eternal, pure and painless, will judge and value all objects improperly. A house, a chair and a pen are something to a man, by which he can satisfy his body and mind. They could not be the same things to a cow. But the question now is: what are all these things to the real man, who is eternal, pure and painless? To look at all things as for the use of such a being is to begin to see them without error. It is to have true motives.

"Egotism" is the tendency to think "I am this," and the desire that other people also should think one to be this or that. Thinking oneself to be a certain object or mind, or the combination of these even in the form of an excellent and useful personality, means attachment to things. We are not a personality, but we possess one, and it is not to be despised if it is useful to the real man.

The error of Self-personality or egotism leads to the next two afflictions which are personal liking and disliking. These two are those unreasoning impulses which lead men to judge and value things by their influence on the comforts and pleasures and prides of the personality, not according to their value for an immortal being.

The fifth affliction is "possessiveness," beginning with clinging to the body, which indicates the lack of that insight which causes a man to regard the body as a mere instrument which he is willing to use, and wear out in the course of time.

In this affliction we have not merely the fear of death, but that of old age as well, for men forget that the bodily life has its phases—childhood, youth, manhood and old age—and each of these has its own perfections, though it has not the perfections of the other stages. In this course there is constant apparent loss as well as gain, because no man can pay full attention to all the lessons of life at once, or exert at the same time all his faculties, any more than a child in school can properly think of geography, history and mathematics in the period which is devoted to music.

In Hindu life, before it was disturbed from the West, men were wise enough in old age to give the family business into the hands of their mature sons, and devote themselves to the study and contemplation of life; and just as in the West it is considered the bounden duty of parents to support their children with every kindness and give them the opportunities that their stage in life requires, so it was always considered in the East the duty of the grown up children to support their old people with every kindness, treat them with honour and dignity as the source of their own opportunity and power, and give them every opportunity that *their* stage of life requires. The material requirements of these retired people were very small—a corner in the home, some food and occasional clothes.

It is not presumed that in the preliminary stages the candidate will completely destroy the five afflictions. His object will be attained if he succeeds in definitely weakening them. Three kinds of practices are prescribed for this purpose in the yoga of action. These are called *tapas*, *swadhyaya* and *ishwarapranidhana*.

It is impossible to translate these terms by a single word each, without causing serious misunderstanding. The first is often translated as austerity, and sometimes even as mortification. The word means literally "heat" and the nearest English equivalent to that when it is applied to human conduct is "effort." The yogi must definitely do those things that are good, even when a special effort is necessary because old habits of the personality stand in the way. Briefly it means this: "Do for the body what you know to be good for it. Do not let laziness, selfishness, or thoughtlessness stand in the way of your doing what you can to make the body and mind healthy and efficient."

Patanjali does not explain the practice of *tapas*, but Shri Krishna says, in the seventeenth chapter of the *Bhagavad Gita* "Reverential action towards the gods, the educated, the teachers and the wise, purity, straightforwardness, continence, and harmlessness are *tapas* of the body; speech not causing excitement, truthful, affectionate and beneficial, and used in self-study is the *tapas* of speech; clearness of thinking, coolness, quietness, self-control, and purity of subject-matter are the *tapas* of mind."

Shri Krishna here gives a wider range to the meaning of *tapas* than does Patanjali, who makes it particularly a matter concerning the body.

How than can any one say that *tapas* is self-torture? It is true that there has grown up a system of painful practices, such as that of holding the arm still until it withers, or sitting in the sun in the midst of a ring of fires, but these are superstitions which have grown up round a valuable thing, as they are liable to do everywhere. Those who follow these methods are few as compared with the true yogi. All over the country there are Indian gentlemen—many of them Government servants who have a routine task with short working hours—who every day spend some time in meditation, deliberately guiding themselves by the "Yoga Sutras."

A great example of *tapas* is that of the modern women. Their willpower in the government of their bodies and in overcoming bodily self-indulgence excites the greatest admiration. And their results are entirely in line with Patanjali's aphorism iii 45 in which he approves of "excellence of body" and refers to it as consisting of correct form, charm, strength and very firm well-knitness, all of which is the very reverse of mortification or self-castigation, which some have erroneously attributed to yoga, because of superstition.

These delightful beings are not even willing to leave Nature just as she is, but consider in many ways how to bring lightness and freedom from earthiness or grossness or clumsiness into bodily living and bodily appearance. Even the artificialities of high heels and very slender figures have the same "spiritual" background, and where excess or unbalance occurs it can at least be credited to good intentions, carried out with great willpower or *tapas*. The proportion of *tapas* is on the increase all the time as seen by the exercises and dietary courses which are extensively advertised and the thoroughness and continuity with which they are carried out.

Man himself, too, it must be said, shares a little in this sort of effort, shaving or at least trimming his beard and whiskers, and padding his shoulders to ridiculous excess, as he used to do his calves in the old days when trousers were worn short and stockings were the vogue.

In all these matters there has been plenty of *effort*, in the main tending away from uncouth and un-mastered living. I know some of both sexes who assiduously perform what our yogis call *uddiyana*, the exercises of the abdominal muscles, with the effect of correct posture and adequate strength, thus attaining the "natural corset," as it has been called, essential to health and good appearance. There is no doubt that such exercises are necessary for those who do not do work involving bending, and it is not a bad thing that this undertaking calls for considerable willpower which then becomes useful also for other purposes as well, and also contributes to the enjoyment of consciousness.

The second practice, *swadhyaya*, means the study of books that really concern yourself as an immortal being. Psychology, philosophy and ethics come in here. Give up indiscriminate reading, and study what bears upon your progress, is the advice.

The third practice, *ishwara-pranidhana*, means devotion to God, but God as understood by the Hindu, as the perfect Being pervading all things, the life of the world, the inner impulse of which each one of us is a *share*. The aspirant must habituate himself to see that Principle in everything, to accept all as from that hand. "Everything that is received is a gift," says a Hindu proverb; more than that, it is a gift from God, presented with perfect wisdom, to be accepted, therefore, with cheerfulness and joy.

Behind the eyes of every person he meets, the aspirant must also see the Divine. The common salutation of the Hindu, with the palms together, looks curious to the Westerner, as resembling prayer. It *is* prayer—the recognition of God within our fellow-man. It is appreciation, the opposite of depreciation. *Ishwara-pranidhana* is in effect the full appreciation of everything. It makes for maximum attentiveness and thus maximum living.

This practice develops right feeling towards everything; the previous one right thought, and the first right use of the will, and the three together, pursued diligently for even a short time, play havoc with the five afflictions.

When the candidate has weakened the afflictions to some extent, he is ready for Patanjali's regular course, the eight "limbs" of yoga. These may be divided into three sets: two moral, three external, and three internal, as shown in the following list:

1.	*Yama,*	Five abstentions.	Ethical
2.	*Niyama.*	Five observances.	
3.	*Asana.*	Balanced posture.	External
4.	*Pranayama.*	Regularity of breath.	
5.	*Pratyahara.*	Withdrawal of senses.	
6.	*Dharana.*	Concentration.	Internal
7.	*Dhyana.*	Meditation.	
8.	*Samadhi.*	Contemplation.	

The two ethical or moral "limbs" of yoga contain five rules each, which the man must practice in his daily life. Put together, they make what we may call "the ten commandments." The first five are; "Thou shalt not (a) injure, (b) lie, (c) steal, (d) be sensual and (e) be greedy."

Explaining this aphorism, Vyasa says that *ahimsa* or non-injury is placed first because it is the source of the following nine. Thus the brotherhood principle is considered as fundamental. Truth, for example, can hardly arise unless there is a motive beyond selfish desires. Vyasa explains that this means word and thought being in accordance with facts to the best of our knowledge. Only if speech is not deceptive, confused or empty of knowledge, he says, is it truth, because speech is uttered for the purpose of transferring one's knowledge to another.

Vachaspati's glossary interprets truth as word and thought in accordance with facts, and fact as what is really believed or understood by us on account of our own direct experience, our best judgment or the accepted testimony of reliable witnesses. So yoga is rooted in virtue, and that in brotherhood, or a feeling for others. Without at least the desire for these five, though perfection in them may not be attained, contemplation cannot yield its richest fruits. We are to be at peace with the world, even if the world is not at peace with us. In this case there is no *desire* to injure, lie, steal etc. Such activities are not sources of pleasure, in any circumstances.

The second five are: "Thou shalt be (a) clean, (b) content, (c) self-controlled, (d) studious, and (e) devoted." Few comments are needed on these. Contentment does not mean satisfaction, but willingness to accept things as they are and to make the most of them. Without dissatisfaction one would not take to yoga. It implies a desire to improve one's life. The remaining three are *tapas*, *swadhyaya* and *ishwara-pranidhana*, the preliminary yoga or yoga of daily life—apart from any private exercises—still carried on.

By the attainment of these five a man can be at peace with the world. It is the end of antagonism *from his side*.

Incidentally, Patanjali mentions that when the ten virtues are firmly established in a person's character definite effects will begin to appear, such as absence of danger, effectiveness of speech, the arrival of unsought wealth, vigour of body and mind, understanding of life's events, clarity of thought, steadiness of attention, control of the senses, great happiness, perfection of body and senses, intuition and realization of one's true self. These can come only after the cessation of all antagonisms to anybody or anything in the world.

Now we come to what some will regard as the more practical steps, though to the understanding yogi nothing can be more practical than the ten commandments. Of these the three external steps are *asana*, *pranayama* and *pratyahara*. The first is right posture, the second right breathing and the third control of the senses. They mean the training of the outer instrument or body so that it will offer no impediment to the serious practices of meditation which are to be taken up.

First, one must learn to sit quite still in a chosen healthy position. "The posture must be steady and pleasant," says Patanjali—that is all. There is no recommendation of any particular posture, least of all any distorted, painful, or unhealthy position. Posture is achieved when it becomes effortless and the mind easily forgets the body. It is chiefly a matter of balance. Some practice of balanced sitting, whether on the ground or on a chair is necessary until balanced musculature is attained. Very often there is fatigue because some of the muscles are weak, yet to sit unbalanced for long is almost impossible.

Next, regulation of breath is necessary. During meditation, people often forget to breathe normally; sometimes they breathe out and forget to breathe in again, and so are suddenly recalled to earth by a choking at the throat. Many people never breathe well and regularly at all; let them practice simple natural exercises, such as those recommended by teachers of singing, and take care that the body is breathing regularly and quietly before they enter their meditation. Sometimes numbers or proportionate times are prescribed, and one of the most authoritative in India is that in which one breathes in with the number 1, holds the breath with the number 4, breathes out with the number 2, and immediately begins again; but it is impossible to prescribe the perfect numbers, because they must differ with different people. The question really is: how long must your breath be so as to provide for enough oxidation? Science will some day say. But one must not hold it in longer than that, for to do so is to deprive the whole system of oxygen. Your body has to carry on all its ordinary sub-conscious activities while meditation is going on.

The only general practical advice one can give is that the breathing should be regular and a little slow, and there should be enough pause between inbreathing and outbreathing. It should also be calm, as may be judged by its not causing much disturbance in the outside air. The student will soon find out what suits him. Stunts such as breathing up one nostril and down the other, or holding the breath for a long time, are not mentioned by Patanjali and should be generally avoided as dangerous.

Pratyahara is the holding back of the senses from the objects of sense. One must practice paying no attention to sounds or sights or skin sensations, quietening the senses so that they will create no disturbance during meditation.

Think of what happens when you are reading an interesting book. Someone may come into the room where you are, may walk past you to get something, and go out again; but perhaps you heard and saw nothing at all. You were in what is sometimes called a brown study. The ears were open and the waves of sound in the air were no doubt agitating the tympanum, from which the nerves were carrying their message to the brain. The eyes were open, and the light waves were painting their pictures on the retina—but you saw and heard nothing, because your attention was turned away from those sensations.

The yogi must try to withdraw attention at will, so that in his meditation no sight or sound will distract him. This is helped by an absence of curiosity about anything external during the time set apart for meditation. One way of practicing this is to sit and listen for a while to the various sounds of nature; then listen to the delicate sound in the ear and so forget the former (though you cannot watch yourself forgetting it); then listen to a mere mental sound conjured up by the imagination, and so forget even the music in the ear.

Then come the three internal steps, to which everything else has been leading up, called *dhurana*, *dhyana* and *samadhi*. They are concentration, meditation, and contemplation.

Concentration is really voluntary attentiveness, but this involves narrowing the field of view, focusing the mental eye upon a chosen object.

When you practice concentration or meditation, always choose the object before you begin. Sometimes people sit down and then try to decide what to concentrate upon, and come to no settled decision before their time is all gone. Then, do not try to *hold* the object in position by your thought. It is not the object that is going to run away; it is the mind that wanders. Let the object be thought of as in a natural position—if it is a pen it may be lying on the table; if it is a picture it may be hanging on the wall. Then narrow the field of attention down to it, and look at it with perfect calmness, and without any tension or sensation in the body or head.

Do not be surprised or annoyed if other thoughts intrude on your concentration. Be satisfied if you do not lose sight of your chosen object, if it remains the central thing before your attention. Take no notice of the intruding thoughts. Say "I do not care whether they are there or not." Keep the emotions calm in this manner, and the intruders will disappear when you are not looking. Calmness—no physical strain—is necessary for successful concentration, and, given this, it is not at all the difficult thing that it is sometimes supposed to be. Detailed methods for practicing concentration are given in my book *Concentration*," and regarding that and the other seven steps as well in my *Practical Yoga: Ancient and Modern*, which contains my translation and explanation of all the Patanjali Yoga aphorisms.

Meditation is a continuous flow or fountain of thought with regard to the object of your concentration. It involves the realization of that object as fully as possible. You must not let the string of thought go so far away on any line that the central object is in any way dimmed. On the contrary, every new idea that you bring forward must be fully thought of only with reference to it and should make it clearer and stronger than before.

Thus for practice you might meditate on a cat. You would consider it in every detail; think of all its parts and qualities, physical, emotional, mental, moral and spiritual; think of its relation to other animals and of particular cats that you have known. When this is done you should know what a cat is much better than you did before. You will have brought into agreement and union all your knowledge or information on the subject. In this meditation there is no clutching, no anxiety, only calm mental reviewing and thinking.

The same method applies to virtues such as truth, kindness and courage. Many people have the most imperfect ideas as to what these are. Make concrete pictures in the imagination of acts of kindness, courage, truth. Then try to realize the states of emotion and mind, and the moral condition involved, and in doing so keep up the vividness of consciousness that has already been attained in the beginning of the practice on account of concentration on the concrete scene.

In meditation you take something up, but it is the opposite of going to sleep, because you *retain* the vivid qualities of reality which belong to the concentrated waking state. Yet it should always be done with perfect calm, and no tension or excitement. It widens, includes and integrates without loss of the quality gained by concentration or specific attentiveness.

Contemplation is another kind of concentration; this time a poise of the mind at the top end of your line of thought. When in meditation you have reached the highest and fullest thought you can about the chosen object, and your mind begins to waver, do not try to go forward, but do not fall back. Hold what you have attained, and poise calmly on it for a little time.

You will find that by contemplation you have created a platform. You have been making a new effort and so have developed or discovered some hitherto latent possibilities. There may be something in the nature of illumination. You must see what comes; never try to predetermine it. Then contemplation opens the door of the mind to intuitive knowledge, and many powers.

The student is told always to begin with concentration, then proceed to meditation. The triple process is a mind-poise called *sanyama*.

If the candidate wants to have what are commonly called psychic faculties and powers, Patanjali explains how he may obtain them—by *sanyama* on various objects having corresponding qualities. He mentions knowledge of past and future, memory of past lives, reading of others' minds, perception of those who have reached perfection, and other powers and knowledge connected with "higher hearing, touch, sight, taste and smell" but remarks that, though these are accomplishments of the out-going mind, they are obstacles to the full or higher *samadhi*. Vachaspati comments on this that sometimes the mind is captivated by these psychic powers, just as a beggar may think of the possession of a little wealth as abundant riches, but the real yogi will reject them all. How can the real man, he asks, who has determined to remove all pain—including psychological or emotional pains—take pleasure in such accomplishments, which are opposed to his true state of being? Only by non-attachment to all such things, however great, may the seeds of bondage be destroyed, and independence or freedom be attained.

True contemplation, poised on higher matters, Patanjali teaches, leads to the complete dispersal of the afflictions, and on to great clarity and insight, culminating in the cessation of the junction of the seer and the sight, the absence of all pain and the uncovering of the inner light.

Shri Krishna's Gita-yoga

We have used the new term Gita-Yoga here because it sums up the titles of all the eighteen chapters of the *Bhagavad Gita*, each of which is called a yoga, such as "The Yoga of Knowledge," "The Yoga of Action," etc.

Gita means song, and the whole title means the song of Shri Krishna, who is referred to as the Bhagvan—the most illustrious being. Shri Krishna is regarded as the most perfect of all Teachers—so much so that he could speak about everything from the divine standpoint and with divine knowledge of the reality beyond mind, so that when saying "I" he spoke as an incarnation of the Divine Being. He is considered to have lived about 5050 years ago, and the *Bhagavad Gita* is regarded as a record of what he said or sang to his devoted friend and disciple Arjuna, who was in a state of despondency because he could not solve a problem of "right or wrong" in which his emotions were very much involved. The problem was whether to fight or not in a certain battle which was about to begin. Arjuna's particular problem does not concern us now. The yoga-teaching it called forth from Shri Krishna is read and meditated upon by millions of people every day.

Shri Krishna's teaching is more a yoga for the emotions than the mind, although he does explain the necessity for mind-control and uses the same two words—practice (*abhyasa*) and uncolouredness (*vairagya*) for describing the means to its attainment as Patanjali does when starting his teaching. Shri Krishna tells Arjuna that though his heart is in the right place his unhappy emotional state is due to ignorance. The first point of the Teacher's instruction is—do not judge right and wrong from the standpoint of bodily appearances, but only from what is of value to the immortal soul, taking into account that actions, emotions, thoughts and decisions all have some effect, some tending downwards or away from self-realization and others tending upwards or toward self-realization. Downwards there is bondage and sorrow; upwards there is joy and freedom or the divine state of being, so let this first point be firmly understood at the beginning. Shri Krishna said: "You have sorrowed for

those who need no sorrow, yet you speak words of wisdom. Those who know do not grieve for the living, nor for the dead. Certainly never at any time was I not, nor you, nor these lords of men, nor shall we ever cease to be hereafter. As there is for the owner of the body childhood, youth and old age in this body, so there comes another body; the intelligent man is not confused by that. Just as a man, having cast off his worn-out clothes, obtains others which are new, so the owner of the body, having thrown away old bodies goes to new ones. Weapons do not cut him; fire does not burn him; waters do not wet him; the wind does not dry him away..."

This point being clear the Teacher goes on to the next. He says in verse ii 39 that what he has given is knowledge, based upon his own supersensuous experience as well as that of ancient Teachers, but now he wants Arjuna to take up something more than mere knowledge-yoga—he wants him to take up *buddhiyoga*. *Buddhi* is wisdom, which comes from doing all things for the benefit of souls, not bodies primarily. It is *buddhi* or wisdom to revalue everything from that standpoint.

It is easy to see that the heart of wisdom is love for the cosouls, which Krishna calls indestructible *jivabhutas*, that is, living beings, as distinguished from temporary states and conditions, which are called *bhavas*. Thus the human personalities, in all their varieties are *bhavas*, or existent conditions, but the real men who are owners of the personalities are immortal beings. The lesson that the heart of wisdom is love—goodwill, brotherhood—is driven home by Shri Krishna in his third discourse or chapter, in which he states that the interdependence of all the living beings in the world is universal, and as this is so one should cooperate heartily, not merely mentally but with love, for the very simple reason that the man who loves cannot abstain from activity. He is in a vigorous state, for love is the great energy of the soul. He is like the typical gentleman of Confucius, who was defined as never neutral, but always impartial.

The man of love looks out upon the world, and feels that he must do what he can, however small the opportunity, for the welfare of mankind. This important fact was also soon placed before Arjuna by his Teacher. After pointing out how all the living beings in the world are related to one another in service, how everywhere there is interdependence, he then declared that the man who on earth does not follow the wheel thus revolving lives in vain. Said Shri Krishna: "The man who performs actions without personal attachment reaches the 'beyond'; therefore always do work which ought to be done, without personal attachment. Janaka and others attained perfection through work, so, having regard to the welfare of the world, it is proper for you to work." There is great significance in the words which have been translated "the welfare of the world." They are *loka-sangraha*, *loka* means the inhabitants; *sangraha* means their holding or combining together, their living in harmony. This means love, and if there must be fighting, it is a regrettable necessity, and is to be done still with love in the heart.

It is in this activity that work and love are brought together. What is called *karma-yoga* thus comes into being. Mere work or karma is not yoga, but when that work is energized by love for mankind, it becomes a yoga, that is, a method for the realization of the unity of life. So *karma-yoga* is one branch of Krishna's great teaching of love. The *karma-yogi* "goes about doing good."

And yet that *karma-yoga* is also devotion to God. Among Krishna's devotees, as among those of Christ, there are two distinct kinds. There are those who admire the teacher because he was the great lover of mankind; and there are those who fall down in admiration and devotion before the greatness and goodness of the teacher, and then learn from his example and precept to spread some of his love around them, among their fellow-men. Some love man first and God afterwards; others love God first and man afterwards. The first are the *karma-yogis*; the second the *bhaktiyogis*.

God himself is depicted in the *Gita* as the greatest karma yogi, the pattern for all who would follow that path. He says: "There is nothing in the three worlds, O Partha, that I ought to do, and nothing attainable unattained, yet I engage in work. Certainly if I did not always engage in work without laziness, people on all sides would follow my path. These worlds would become lost if I did not work; I would be the maker of confusion, and would ruin these creatures." No reason can be given why he should thus work, except that he loves the world.

But let no man be discouraged in this work because he himself is small. Let not his vision of great things and devotion to great beings cause him to sink down disconsolate, thinking, "There is nothing that I can do that is big enough to be worth the doing." Let him remember that spiritual things are not measured by quantity but their greatness consists in the purity of their motive.

It is the love that counts—not the action. It is one of the greatest glories of this universe that the common and inconspicuous life of ordinary men contains a thousand daily opportunities of spiritual splendour. Says Shri Krishna: "Men reach perfection, each being engaged in his own *karma*. Better is one's own *dharma* though inglorious, than the well-performed *dharma* of another. He who does the duty determined by his own state incurs no fault. By worshipping in his own *karma* (work) him from whom all beings come, him by whom all this is spread out, a man attains perfection."

The words *dharma* and *karma* here require explanation. *Dharma* means where you stand. Each man has to some extent unfolded the flower of his possibility. He stands in a definite position, or holds definite powers of character. It is better that he should recognize his position and be content with it, true to the best he knows, than that he should try to stand in the position of another, or waste his powers in mere envious admiration. To use his powers in the kind of work he can do, upon and with the material that his past karma has provided for him in the present is not only the height of practical wisdom—it is worship of God as well. All life lived in this way is worship; ploughing and reaping, selling and buying—whatever it may be. Conventional forms of kneeling and prostration are not the sole or even the necessary constituents of worship, but every act of the *karma-yogi* and of the *bhakti-yogi* is that. The word bhakti does in fact contain more of the meaning of service than of feeling.

The Lord does not ask from his devotees great gifts. Says Shri Krishna: "When anyone offers to me with devotion a leaf, a flower, a fruit or a little water, I accept that, which is brought with devotion by the striving soul. When you do anything, eat anything, sacrifice anything, give anything or make an effort, do it as an offering to me. Thus shall you be released from the bonds of karma, having their good and bad results, and being free and united through *sannyasa* (renunciation) you will come to me. I am alike to all beings; none is disliked by me, and none is favourite; but those who worship me with devotion are in me and I also am in them. Even if a great evildoer worships me, not devoted to anything else, he must be considered good, for he has determined well. Quickly he becomes a man of *dharma* and attains constant peace." 5 It is clear, then, that this yoga is a way of thinking, and acting, inspired by love, which releases a man from bondage to his own personality.

As there is community of work between God and man, so is there community of interest, and indeed, community of feeling. "All this is threaded on me," says the Divine, "like a collection of pearls on a string." And the reward of the path of yoga is the full realization of this unity: "At the end of many lives the man having wisdom approaches me. By devotion he understands me, according to what I really am; then, having truly known me, he enters that (state) immediately. Although always doing work, having me for goal, through my grace he obtains the eternal indestructible goal."

The love of man for God is more than reciprocated; "He who has no dislike for any being, but is friendly and kind, without greed or egotism, the same in pleasure and pain, forgiving, always content, harmonious, self-controlled and resolute, with thought and affection intent upon me, he, my devotee, is dear to me. He from whom people are not repelled, and who does not avoid the world, free from the agitations of delight, impatience and fear, is dear to me. Those devotees who are intent upon this deathless way of life, thus declared, full of faith, with me as (their) supreme—they are above all dear to me."

Some of the devotional verses suggest a great absence of self-reliance *if* they are taken out of their general context, as, for instance: "Giving up all *dharmas* come only to me as your refuge. Do not sorrow; I will release you from all sins." This "I" to whom reference is so often made, is the one Self, the one life, and therefore it advocates the giving up of selfishness and taking interest in the welfare of all. There is in all this no suggestion anywhere that man should lean upon an external God, an entity. This devotion is required to the "me" which is *all* life, and not a portion of life in some external form, however grand. Shri Krishna speaks for that one life "equally present in all."

The objective side of this is by no means ignored in this teaching of the importance of the soul, indeed, of all souls. While the souls bring themselves more and more into harmony through the power of love or wisdom or *buddhi*, certain material standards are recognized. The material side, consisting of all the *bhavas* or conditions, must be brought into a state of orderliness and appropriateness called *sattwa*. In the teaching of this part of the subject Shri Krishna says that everything in Nature can be classed under one of three heads—it is *tamasic*, that is, material and sluggish, or *rajasic*, that is, active and restless, or *sattwic*, orderly and harmonious. This is in agreement with both ancient and modern thought.

Modern science recognizes three properties in Nature, or three essential constituents in the objectivity of the external world. One of these is materiality, or the ability of something to occupy space and resist the intrusion of another body into the same space. The second is natural energy or force, and the third is natural law and order. There is no object to be found anywhere, be it large or small, which does not show something of all these three, as it occupies space, shows internal or external energy, and "obeys" (or operates) at least some of Nature's laws. These three qualities of Nature were also well known to the ancient Hindus under the names of *tamas*, *rajas* and *sattwa*, and they held that things differed from one another according to the varied proportions of these three ultimate ingredients. Thus an object in which materiality predominated would be described as *tamasic*, and one in which energy was most prominent would be spoken of as *rajasic*.

The same adjectives are applied very fully in the *Gita* to the personalities of men. In the early stages of human awakening we have the very material or *tamasic* man, who is sluggish and scarcely cares to move, unless he is stirred by a strong stimulus from the outside. Next comes the man in whom *rajas* has developed, who is now eager for excitement and full of energy. Perhaps the bulk of people in the modern world are in this condition, or beginning to come into it. *Rajas* sends them forth into great activity with every kind of greed, from the lowest lust of the body to the highest forms of ambition for wealth and fame and power. Men of this kind cannot restrain themselves—to want is to act.

Thirdly come the people who recognize that there is such a thing as natural law, who realize, for example, that it does not pay to eat and drink just what they like and as much as they like, but that there are certain regulations, about kind and quantity and time, which pertain to eating and drinking, and that violation of these regulations leads to pain.

In time that pain draws attention to what is wrong and the man begins to use his intelligence, first to try to thwart the pain and avert the law, but later on to understand the law, and obey. And then, in that obedience he learns that life is far richer than ever he thought it to be before, that there is in it a sweet strong rhythm unknown to the man of passion, and that alliance with the law can strengthen and enhance human life beyond all the hopes of the impassioned imagination. All good, thoughtful people are in this third stage, obedient and orderly, and they deserve the name of *sattwic* people.

The disciple has to see that his material and personal life or *bhava* is kept in the *sattwic* condition, as regards body, emotions and thoughts. This is a great yoga undertaking. In this there is plenty to do resembling Patanjali's first five steps. At the same time the disciple must go further than the ordinary good man; he must hold himself above all the qualities of Nature (*tamas*, *rajas* and *sattwa*), *using* the *bhava*, not being immersed and lost in it. "Be thou above the three attributes of Nature, O Arjuna," says the Teacher, "without the pairs of opposites (such as heat and cold, praise and blame, riches and poverty), always steadfast in *sattwa*, careless of possessions, having the (real) self."

These laws work out in a multitude of ways in life, but there are three main principles behind them all—principles of the evolution of consciousness. They express themselves in the powers of will, love and thought, creative in the world, and self-creative in the man. There are only three things that the man must now not do. He must never cease to use his will in work. In that work he must never break the law of love. And in that work of love he must never act; without using his intelligence. These are *principles*—greater than all rules and regulations, because they are the living law of the true self; and not much consideration is required to see that he who follows this law must necessarily show in his practical life all the virtues that are admired by good men of every religion. Indeed, we can adopt from the Greeks the three eternal valuables—goodness, truth and beauty—and say that a man is truly a man only when he is operating these.

These teachings condense down to three practical exercises, which convert experience into soul-knowledge. Shri Krishna does not value life for its own sake, or even brotherhood for its own sake, or even love for its own sake. All actions are valuable only because they lead to knowledge of realities of the soul and the ultimate self. Regarding the aspirant's work or living in the world as stimulating a hunger for something better, which, did he but know it, causes the awakening in himself of a deeper knowledge, and regarding all *buddhi-yoga* and *karma-yoga* as an offering on the altar of world-welfare, valuable also because they are a means of true self-education, useful to everybody, Shri Krishna says: "Better than the offering of any material object is the offering of knowledge, for all work culminates in knowledge. You should learn this by reverence, enquiry and service, and those who know and see the truth will teach you the knowledge.

By this you will see all beings without exception in the self, and thus in me. Even if you were the most wicked of evildoers, you would cross over all sin by the raft of (this) knowledge. As fire reduces fuel to ashes, so does the fire of knowledge reduce all *karmas* to ashes. There is indeed no purifier in the world like knowledge. He who is accomplished finds the same in the self in course of time. Having attained (this) knowledge he very soon goes to the peace of the Beyond." 12 The word "knowledge" (*jnana*) in the *Gita* means always something known—high or low. "Wisdom" is *buddhi*, meaning the faculty of understanding the life side of the world.

This passage introduces us to a portion of the definite path of training—the equivalent of Patanjali's practical yoga. It was not sufficient for Arjuna to have great love. If he would tread the path, he must express it in work in the form of service, and must also have an enquiring mind, so as to gain some understanding. The unbalanced character is unfit for the higher path, no matter how great the progress it may have made along one line. Three practices are prescribed; reverence, enquiry and service—in the original, *pranipata*, *pariprashna* and *seva*. The first means bowing, or respect for the Divine in all beings and events, which is the same thing as Patanjali's *ishwara pranidhana*. The second is enquiry or questioning, resembling Patanjali's *swadhyaya*. The third is service, another form of practical effort, the equivalent on this path of Patanjali's *tapas*. The requirements are thus the same in each school, but the order and emphasis varies.

When speaking of service, it is necessary to emphasize broad conceptions. Some would narrow it down to personal service to a particular teacher, but the whole *Gita* points to that brotherhood which is the doing of one's best duty to all around, in one's own limited sphere of circumstances and ability. The aspirant should desire the welfare of the world. This does not imply that we should merely engage ourselves with those who are in need, who are weak or poor or ignorant, and bestow our assistance upon them. That is a dangerous pastime, as it tends to a habit of superiority, and often ends in the production of a missionary spirit which is fatal to occult progress. Right association with those who are approximately one's equals is, on the whole, the best means for rendering the greatest help to others and oneself. Life does not flow harmoniously across big gaps. The beginner does not become an expert tennis player by playing against great experts, but with those just a little better than himself, and it is not the business of the greatest expert to teach the mere beginner, just as it is not the business of the chief professor of a college to teach the infant class. A good, sensible, brotherly life, in which one does not embarrass others by making conspicuous sacrifices on their behalf, is always the best. The teaching does not ask for *rajasic* efforts, but a *sattwic* fitting in of oneself into the social welfare.

We may see all mankind in process of evolution or self-unfoldment in seven degrees or stages, according to Shri Krishna's teaching. In the first three stages the man's life is energized from the personality; in the last three, from the real self. In the middle stage there is a conflict between the two, while the man is beginning to work at the three practices mentioned above.

There is one term which Shri Krishna applies to all those who are renouncing allegiance to mere pleasures and self-satisfactions and personal attachment to the objects of the world. He calls them *sannyasis*. In the final discourse of the *Gita*, the eighteenth chapter, there is a long explanation of the meaning of the term *sannyasa*. It is compared with another—*tyaga*. *Tyaga* means abandoning, giving up, leaving behind, and a *tyagi* is therefore one who has renounced the world, given up all possessions, and taken to the uncertain life of a religious mendicant, except perhaps that the term mendicant is not quite appropriate, since this man does not positively beg. *Sannyasa* is the same thing in *spirit*. The *sannyasi* does not necessarily give up the material things, but he gives up personal attachment to them. There is still plenty to do for the man who is becoming more and more conscious of the life around him, and therefore less liable to merely personal interests and motives. The things that he must do are described by Shri Krishna as follows: "Acts of *yajna*, *dana* and *tapas* should not be given up, but should be done without personal attachment or desire for results." These three kinds of action which alone the *sannyasi* is permitted to do, and which in fact he must do, are sacrifice, gift and effort.

It is always unsatisfactory to try to translate these technical Sanskrit words into one-word equivalents in English. Sacrifice (*yajna*) does not mean the mere surrender of things, but it really means to make all things holy. This occurs when they are offerings. Any action done with an unselfish motive is thus holy. The *sannyasi* does not, however, need to make any ceremonial offerings, because he sees the one life everywhere, and all his actions are direct service of that life.

In the West it is significant that "holy" is connected with "whole," and so what is done not for selfish gain but in the interests of all is holy. Sacrifice is thus a law by which living beings are related into one great brotherhood. A very important part of the teaching of the *Gita* is that one should recognize, accept and like the great fact of the mutual support of all living beings, and act or live accordingly. This is called the law of sacrifice.

The *sannyasi* gives freely; leaving it to the law to repay. He also consents to receive only freely, and should any one offer food or anything else for his use, he declines it if the gift is not sincere and free from any suggestion of obligation. His life is one of giving (*dana*). All his powers are completely at the service of mankind. And he must strive also, by *tapas*, to increase those powers. There is plenty to do for the man whose life is only sacrifice, gift and effort, whether he be a wandering monk in India or a railroad magnate in the United States.

This yoga does not exclude meditation. On the contrary it recommends it, but we need not study that here as it has been so fully dealt with in our previous chapters.

In all this teaching one seems to hear the echo of the words of all the spiritual guides of mankind: "We are not interested in the outer man, but in the real man in you. Cling to the real man. That is union with yoga. Let this be a matter for frequent reflection and all else will be purified." The practice of this meditation is essential, but only brings its effect in combination with the practice of true valuation of things in our material living—which is estimation of their value by love, their value *for* somebody.

This love leads on to spiritual insight which, as it combines knowing and being, can be called unification—through purification—with the ever present Divine reality.

Shankaracharya's Gnyana-yoga

This Teacher, who founded monasteries in India for the study of Vedanta philosophy, is believed by many of his followers to have lived several centuries before Christ, though other scholars place him much later. The date does not matter to us today, but his philosophy does, for it is regarded by some millions of people, and especially by the intellectuals, as the very pinnacle of Aryan thought. It was not that he originated a new philosophy, though he did propound a self-culture or discipline necessary to the understanding of it.

Shankaracharya expounded with great clarity and completeness the already existing philosophy of the Upanishads—a section of the Vedas often called the Vedanta, or end of the Veda, containing the "last word" or highest teaching about the nature of Brahman (God), man and the world. This teaching summed up its conclusions in a number of Great Sayings, including "There is one reality, but the intellectual persons speak of it variously," "All this certainly is Brahman," "*That* is the reality," "*That*, thou art" and other similar sentences to be (1) listened to, (2) thought about and (3) meditated upon, for the attainment of knowledge of the deepest truth, the very secret of life, the discovery which reveals the unalloyed freedom and happiness of our true self, when false ideas are put aside.

Gnyana or *Jnana* is knowledge. The central doctrine of this philosophy is that everything is one, and it can be known. But that knowing is only by being. We know ourselves not by words but by being ourselves, do we not? And this is happiness, for it seems that though this consciousness of self that we find ourselves to be is troubled, we always ascribe that trouble to something else—something outside—which restricts or annoys us. Who is there who blames himself for his sorrow? Even the thoughtful person who calls himself imperfect ascribes his troubles and sorrows to the imperfections, and says that if he could be without them he would be happy. Generally he tries to get rid of them. So it is by the study of the self that this philosophy proceeds to disclose the occult or secret truth which removes the imperfections and leaves the self free and joyous. Shankaracharya says in one word what all these imperfections are, what it is that we suffer from—it is ignorance, *avidya*. It will be, then, the very height of practical occultism to dispel that ignorance. Because of wrong assumptions we make mistakes, even with the best of intentions—even the intentions are imperfect because of ignorance. So thoughts, intentions and actions are all clouded by ignorance. Finally, even actions are tremendously confused, and without power, because of ignorance.

This is true occultism, then—the dissolution of ignorance at its source, not any small potterings for the gaining of petty pleasures or for the removal of petty pains, but to look behind the veil and find the pure self and no longer play about in the fields of ignorance. This is the real business of life, the Upanishads assert, which can be done, and has been done by successful human beings, who have seen the error and mastered it. At the very least it is better not to walk into new trouble than to busy oneself merely with removing the old.

First of all, Shankaracharya makes a distinction between people who want to *have* and those who want to *know*. To have is connected with external things. The whole world consists of things to have. Shankara does not deny the infinity of worlds or the existence of "higher planes," containing lofty and glorious beings or gods, or that by desiring things of higher planes or heavens and by worshipping the gods people may obtain centuries and even millennia of delight in various lofty heavens; but he affirms that all those things are the playthings of children or the tinsel of fools, who are making them all for themselves because they have not thought about the eternal realities.

He therefore draws a decided distinction between *dharma-jignasa* (the desire to know what should be done in order to obtain better conditions on earth and in heaven) and *Brahma-jignasa* (the desire to know that which is eternal). This is discussed very decisively in Shankara's commentary on the first of the *Brahma-Sutras* or aphorisms. The desire for the "heavens" must be preceded by sense-experience, and confidence in the Vedas, which declare that the heavens exist; but the desire for Brahman must be preceded by thought, thought and more thought (*vichara*), especially with reference to an understanding of the distinction (*viveka*) between the eternal (*nitya*) and temporary (*anitya*) realities. In emphasizing thought, however, Shankara does not leave out study of the Vedanta, which contains much information and advice about seeking the eternal. Shankara's emphasis on thinking is very clear in his *Aparokshanubhuti*: "Thinking should be done for the sake of attaining knowledge of the Self. Knowledge is not attained by any means other than thinking, just as objects are never seen without light. 'Who am I?' 'How is this world produced?' 'Who made it?' and 'What is the material?' — such is the enquiry."

It is well known that we do not see things as they really are, because of our limited point of view, and yet there is in us the craving for greater understanding, because the human soul is one with the divine or universal soul. Each one of us reflects that, just as the disc of the sun may be reflected in many little pools of water. We have thus a dual nature, and though the lower may be satisfied, still the higher makes its claim in a ceaseless desire to understand. If human power and love were to grow so great, as to make our life on earth a perfect paradise of peace and plenty for all, still men would say, "Now, we want to know why all this is so." There are the needs of the personality—food, clothing and shelter, amusement and education, exercise and rest—but beyond these there are spiritual needs, and among them is the real hunger for understanding.

It is not supposed by Shankara that the average or ordinary man can think straight in these matters. He prescribes a course of what may be called purification as a preparation. This is called the *sadhanachatushtayam*, the "group of four accomplishments." They present three departments of self-training, and a concluding condition of mind, as will be seen in the following table:

Name of Accomplishment		***Functioninvolved***
In Sanskrit	In English	
1. Viveka	Discrimination	Thought
2. Vairagya	Uncolouredness	Feelings
3. Shatsampatti	6 Successes	The Will
4. Mumukshatwa	The State of Longing for Liberation	

Viveka is the practice of discrimination between the fleeting and the permanent. This is the first of three preliminary yogas in this school. It is here that the thinking, thinking, thinking, begins. It is to be applied to oneself, to others and to the whole business of life. It is an inspection of the contents of one's ordinary self, to discriminate between the relatively temporary and permanent. First one may dwell upon the body and realize that it is only an instrument for the conscious self to play upon.

Then, one may dwell on the habits of feeling and emotion which have been accumulated during the present lifetime (or, strictly, bodytime), and realize these also to be part of the instrument—"I am surely not my feelings and emotions towards things and people." Thirdly, one must meditate upon the fact that the lower mind, the collection of information, ideas and opinions that one has acquired up to this period, is also not the self, but merely an internal library more or less imperfectly indexed, in which the books have a tendency to open at certain places because they have been opened there many times before.

This meditation may then be applied to other people, so that one comes to think of them as the consciousness beyond the personality, and in dealing with them to assist and further the higher purposes of the Self within them rather than the desires rising from the personality. Being a material thing, even up to the mental plane, that personality has its own quality of inertia, and dislikes the discomfort involved in new thinking and willing and feeling, until it is well trained and learns to rejoice in the sharing of a life more than its own. But we must also help to bring the day of triumph nearer for all whom we contact, as Shri Shankaracharya did, for he was one of the world's busiest men.

This meditation must be extended still further to all the business of life, to the family, the shop, the field, the office, society. All these things must be considered as of importance not as they minister to the laziness, selfishness or thoughtlessness of the personality, but as they bear on the advancement in power of will, love and thought of the evolving consciousness in all concerned. It will be seen that works and their objects pass away, but the faculty and ability gained by them remains in the man.

Fifteen to thirty minutes of this kind of meditation each day is sufficient to establish very soon an entirely new outlook in the personality. Emerson speaks of something of the same kind in his essay on "Inspiration," as the way to an altogether richer life than any of us can possibly reach without it. It can often be practised to some extent under unfavorable conditions, as for example in the railway train, if one makes up one's mind to take the various disturbances of it with a sweet temper, and lend oneself to the rhythm of its noise.

The second requirement is *vairagya*, an emotional condition in which one does not respond at once to impressions coming from the outer world, but first submits the matter to the discriminative power rising from viveka. If you strike an ordinary man, he will get hot and strike back, or run away, or do something else spontaneous and scarcely rational; but a man having *vairagya* would use his spiritual intelligence before responding. The literal meaning of the word *vairagya* is "absence of colour," and in this connection it means absence of passion. *Raga* is coloring, especially redness. People everywhere take their emotional coloring from their environment, according to well known psychological laws; like pieces of glass placed on blue or red or green paper, they change their colour. Likes and dislikes rise up in them without reason, at the mere sight of various objects, and the appearance of different persons calls up pride, anger, fear and other personal emotions.

They are constantly judging things not with their intelligence but by their feelings and emotional habits. "This is good, that is bad," means generally nothing more than, "I like this; I do not like that." A man dislikes a thing because it disturbs his physical or emotional convenience or his comfortable convictions, "I thought I had done with thinking about that—take it away, confound you," grumbles the man comfortably settled in his opinions, as in a big armchair.

Vairagya is the absence of agitation due to things outside. A mistaken idea which is sometimes associated with this word is that it implies absence of emotion. That is not so. The purified personality responds to the higher emotions, the love emotions that belong to the real self. Those emotions come from that aspect of the indwelling consciousness which feels other lives to be as interesting as one's own.

This is the root of all the love emotions—admiration, kindness, friendship, devotion and others—which must not be confused with any sort of passion, which is personal or bodily desire. If a man has *vairagya* and he is still at all emotional, his emotion must express some form of love. *Vairagya* may be developed by a form of meditation in which the aspirant should picture and turn over in mind the various things that have been causing him agitation, or the disturbing emotions of pride, anger and fear. Having made a picture of the cat spilling the ink on the best tablecloth, or of your enemy putting in a bad word for you with your employer or superior behind your back, you calmly look at it, meditate on it, and the light of your own intelligence will see the real value of the experience and this removal of ignorance will also remove the agitating emotion. This is a question of feeling, not of action. Do not here substitute the deadly coldness that some people sometimes feel instead of anger, and imagine that to be the calm state.

The calmness obtained in this way will soon make all the other meditation far more effective than before, because meditation best opens the door to the inner world and all its inspiration when the body is quiet, the emotions are calm, and the attention is turned to the subject of thought without any muscular or nervous strain or physical sensation whatever. Incidentally it should be said that meditation with physical sensation or strain may prove injurious to health, but meditation rightly done in this way can never do the least harm.

The third requirement is called *shatsampatti*, which may be translated "the six forms of success." The will is now used to make all conditions favorable for the further development of *viveka*. To understand the function of the will, it is necessary to realize that it is the faculty with which we change *ourselves*. Thought is *kriyashakti*, the power of mind that acts upon matter; but it is the will with which we change our thoughts and other inward conditions. Now willpower is to be used to bring the whole life of the man within the purpose of *jnanayoga*. This work is the equivalent of the *tapas* of Patanjali and the *seva* of Shri Krishna.

The six forms of success are: (1) *shama*, control of mind, (2) *dama*, control of body; (3) *uparati*, which means cessation from eagerness to have certain persons and things around one, and therefore a willing acceptance of what the world offers—contentment with regard to things and tolerance with regard to persons, a glad acceptance of the material available for a life's work. The fourth is *titiksha*, patience, the cheerful endurance of trying conditions and the sequence of karma. The fifth is *shraddha*, fidelity and sincerity, and therefore confidence in oneself and others. The sixth is samadhana, steadiness, with all the forces gathered together and turned to the definite purpose in hand.

Every one of these six practices shows the will at work producing that calm strength which is its own special characteristic. This is necessary for yoga, and anything in the nature of fuss or push, or excitement is against it. In no case does this calmness mean the reduction of activity or work, but always that the work is done with greater strength but less noise. Success is marked by quietness, the best indication of power. Thus the mind and body will be active but calm; and there will be contentment, patience, sincerity and steadiness.

The three branches of training already mentioned make the entire personality exceedingly sensitive to the higher self, so that a great longing arises for a fuller measure of realization. This is called *mumukshatwa*, eagerness for liberation.

To complete this occult knowledge one must combine the *maya* doctrine with the self-realization doctrine. It is, of course, the self-realization of itself that is the full achievement. And since *maya* does not mean something unreal but something outside the categories of both the real and unreal, and is in fact nothing but error, we shall have to say that the power of *maya* is a power of the self itself, and that all that is not unreal in the *maya* is beyond time and space, a part of the self itself, whatever "parts" may mean-in the indivisible. The general dictum of all the yogas is fulfilled here—that never will the yogi find something that could be anticipated, but only something unknown before, which, however, by universal testimony, is true being, pure consciousness and incredible joy. All the explanations given in this chapter and much more will be found in my book on Vedanta entitled *The Glorious Presence*.

It will be useful now to see that the same three means of self-guidance are employed in all the three schools we have studied so far—of Patanjali, of Shri Krishna and of Shankaracharya. It becomes obvious when we thus compare them that all are aiming at maturity of mind, the ripening of the three functions of will, love and thought. They put these three in different order, however, indicating the different temperaments of those who take to the different schools of occult practice and thought. The following table will make the comparison clear.

Patanjali

1. *Tapas* (Will)
2. *Swadhyaya* (Thought)
3. *Ishwara-pranidhana*

Krishna

1. *Pranipata* (Love)
2. *Pariprashna* (Thought)
3. *Seva* (Will)

Shankara

1. *Viveka* (Thought)
2. *Vairagya* (Love)
3. *Shatsampatti* (Will)

When the student has followed this preliminary training with some success he will be ready for two things (1) the understanding of the doctrine of *maya*, and (2) the direct visioning of the Self.

Maya has often been translated "illusion," whence it has been thought that Shankara teaches that all this world does not exist, and people only imagine that it does so—that there is nothing there. That is not so. He does not deny the existence of objects, but affirms that we see them wrongly—just as a man may see a piece of rope on the ground and mistake it for a snake, or as he may see a post in the distance and think it to be a man.

It is necessary to know that *maya* has two functions: "covering-up" (*avarana*) and "throwing-out" (*vikshepa*). The first is declared to be the effect of *tamas*, which hides or obstructs the life, and the second the result of *rajas*, or energy. "Covering-up" implies that although we are—every one—universal in our essential nature, our attention is now given to less than the whole.

Most of the reality is covered up, and since we see only the remainder, it must necessarily become unsatisfying and stupid and even painful, when we have played with it long enough to exhaust its lessons for us. When we have read a book and absorbed the ideas in it, we do not want to read it again. If it is forced upon us, the experience will be painful. We may laugh at a good joke told by a friend today, but if he persists in telling us the same story again and again it will be far from a joke. Our life must be moving on, and overcoming the *avarana*; there is no long-lasting pleasure or gain in standing still on any platform of knowledge that we may have gained at any time or stage.

"Covering-up" does not mean that objects of experience lack reality. The *maya* or illusion is that we do not see their *full* reality; we see too little, not too much. So far as they go they have an excellent flavour of reality, but their incompleteness is unsatisfying.

The second function of *maya*, "throwing-out" (*vikshepa*), means that we put forth our thought and energy in reference to that part of reality which for us individually has not been covered up, and thereby we produce the world of *maya* or created things, which are only temporary (*anitya*).

The power of "throwing-out" is not merely of the mind, but is actually creative, and this it is which produces all the *forms* around us, the world of manifestation. The objects therein are very much like pictures painted by an artist. They represent his expression of such part of the reality as is not covered up. As he looks at the picture and realizes how defective and even nonsensical it is, the hunger arises in him for something more satisfying, which then works at removing the "covering-up." Thereby arises what is called intuition, which always comes as the result of a complete study of any fact or group of facts in the world of experience. It is in this manner that experience is educative. It gives us nothing from the outside, but enables us to introduce ourselves to a fuller part of reality. So *avarana* resembles concentration, and the result of experience can be compared to contemplation. Thus *maya*, while not reality, is also not unreality.

Shankara speaks in very strong language about the effect of *avarana* and *vikshepa* in practical life: "The function of *avarana*, made of *tamas*, covers up the shining Self, which has unlimited faculties, just as the shadow of the moon hides the disc of the sun. When there is thus the obscuration of a man's real and stainlessly radiant Self, he thinks he is the body, which is not the Self. Then the great power of *rajas* called *vikshepa* afflicts him by the binding qualities of passion, anger, etc., so that this unintelligent man, deprived of real knowledge of the Self, through being swallowed by the crocodile of the great delusion, wanders about, rising and falling in the ocean of limited existence. As clouds produced by the sun obscure the sun as they develop, so does egotism arising from the Self obscure the Self as it flourishes. And as on a bad day when thick clouds swallow the sun, and they also are afflicted by sharp cold winds, so does the power of acute *vikshepa* annoy the man of confused intelligence with many troubles. By these two powers the man is bound; deluded by them he wanders about, thinking the body to be himself."

Then comes the question how to remove these two: "Unless the *avarana* function ceases completely, vikshepa cannot be conquered. When subject and object are separated, like milk from water, then *avarana* disappears on its own account in the Self. Perfect discrimination, arising from clear perception, having distinguished the subject and the object, cuts away the bondage of delusion made by *maya*, and then for the free man there is no more wandering about."

The substance of material things is called *sat*, or being. Consciousness, with its powers of will, love and thought, is called *chit*. Beyond those three aspects of consciousness is *ananda*, the true life that is sheer happiness. The being of true life is happiness. First a man must get over the delusion that he *is* the body, and realize that he is consciousness using the body. He *has* a body. Then, later on, he must realize that he *is not* the powers of consciousness, but that he simply *uses* these. Then he will be his own true self, *ananda*, happiness, which is the nature of our pure being. But that happiness is one with consciousness (*chit*) and being (*sat*), as the man will find on reaching illumination; so the world of sat is real, part of his own true life, and not illusion. *Maya* was the practical effect of the mistake (*avidya*) by which he confused together, first consciousness and external being, and then consciousness and his psychological or internal being.

The analogy of dreaming is employed to illustrate these points. Just as on waking we realize that our dream was irrational, so on waking from the dream that we now call waking we shall realize the truth that will make our present outlook appear irrational. Not that it is irrational, but that the true vision has the correct data or perception. Even our present knowledge, it is said, is ignorance, or better unwisdom, because we are always looking at things with the eyes of the flesh, while we ought to look at them with the eyes of the spirit, that is, from the standpoint of the imperishable consciousness.

The question then arises—what is the best practical way to attain reality. To this two answers may be given: (1) Realize the infinite possibilities of every finite experience, and (2) do not mix yourself with your objects of experience. As to the first, it means simply that we can learn from one thing what we can learn from many things. For example, a man has one mother. If he has learnt to love that mother, then he is predisposed to love any mother whom he may meet. He does not need to learn the lesson all over again in connection with those other mothers.

As instructed in the *Gita*, by attending to his own experience a man reaches perfection.

Another instance of the same principle is the use of the human body. If we had to attain some kind of perfection which involved knowledge of all things which people are making for themselves by their "throwing-out," this body would not be enough. In such a case we should need seven-league boots and a hundred or a thousand arms and legs instead of only two of each. But this is not the way of the evolution of life. It can reach its perfection through an ordinary body with two arms and two legs. It need not have the muscular system of a professional athlete or the mental capacity of a German chemist or lexicographer. Realize the infinite possibilities of the moment's experience, cease to resent any of the experience, and immediately most of the pain and sorrow that it may contain is emptied out of it, and it becomes immensely fruitful.

There are two ways in which we may live our lives amidst events of the world, without retiring at all from that world. In both cases the mixing with the world will be the same, but in one there is real confusion (that is, fusing together) and in the other merely mixing. For example, if milk and water are put together it is very difficult to separate them, but if oil and water are mixed together, although they are together they retain their individuality. So in relation to the world we are to be like oil in water, not milk in water. We must distinguish between "the world," "my world" and "myself"—three things, not two. It is like a person playing a game of chess. The board is there—my world. The pieces have been moved into a certain position. A good player does not become excited and flustered, whether he is winning or losing. He cannot, in fact, really in himself either win or lose. Even if his pieces are captured one by one, if he has played the game to the best of his ability he has developed his faculties, and on the whole he is a little more likely to profit by a lost than by a won game.

These facts being established, people sometimes raise the academic question: "Whence comes this ignorance which hides the full reality?" With regard to this Buddha's advice was: "Sink not the string of thought into the fathomless." The fact is that we have to begin our reasoning and our activity from the place in which we find ourselves. We are apparently on a ladder, which goes upwards out of sight. The important thing is that it goes upwards. But one would not avoid the ultimate question. The answer to it is that space and time are a creation of ignorance—they come into being through the "covering-up," and disappear for us when the covering is removed. How, then, can the questions, "where" and "whence," which ask for an answer in terms of time and space, be applied to this matter? Evidently there is some sort of evolution or unfoldment, but it is not a change in time and space. That this is so is indicated by the unchanging character of our feeling of "I" which is the same point of reference in youth and age, and whether we be here or there, and standing on our heads or on our feet.

The meditations of Shankara are practical, because they are not merely thoughts about things, considered as objects, dwelt upon in the third grammatical person. First, the student must say to himself, "I am not *it*"—"it" being the personality, physical and psychological, composed of body, personal emotions and fixed ideas. This means not simply the set of "vehicles" as they stand, but also their habits of action, emotion and thought—the entire personality. He must put that outside himself. Secondly, he must say, "I am not *you*," referring now to that in himself which he would call "you" in another person—the collection of thinkings, lovings and willings or powers of consciousness. The personality is something that you *use*—not something that you *are*. So also the conscious powers are something that you *use*, not something that you *are*. Thirdly, he must say, "I am I. I can take up and put down these powers of consciousness. I can enlarge or reduce them." But in the second stage he must take care to think of his own ordinary consciousness always as *you*, never as *it*, nor as *I*, otherwise he will remain in the *you*, and not reach the *I*.

All happiness in life is beyond the limited consciousness and is experienced when that activity is forgotten. All the delight that comes from response to beauty, love and truth in the world, and from the powers of will, love and thought in consciousness, lie in the Self beyond, when the world and the limited self are forgotten, and time and space have been swallowed up in something greater, beyond their limitations. Beyond common consciousness, in a state better than that limited consciousness, we are, and all clinging to mental ideas about oneself, pleasurable or not, bars the realization of that truth. That unchanging *I* is *ananda*, happiness, the one reality. To know this directly, not by logic, is the high purpose of the Vedanta.

The Hatha and Laya Yogas

The practice of *hatha-yoga* is composed chiefly of *pranayama*, which is regulation of breath, *asana*, the practice of various postures, and a set of six *bandhas* or body-purifications. Although the writer of these words holds to the opinion that these physical practices cannot develop the mind at all, or contribute to its yogic or occult experience, he agrees that when the *hatha-yoga* exercises are properly done they are very beneficial to the body. As long as people have bodies they should treat them if possible as prize animals, but if that is too much to ask they should at least give them good exercise as well as good rest and good food. In this sense only one should understand the well-known maxim: "No *raja* without *hatha*; no *hatha* without *raja*."

The *asanas* or postures have some advantages over ordinary physical exercises intended for muscular development. Although these latter do also stimulate good breathing and benefit the nervous system to some extent, especially if used in conjunction with proper relaxation at suitable times, the *hatha-yoga* postures do in addition provide suppleness and slenderness, and give massage to the internal organs. Besides this, when allied to suitable and not excessive breathing exercises, the entire body benefits. None of the yoga schools aims at abnormal strength—a reasonable standard such as is suitable for the ordinary purposes of life is regarded as sufficient, and more than that may often be just a matter of personal satisfaction or pride, not the spiritual attainment which the *hatha-yogis*, *raja-yogis* and all other yogis are aiming at, which contains no self-satisfaction. Incidentally, one must remark, great mental muscularity—to use a metaphor—is also not sought by any of them. If there are mental giants among them, this must be put down to some work of supererogation in that line in their previous lives.

In an earlier chapter we have spoken of *hatha* as the "sun" and "moon" breaths. It comes in, say some works, with the sound of ha and goes out with the sound of tha. Another explanation is that the "sun" and "moon" correspond to the breaths travelling through the right and left nostrils. Still a third view is that as the whole word *hatha* ordinarily means forcefulness, the system of *hatha-yoga* is one which, at least as compared with other yogas, requires considerable energy. It has already been stated that in those yogas the thinkings and meditations are intended to be done without allowing any tension in the body.

We may introduce the picture of a typical form of *hatha-yoga* breathing by quoting from the *Shiva Sanhita*:

"The wise man, having closed the right nostril with the thumb of the right hand, and having drawn air in through the left nostril, should hold his breath as long as he can, and then let it out through the right nostril slowly and gently. Next, having breathed in through the right nostril, he should retain the air as long as possible, and then breathe it out gently and very slowly through the left nostril.

"Let him thus practice regularly, with twenty retentions, at sunrise, midday, sunset and midnight, every day, keeping a peaceful mind, and in three months the channels of the body will have become purified. This is the first of four stages of *pranayama* (regulation of breath), and the signs of it are that the body becomes healthy and likeable and emits a pleasant odour, and there will be good appetite and digestion, cheerfulness, a good figure, courage, enthusiasm and strength.

"There are, however, certain things which the *swarasadhaka* (breath-practiser) must avoid: foods which are acid, astringent, pungent, salty, mustardy and bitter, and those fried in oil, and various activities of body and mind, bathing before sunrise, stealing, harmfulness, enmity, egotism, cunning, fasting, untruth, cruelty to animals, sexual attachments, fire, much conversation and much eating. On the contrary, he should use and enjoy *ghi* (butter clarified by simmering), milk, sweet food, betel without lime, camphor, a good meditation-chamber with only a small entrance, contentment, willingness to learn, the doing of household duties with *vairagya*, singing of the names of Vishnu, hearing sweet music, firmness, patience, effort, purity, modesty, confidence and helping the teacher.

If there is hunger, a little milk and butter may be taken before practice, but there should be no practice for some time after meals. It is better to eat a small amount of food frequently (with at least three hours' intervals) than much at once. If the body perspires it should be well rubbed (with the hands). When the practice has become well established, these rules need not be so strictly observed."

One does not wish to put any of these *hatha-yoga* practices into print, to be read by various kinds of people, without sounding a warning. Many people have brought upon themselves incurable illness and even madness by practising them without providing the proper conditions of body and mind. The old yoga books are full of such warnings, and they tell the would-be practicer to go to a teacher who really knows all about these things, to receive personal inspection and instruction. For example, the *Gheranda Sanhita* announces that if one begins the practices in hot, cold or rainy weather, disease will be contracted, and also if there is not moderation in diet, for only one half the stomach must ever be filled with solid food. When the present writer tried, as a boy of fourteen or fifteen, the long alternate breathing for three quarters of an hour, he found when he stood up that he had lost his sense of touch and weight. He handled things without feeling them, and walked without any sense of touching the ground. The sense returned only after ten or fifteen minutes.

The *Hatha Yoga Pradipika* states that control of breath must be brought about very gradually, "as lions, elephants and tigers are tamed," or else "the experimenter will be killed," and by any mistake there arises cough, asthma, head, eye and ear pains, and many other diseases. The *Shandilya Upanishad* gives the same warning. On the other hand, right practice may be undertaken by anybody, even the young and the old, the sick and the weak, and will result in slenderness and rightness of body.

The theory behind these breathing exercises is that between the mind and the body comes *prana*. This word is translated "principle of life"—referring to life in the body. Five vital airs are mentioned extensively in the Sanskrit literature which touches on the physiology of the human body. *Prana* is always referred to as the chief of these vital airs. The word comes from a verbal root "an" meaning "to breathe," and thus "to live." Patanjali in his aphorism on *Pranayama* calls it regulation of the manner of movement of *shwasa* and *prashwasa*, that is, breathing.

The late Dr. Vaman R. Kokatnur, noted scientist and Sanskrit scholar, in a paper read at the American Chemical Society's meeting in Detroit in September 1927, quoted a text which says that what is inhaled is *prana* and what is exhaled is *apana*. On various grounds he made out a good case for these being oxygen and carbon dioxide, a third "air," *udana*, being hydrogen. Of the other two of the five, *samana* is generally spoken of as essential to digestion and *vyana* "pervades the whole body." Many speak of these five airs as being something else, fine or "etheric," but all agree that various ways of breathing affect them all. Many of the teachers recommend the traditional proportions of one unit of time for inbreathing (*puraka*), four units for holding the breath within (*Kumbhaka*), and two units for out-breathing (*rechaka*).

The *Shiva Sanhita* speaks of the units being gradually lengthened, as seen in verse iii 57: "When the yogi is able to practice holding the breath for an hour and a half, various *siddhis* (faculties and powers) arise, including prophecy, travelling at will, sight and hearing at a distance, vision of the invisible worlds, entering others' bodies, turning various metals into gold, invisibility at will, and moving in the air."

Various teachers and books offer more elaborate, as well as some simpler, breathing exercises. The following eight are often mentioned: (1) Practice *kumbhaka* (holding the breath) until the pressure of air is felt from head to foot, then breathe out through the right nostril; (2) breathe in deeply and noisily, hold as before, and exhale through the left nostril; (3) putting the tongue between the lips breathe in with a hissing sound; exhale through both nostrils; (4) breathe out as fully as possible, then in with a hissing sound, and go on very rapidly like bellows, until tired; then exhale by the right, or (5) the left nostril; (6) breathe in with the sound of a female bee; (7) after breathing in, contract the throat, place the chin on the chest; breathe out very slowly; (8) simply hold the breath, without inbreathing or out-breathing, as long as you like.

While issuing warnings about these exercises, I would like to add that many have found benefit from the following simple practice. Breathe in fairly fully while saying mentally to yourself "*puraka*;" hold the breath in without any muscular effort while saying "*kumbhaka, kumbhaka, kumbhaka, kumbhaka*;" breathe out quite fully while saying "*rechaka, rechaka*." This may be done at odd times as a pick-me-up, with generally about ten repetitions. The best slowness or quickness of the words should be found by the student for himself, but all the words should be of the same length. A tendency to lengthen them a little may gradually and rightly appear.

Some teachers maintain that all the impurities of the body may be removed merely by control of breath, but others hold that it is necessary to practice also certain cleansings, especially in the case of persons who are flabby and phlegmatic.

The six principal purifications are: (1) slowly (under the direction of a teacher) learn to swallow a clean, slightly warm, thin cloth, four fingers broad and fifteen spans long; hold on to the end of it, and gradually draw it out again; (2) take an enema sitting in water and using a small bamboo tube; shake well and dispel; (3) draw a fine thread, twelve fingers long, in at one nostril and out at the mouth; (4) look at something without winking, until tears come; (5) with the head bent down, slowly massage the intestines, round and round both ways, and (6) breathe rapidly, like the bellows of a blacksmith. These acts are said to remove corpulence and many other diseases.

The *Gheranda Sanhita* has a much bigger collection—about twenty-four purifications—which includes swallowing air with the lips formed "like the beak of a crow," and expelling it from below; doing the same with water; gently pressing the intestines towards the spine one hundred times, massaging the depression at the bridge of the nose (especially after waking and after meals); vomiting by tickling the throat; gargling; drawing air softly in at one nostril, and sending it out softly at the other, alternately; drinking water in at the nostrils and letting it out at the mouth.

Closely connected with the elaborate practices of *pranayama* are the postures (*asanas*). Quite often eighty-four of these are enumerated, but the *Shiva Sanhita* contents itself with recommending four, which are called "The Adept Seat," "The Lotus Seat," "The Powerful Seat," and "The Swastika Seat." These are briefly as follows: (1) body straight, legs crossed, one heel at the anus, the other at the front, gaze between the eyebrows, chin on breast; (2) legs folded with feet, soles upwards, on opposite thighs, arms crossed, hands on thighs, tongue pressed against teeth, chin on breast or held up, gaze on tip of nose (or straight in front); or arms may be crossed behind, hands holding great toes; (3) legs stretched out, apart, head held in hands and placed on knees; (4) feet between calves and thighs, body straight. The *Hatha Yoga Pradipika* also advocates four *asanas* especially, two being the same and two different.

An excellent modern book on *pranayama*, *asanas* etc., is *Yoga Asanas* by Swami Shivananda, of Rishikesh, in the Himalayas. In this the Swami explains with illustrations a large number of postures, including the *Sukhasana*, or "pleasant posture" described and recommended for the West in my *Practical Yoga: Ancient and Modern*. He also gives very useful simple breathing exercises as well as the more elaborate ones.

We come now to another school of yoga called the laya yoga. Laya means "latent" or "in suspense." The especial features of this yoga are its study and practice of *kundalini* and the *chakras*. *Kundalini* is described as a force lying in three and a half coils like a sleeping serpent, in a cavity near the base of the spine. This is regarded as a goddess or power, "luminous as lightning," who, even though sleeping, maintains all living creatures. She lies there with her head blocking a fine channel which goes straight up the spine and is known as the *sushumna*. Some, to link this up with modern thought, have called it the fount of bodily electricity.

The purpose of the laya-yoga practice is to awaken the *kundalini* (or "coiled one"), who will start up hissing, and can then be carried through the series of six *chakras* (literally, "wheels"), which are threaded upon that channel at various points in the body, which are situated at the level of the base of the spine, the root of the penis, the navel, the heart, the throat and the eyebrows.

These *chakras* are depicted somewhat as flowers rather than wheels, and have petals respectively numbering four, six, eight, twelve, sixteen, and two. The works describing these *chakras*, and the effects of meditation upon them or in them, are altogether too numerous even to mention. They are depicted with very much symbology. For example, the *anahata chakra* (at the heart) has a *yantra* or design showing twelve petals, each one bearing a certain letter of the alphabet. In the center circle there is a pair of interlaced triangles, having written in the middle of them the syllable "*yam*" (which is a *mantra* or sound which can produce some effect when properly repeated). This *yam* is pictured as riding on a black antelope, and, in its final sound *m*, which is written as a dot, a figure representing the male divinity is placed. He is styled Isha, has three eyes, and holds out his hands with gestures of dispelling fear and granting boons.

Near by, in the pericarp of the lotus (for the *chakras* are also called lotuses) is the female divinity Kakini, seated on a red lotus, having golden colour, dressed in yellow clothes, wearing all kinds of jewels and a garland of bones. She has four arms, two hands bearing a noose and a skull, and the other two showing signs of dispelling fear and granting boons. In the center, above the interlaced triangles, is an inverted triangle as bright as lightning, and in that a symbol of Shiva of a golden colour with a crescent moon surmounted by a dot upon its head. This *chakra*, like all the *padmas* (lotus flowers) is brightly coloured, the petals and pericarp being red. One cannot attempt in this brief space to unravel the significance of all these letters, colours and symbols, or to give the symbols of the other five *padmas*. Each *chakra* has its own diagram, colours, animal, divinities, letters, etc.

It will be evident that the yogi, as he meditates in each of them in the course of his progress, will have plenty to think about. Arthur Avalon's excellent translation of the *Shatchakra Nirupana*, with comments thereon, is a mine of information on the subject, but the thorough student should also read various minor Upanishads, Puranas and general works on yoga touching on this subject. There is a certain amount of conflicting testimony on the subject of colours, divinities etc., but this does not mar the general unity of information as regards all the main features.

There is in all the literature on the subject a poetical rather than an exact description of what happens as *kundalini* rises. The spine is called "the axis of creation" for the body. In that is the channel *sushumna*; within that another, named *vajroli* and within that again another, called *chitrini*, "as fine as a spider's thread." On this tube the lotuses are said to be threaded "like knots on a bamboo rod." Kundalini rises up little by little, as the yogi employs his will. In one practice he brings her as far as he can, and, as she pierces any one of the lotuses, its face, which was turned downwards before, turns upwards, and when the meditation is finished he leads her back to her home near the base of the spine.

It is further explained that as she leaves each *chakra* on the way up, she withdraws the functions of that center, and so makes them latent, hence the term laya-yoga, or the Yoga of Suspension. It is, of course, natural that in such a process, as attention is given more and more to the higher thought, the lower responses should become latent, as, for example, when we are reading and do not hear or see a person who enters the room.

Kundalini proceeds upwards until she reaches the great "thousand-petalled lotus" at the top of the head, beyond all the six *chakras*. There she enjoys the bliss and power of union with the source of all life, and afterwards, as she returns through the centers she gives back to each its specific powers, purified and enhanced. The process of bringing *kundalini* to the highest point is usually considered to require some years, but there are exceptional cases in which it is done quickly.

The hatha-yoga books take up a curious view of the mind in relation to all these matters. It is expressed in a few verses of the *Hatha-Yoga Pradipika*. "The mind is the lord of the senses; the breath is the lord of the mind; and that depends on *nada*." "There is talk of *laya*, *laya*, but what is its character? *Laya* is the non-arising of further vasanas, and the forgetting of external things." Some of the minor Upanishads, such as the *Muktika* of the *Shukla-Yajurveda*, have a similar idea.

Even so brief an account of these practices as this is would be incomplete without mention of the *mudras*, or physical practices, and the *nadas*, or internal sounds. The *mudras*, although in some cases similar to the purifications, are intended for a different purpose—to obtain some delight or power, and to awaken *kundalini*, for it is held that the awakening can take place through *asanas* (postures), *kumbhakas* (holdings of the breath) and *mudras*.

Though there are many *mudras*, only ten are usually recommended. Among the most popular ones intended to awaken *kundalini* is that of supporting the body on the palms of the hands and softly striking the posteriors on the ground, which is also considered to remove wrinkles and grey hair. In another, very highly recommended, the membrane under the tongue is gradually cut ("one hair's breadth every seven days"), and rubbed with salt and turmeric, so that the severed parts will not join.

The tongue is also gradually lengthened by a process resembling milking, so that after six months the yogi can turn it upwards into the cavity at the back of the palate, and thus, with the hole closed and the breath suspended, contemplate *kundalini* and "drink the nectar" flowing there. Another physical method requires a sort of massage for an hour and a half morning and evening, for up to forty-five days. Still another requires the feet to be crossed behind the neck.

It must be mentioned that those raja yogis who do not approve of the awakening of *kundalini* by these external methods, nor even by meditation upon it, nevertheless usually believe that *kundalini* naturally awakens and rises as a result of the purely internal meditations which they practice. This takes place a little at a time so that there is no strong feeling or pain in the body, as is often the case when it is done by the *hatha-yoga* methods.

The purifying and subliming effects of the return journey through the *chakra* in all cases awakens some degree of clairvoyance and similar powers, but what the yogi sees will depend upon his state of mind, and even then the understanding of what he sees will depend upon his evolutionary status. There is plenty of room for error, inasmuch as his own thoughts and those of others may easily be mistaken for objective realities, as in dreams.

Some of the books prescribe an "elephant *mudra*," which is performed by standing up to the neck in water, drinking it in through the nostrils, sending it out through the mouth and then reversing the process. This resembles the action of elephants in the pools and rivers, though they use the trunk only, not the mouth.

Now we come to the *nadas* or sounds. The *Shiva Sanhita* instructs the yogi to close the ears with the thumbs, the eyes with the index fingers, the nostrils with the middle fingers and the lips with the remaining four fingers. After some practice, he will begin to hear the mystic sounds. The first will be like the hum of a bee, then a flute and then a *vina*. With more practice there comes the sound of bells, and afterwards thunder. The mind of the yogi becomes absorbed in these sounds, and he forgets the external things which could distract him. These sounds are usually called *anahata*, or belonging to the heart center.

According to the *Hatha Yoga Pradipika*, when the ears, eyes, nose and mouth are closed, a clear sound is heard—first like the tinkling of ornaments, and later like kettle-drums; later still there is the sound of the flute and the *vina*. In the middle stage there may be the sound of bells and horns. The yogi must give his attention to the subtler sounds. The *Nadabindu Upanishad* also gives much the same order of sounds as the *Hatha Yoga Pradipika*, mentioning in stage one the sound of the sea, clouds, waterfalls and kettledrums, in the second stage that of drums, bells and horns, and thirdly, that of tinkling bells, flutes, *vinas* and bees. The *Hansa Upanishad* gives the order more in agreement with the *Shiva Sanhita*. First come soft chattering sounds, then that of the bell, conch, lute, cymbals, flute, drum, double drum, and, lastly, thunder. The *nada laya* or "absorption through sound" is regarded as a great aid to concentration.

Samadhi, the highest practice of yoga, is conceived in a very material manner in the *hatha-yoga* books. The idea is that the yogi in *samadhi* is uninfluenced by anything external, because the senses have become inactive, and he does not even know himself or others. Although the *Gheranda Sanhita* says that *samadhi* involves union of the individual with the supreme Self (*Paratman*) so that "I am Brahma and no other; Brahma am I, without any sorrows; I am of the nature of fundamental existence, knowledge and bliss, always free and self-supporting," it also prescribes, for the attainment of this, various *mudras* or physical practices, such as that of turning the tongue into the nasal cavity and stopping the breath, the theory being that all you need to do is to cut off contact with this world, and the other state will be there.

The Bhakti and Mantra Yogas

Bhakti, or devotion, arises from the appreciation of goodness. There will be no devotional feeling towards what is not good. If some persons were to worship or rather propitiate a dangerous deity it would not be devotion. So devotion implies goodness and is towards goodness. It is a form of love, but essentially love of something or some person who is "good."

Merchants, who speak of goods, not of mere things or articles, are in this particular excellent psychologists. Goods are things which are good for us, or we might better put it, good to us. We go further as our intelligence or knowledge increases and recognize that some things which are not good to us are good to others. "The farmer prays for rain, the washerman for sun," says the Japanese proverb. On this basis, everything is seen to be good because everything is good to some being.

When men ask themselves where all these goods come from they easily ascribe them to a goodness which has the nature of a superior mind. They find that the good man is one who positively produces goods of some kind and passes them on to others. Not only the things he produces but he himself is thus a manifestation of goodness. From such thoughts it is easy to pass on to the idea of a deity or deity who is goodness, and, in the height of this idea, is good to all and always, even when the goodness of his gift of the moment is not understood and felt as such.

In this way the intellect permits the goodness to be universalized, and prevents the judgment of goodness from being based on one's own personal pleasure or one's own material welfare. Thus devotion, which arises at first from the reception of some goods, ends up by declaring that all is good, and this devotion then makes logical a predisposition towards appreciative feelings, even when there is not understanding.

That is true and complete religious devotion, which never questions but always appreciates everything, or judges all things and their Giver as expressions and sources of that goodness. In the West philosophers have said that it is possible to get good out of every experience, so one should "look for the good in everything"; but in India they always went one better than that by saying one should "look for the God in everything," because in this way the feelings as well as the intellect had their play. In looking for the good in everything there is usually a somewhat antagonistic feeling. This philosopher says he will face all situations boldly and extract some good from them. But in accepting the God in everything there is a glad meeting and full attentiveness and openness of heart. It is a perfectly happy condition, in which the poet could say:

Hither! take me, use me, fill me,
Vein and artery, though ye kill me!

Another way of approaching a knowledge of the heart of the devotee is to ask oneself where the philosopher gets his truth, which is a good. Did he make it? No, he found it. Where did the artist get his beauty? Did he make it? No, he found it. Since it takes the best and greatest men merely to find these goods and present them to others in, at best, an imperfect form, what shall be thought of the original Cause of all the truths and beauties? We naturally bow with great joy before the thought of that Cause.

The *bhakta* or devotee is satisfied with the joy of the consciousness of the presence of Goodness. But he still has also a touch of philosophy—the thought that his own joyous devotion—imperfect as he knows it to be and rejoiceful as he is that he has even a little of it, and perhaps even then only sometimes—will ultimately increase to fill the whole of his life and then be present at all times. Thus devotion is itself another good, and a source of joy.

It is only one step more to the formation of *bhakti-yoga*, a method for increasing the *bhakti*. Religious services are usually a mixture of this with what we shall presently study as the mantra-yoga. They aim at the direction of the feelings, and mix it with ceremonial words and actions. In India there is no collective or congregational worship, but still there are occasional gatherings at which stories are told and songs are sung extolling the exploits of divine Incarnations, or there is singing the names or appellations of Deity. In country places there are often *bhajanas* in which songs are sung containing mostly the names of the deities, to the accompaniment of drums and music, before a statue or a picture representing the divinity. Individual worship appears in daily prayers and in yoga practice.

Why is a separate or outside God adored, reverenced, worshipped? Because he is regarded as the source of wealth and bounty, considered either as an example, or as a giver of material benefits, or at least of divine "grace." It is a question whether the raja-yogi could allow himself this form of devotion, which leans on "goodness." The goal of his being is upright, strong life, happy and free because it is illuminated as to *its own* divine nature and that of *all* the other lives seen around, using other forms. If, then, his goal of life is this happiness, which is the joy of upright, strong life, master of its own small world of body and circumstances, how can he look for help towards that freedom at any stage by what he would call the intoxications or consolations or refuges of religion? Let a man do his small daily task according to his strength of will, love and thought, and all will be well with him. He can be immensely devoted to all the life around him, regarding his neighbour as himself. His refuge from selfishness and the fear it brings exists, but he will not bring into it the unnatural considerations of another and separate life governing or uplifting his own. To him this devotion is a *hatha-yoga*, inasmuch as it depends on another "good," external to himself.

Therefore this devotion is often found along with the *hatha* schools of yoga. It comes in also along with concentration in the various *chakras*. The *Gheranda Sanhita* mentions it as one of the means to *samadhi*: "Let him meditate in his own heart upon the proper form of his desired deity; let him meditate with the *bhakti-yoga*, full of the greatest gladness; let him shed tears of happiness."

The flow of unrestrained feeling, even if it means self-abandonment before the recognized glory of the divine, also has its dangers if not balanced by thought and knowledge, as insane asylums testify all over the Western world, and a red record of fanaticism and cruelty witnesses in history; though it is a path that may be followed without special guidance, provided the development of intelligence and will in practical life is not neglected. Many churches and other organizations are busy on this line, but for the most part they miss the point of it because they direct attention to God or his representative as something for the weakling to lean upon or as a fountain of blessing for personal gratification, rather than as something so splendid—a Good beyond all goods—that at the mere sight of it one loses personal desires completely, forgets oneself in the contemplation of it, and adds a new form of ecstasy to the permanent treasures of the soul.

From the Hindu point of view there is an error in the Western idea that grace can come down from above in response to devotion, or, still worse, that higher forces can be brought down by it and by ceremonials. Their view is that by grace we are lifted up, not that anything is brought down. It is akin to the doctrine of intuition. If there is intuition, following upon much thought on a given subject, the field of thought is clarified. Yoga, however, aims at the raising of consciousness above the mind into the clarifier. A crude simile may make this clear; a man owns a car, looks after it and drives it along the road to some destination, and because of that the car is both preserved and used. If the car were left to itself it would rot. Or if it were started up and sent off by itself it would soon meet with an accident.

But when it is properly used, the car is still a car; it does not become a man, and the man is still a man and does not become a car. So with the mind. If left to itself it will rot or produce an accident. But what is above mind—the ethical and moral principles—will preserve it and use it well, will harmonize its parts and contents and illumine its path. All are glad of the intuition, but the yogi wants more than that—his consciousness must be raised into the very source of that intuition. One is speaking of the *bhakta*, who is to be himself raised up, not to have his material nature glorified.

The use of *mantras* constitutes another very definite department of occult practices, known in India from the oldest times. *Mantras* are charms, spells, magical formulas, incantations. *Mantra-yoga* is the employment of words so arranged as to produce these effects. It is not usually considered that ordinary people are qualified to make *mantras*, but that the *mantra-yogi* is a person who knows the *mantras* which have been made by great *mantra-karas* (*mantra*-makers) in the past.

All the hymns of the Vedas are called *mantras*; those which are metrical and meant to be recited loudly are called "*rich*" (hence *Rig-Veda*), those in prose and to be uttered in a low voice are called "*yajus*" (hence *Yajur-Veda*) and the metrical ones intended for chanting are called *saman* (hence *Sama-Veda*). Mantras are formularies which are meant to produce an effect on people and sometimes on things, which will be so affected that they would then affect people. Thus, for example, *mantras* are useful for consecrating shrines, instruments, vestments and other things. People of Western countries are familiar with the idea, as it occurs not only in their stories or folk-lore about wizards and witches, but also in the practices of some of the churches, in which it is imperative that the priest shall conduct the ceremonies with the words exactly as prescribed, and shall also wear the vestments and make the gestures or movements traditionally associated with them and use the instruments according to rule.

It is to be noted that the prescribed wording and chanting must be accompanied by the right intention and belief in the mind. The *mantra* is not supposed to be effective without the thought which is called the intent or purpose; nevertheless the incantator need not know the meaning of the words employed—it makes no difference to the mantric action whether he knows them or not. But the correct *intention* must be used with the *mantra* belonging to it. This implies that one cannot use a *mantra* for any purpose other than that originally intended. It also indicates that the use of *mantras* is not passive (such as that of prayer-wheels or prayer-flags), but they are considered as tools. Thus the reproduction of a recited *mantra* by gramophone record would have no effect beyond that of its mere sound or music.

There are many different *mantras* associated with different schools of activity. But in all of them the chief feature is the repetition (*japa*) of certain fixed forms of words, often with a definite intonation, and always with the thought of their meaning and intention. We find this practice frequently combined with *bhakti-yoga*, as in the following example, from the *Gopalatapani Upanishad* and the *Krishna Upanishad.* Of all the mantras of Shri Krishna, none is considered more powerful than this five-divisioned, eighteen-syllabled one, which is: "Klim, Krishnaya, Govindaya, Gopi-jana, Vallabhaya, Swaha!" The following is the explanation, translated in my book on Concentration:

"Once the sages came to the great Brahma and asked: 'Who is the supreme God? Whom does Death fear? Through the knowledge of what does all become known? What makes this world continue on its course?'

"He replied: 'Shri Krishna verily is the supreme God. Death is afraid of Govinda (Shri Krishna). By knowledge of the Lord of Gopi-jana (Shri Krishna) the whole is known. By Swaha the world goes on evolving.'

"Then they questioned him again: 'Who is Krishna? Who is Govinda? Who is the Lord of Gopi-jana? What is Swaha?'

"He replied: 'Krishna is he who destroys all wrong. Govinda is the knower of all things, who, on earth, is known through the great teaching. The Lord of Gopi-jana is he who guides all conditioned beings. Swaha is his power. He who meditates on these, repeats the *mantra*, and worships him, becomes immortal.'

"Again they asked him: 'What is his form? What is his *mantra*? What is his worship?'

"He replied: 'He who has the form of a protector of cows. The cloud-coloured youth. He who sits at the root of the tree. He whose eyes are like the full-blown lotus. He whose raiment is of the splendour of lightning. He who is two-armed. He who is possessed of the sign of wisdom. He who wears a garland of flowers. He who is seated on the center of the golden lotus. Who meditates upon him becomes free. His is the *mantra* of five parts. The first is *Klim Krishnaya*. *Klim* is the seed of attraction. The second is *Govindaya*. The third is *Gopi-jana*. The fourth is *Vallabhaya*. The fifth and last is *Swaha*. *Klim*—to Krishna—to the Giver of Knowledge—to the Lord of the Cowherds—*Swaha*!'

"Om. Adoration to the Universal Form, the Source of all Protection, the Goal of Life, the Ruler of the Universe, and the Universe itself.

"Om. Adoration to the Embodiment of Wisdom, the Supreme Delight, Krishna, the Lord of Cowherds! To the Giver of Knowledge, adoration!"

Such *mantras* as this are full of symbology, which helps the intent. The word *krishna* means the colour of the rain cloud, a symbol of protection and beneficence. The cows are the verses of scripture, *Vallabha* means Lord and also Beloved, and the "cowherd people" are the great sages. The tree is creation or evolution.

Favourite among the *laya-yogis* is the mantra "*Om, aim, klim, strim.*" "*Om*" is introductory; the other three are called "seed" *mantras*; *aim* being the seed of speech or intelligence, in the first lotus, *klim* the seed *mantra* of love, in the heart lotus, and *strim* the seed *mantra* of power, in the eyebrow lotus. On the *chitrini* canal at these points there are *granthis*, or "knots," which obstruct the advance of *kundalini*. With the aid of these *mantras*, they are broken through. Great results are said to accrue from many repetitions of this *mantra*, which must be said neither too quickly nor too slowly.

The *mantra Om*, which is used at the beginning and end of all prayers, needs special mention. It is considered to have a harmonizing effect, as being the word, or true name, not merely the appellative name, of the "one life without a second." It is composed of three letters, a, u, and m, and can be pronounced with the a and u both distinctly heard, or, as is more usual, with the two blended together as O. The meaning may be derived in the following way. As a is sounded from the throat, it is the beginning of all sounds, and as m is formed by the closing of the lips, it is the end, u being in the middle. Therefore when *Om* is properly sounded with a glide from one letter to the next, it is the complete word. And since sound is creative power, *Om* is not only the natural name of God, but pronunciation of it is a means to harmony with the divine.

The same idea is symbolically represented in the *Shandilya Upanishad*, where the yogi is told to meditate, using the *pranava* that is, *Om*, at the same time thinking of three goddesses: Gayatri, a girl of reddish colour, seated on a swan and carrying a mace, who represents the letter a; Savitri, a young woman of white colour, mounted on an eagle and carrying a disc, who represents the letter u; and Saraswati, a mature woman of dark colour, riding on a bull and carrying a trident, who represents the letter m. Those goddesses are the wives and *shaktis*, or powers, of the three members of the Trinity—Shiva, Vishnu and Brahma—who together constitute the one Brahman.

The yogi is told to use the proportions sixteen, sixty-four and thirty-two for breathing during this meditation.

Very closely allied psychologically with the *mantra-yoga* is the practice of art in connection with religious matters. Just as the repetition of certain words helps the devotee to keep his mind well concentrated, so in the case of the temperament which runs to external creativeness, painting and sculpture is a means of holding up and preserving the desired emotional and mental states. The whole process is like damming up a valley and so conserving the water for the constant use of the countryside. Art may be looked upon as a form of yoga. Shukracharya says: "Let the image-maker establish images in temples by meditation on the deities who are the objects of his devotion. In no other way, not even by direct and immediate vision of an actual object, is it possible to be so absorbed in contemplation as thus in the making of images."

Out of this inevitably comes beauty, even when the intention to do so is not intellectually formulated, for action well done always produces that effect in some natural way. Thus, for example, the limbs and figure of the racehorse are wonderfully beautiful because of the skill developed in running, and also the running is beautiful to see. When an artist does his best, the same effect is produced, both in the man and in the work. This itself constitutes a kind of union with the divine, for if it can be said that God is expressible in material form, it must be in beauty, since that is the one thing in the material world of which the soul never tires.

To understand all this theoretically one has to remember that in the use of the senses there are three factors—the conscious being, the sensations (as of colour, or sound) and the sense-organ (including the whole mechanism from the eye or the ear to the brain-center). Occultly, the sensations are something in themselves, which the mind carries within itself even away from the body. The objects of the world with their colours etc., are expressions of these sensations in innumerable combinations, brought about through action-organs, and then those objects can arouse the sensations again through the sense-organs.

These sensations are vastly important, because they arouse the attentiveness of the consciousness, and assist its concentration or attentiveness and so enrich its content and power. When consciousness is stronger, clearer, its power is greater. Thus sensations are carriers of the will, both ways—from man to the world and from the world to man.

It is easy from this principle to see how all that is going on in this world is a sort of magic. In that magic we get our most formative and delighting effect in what we call beauty, and all things affect us through the shock of beauty or through the lesser process of repetition. Deliberate use of this process is a form of yoga; in the case of the latter method, repetition, we have the mantric effect.

The Occult Path of Buddha

Always the Buddha spoke of two ways of life—one being the ordinary thoughtless course in which people seek happiness through various pleasures, always hoping that they can obtain conditions which will give them satisfaction, the other being called the Path (as distinguished from the former, which is wandering about), a progressive determination to cease such seeking for pleasure in material things.

There is no travelling on this Path, it is stated, for one is not going from one place to another, or even from one mental condition to another. The goal on this path is most occult, hidden from both sense and mind, but is revealed when there is cessation of the ordinary manner of life, which could well be called the way of error and sorrow. The goal is indeed called a ceasing, not a gaining; it is a ceasing of the error or ignorance of desiring and seeking—lo here, lo there. This is called *nibbanna* or *nirvana*.

Before describing the Path we must see what Buddha's great discovery was. It was the discovery that great indescribable joy comes to the man who realizes the universality of sorrow. It comes because he is thereby released from the sense of dependence upon material things and the craving for them. You are clinging to sorrow and suffering. In your ignorance you hug and kiss the spokes of this wheel of agony.

This doctrine was formulated as Four Noble Truths: The Universality of Sorrow or Suffering; The Cause of Sorrow; The Ceasing of Sorrow; and The Way of the Ceasing of Sorrow. We are a little handicapped in using the English language to express the central idea of this doctrine, for we have not one single word, as Buddha had, to express both bodily and psychological suffering, both pain and sorrow. Perhaps suffering will be the best word to use. Perhaps we shall see, if we examine our heart's desire closely, that if we had it fulfilled there would still be suffering.

Some may say that they will accept suffering if they can have some pleasure as well. Shelley said that man looks before and after, and longs for what is not, and Shakespeare went further and pointed out that even if man has what he wants, the thought of time with its changes and uncertainties destroys his happiness. And Robert Burns mentioned that in one respect the life of a mouse was happier than that of a man—the present only troubles it. It is here that the revelation of Buddha came in—the assertion that from his own experience there is the incredible joy of nirvana for those who put aside this error of seeking or expecting happiness from circumstances.

Buddha did not leave people to grope their way out of error and craving. His fourth Truth is called a Path—the Noble Eightfold Path. This means that there are eight things to do which, if successfully done, are ways of living without sorrow. We have now to examine this path, remembering always that there can be no cheating, that this path cannot be used for the purpose of attaining something that is within the wheel of sorrow, whether an object of the body or a quality of the mind.

In the naming of the eight requirements of the Path there is a reiteration of the word "correct" or "proper" at the beginning of each. The first four answer the question, "How does the pilgrim comport himself in thought, speech and action on all occasions?" The second four point to special efforts he must make in his life. The first four are as follows:

1. Correct understanding, views, outlook, appraisal, judgment.

2. Correct aims, motives, plans, considerations, decision.
3. Correct use of speech.
4. Correct behaviour, conduct or actions.

Analyzing these and other modes of living in my book *Character-Building* many years ago, I reduced all the defects of human nature to three: laziness, selfishness and thoughtlessness, and all virtues to three, action, goodwill and thoughtfulness. These three touchstones are implied in the word "correct" in each of the four requirements. No. I implies that one has at the outset adopted the outlook described by Buddha, what is called the *dhamma* (*dharma*), law, rule, or proper way of life. *Dharma* means maintenance—the maintenance on all occasions, in all matters of life, small or great, of the resolution to put an end to pain, which is the basis of the three virtues of action, goodwill and thoughtfulness. These three are to be followed regardless of pain or trouble. Much stress is laid on speech for it is in this that dissipation of life most commonly occurs—idle chatter, cruel gossip and talk without information.

The second group of four requirements assigns the tasks:

5. Correct mode of livelihood—the fulfilling of a definite role in life, which shall be unselfish, sensible, useful.
6. Correct effort—some work of doing good.
7. Correct intellectual activity—some study.
8. Correct contemplation—the expectant poise of the mind which allows intuition and insight to begin.

All these eight have to do with daily life and the use of personal abilities and energies in the world. They may be pursued with less or greater determination and constancy; as Edwin Arnold puts it in his beautiful poem *The Light of Asia*:

Strong limbs may dare the rugged road which storms,
Soaring and perilous, the mountain's breast;
The weak must wind from slower ledge to ledge,
With many a place of rest.
So is the Eightfold Path which brings to peace;
By lower or by upper heights it goes.

The firm soul hastes, the feeble tarries. All
Will reach the sunlit snows.

Now we have to look at the inner or esoteric aspect of all this, and answer the question: "What is happening to the pilgrim himself?" For this purpose Buddha gave the four stages of the Path, and showed what are the defects or "fetters" which bind the ordinary man, and how they are to be thrown off one after the other. The first result of practicing the eightfold way is the weakening and disappearance of the error that the body is itself important. All the eight efforts lead one to be intent upon the life-side of living.

It is not a mere intellectual discovery or piece of psychic science which is proposed here. The man will instinctively stop placing bodily interest first in his thoughts. Pleasures and pride in body and personal qualities will be replaced by the eight general life interests. The *second* fetter to go is uncertainty or doubt about this path. The life proves its value as it goes along and great confidence or faith arises from this knowledge and experience. *Third* comes the cessation of dependence upon outward forms or rules or ceremonies. It is the *life* that will speak in this man on all occasions. On life he will depend, and to life he will respond with life. His action will then face the problems which arise, and will be full of both love and thought. Outer rules and forms are for those who are not on this path.

Then fade away the two terrible "fetters" which hold back the ordinary man from almost any semblance of true living: ignorant likes and dislikes—one should say more than this, passionately ignorant likes and dislikes, producing an inflexibility of mind and living which in most cases borders on the psychopathic. Doctors are acquainted with the fact that many people go about in wheel chairs; not because of inability to walk, but inability to think they can; here we have masses of inabilities and dependencies among mankind, including negativeness and fears. But the grip of fixed likings and dislikings loosens its hold on those who are treading the Noble Eightfold Path, and they become ready to meet everything appreciatively according to its nature. All their troubles are then real or material ones; they have ceased making psychological ones in addition—psychological troubles such as discontent, envy, jealousy, resentment, malice, anxiety, worry, impatience, irritability, etc., which do no good, and only hinder the use of the powers of the life in their dealing with the real troubles.

When these five fetters lie in the dust, as the poet puts it, there are still five more. This situation marks the half-way house of the upward Path. The man is now called an Arhat, a word which means "ready" or "qualified." He now knows what he wants and he is competent to go after it. In a secondary meaning he is worthy, admirable, deserving. The five remaining fetters are:

6. Desire for life in form.
7. Desire for formless life.
8. Pride.
9. Self-love.
10. Ignorance.

It would not be fitting here to attempt to say what this final ignorance is, except negatively—it is the conception of oneself as anything conceivable. Perhaps we had better leave it at that, for it is fundamental in Buddha's thought, as in that of Krishna, Shankaracharya, Jesus and all great *gurus* or teachers, that our final union is with something Beyond—beyond the limitations of mind, thought, feelings and the will, all these, as well as bodily things, being limitations. Buddha more than all others impressed this thought constantly upon his hearers, and emphasized the use of the word *nirvana*—which means "to extinguish" as, for example, the blowing out of a candle. But this includes even the extinction of extinction. In Edwin Arnold's words:

Seeking nothing, he gains all;
Foregoing self, the Universe grows "I";
If any teach Nirvana is to cease,
Say unto such they lie.
If any teach Nirvana is to live,
Say unto such they err; not knowing this,

Nor what light shines beyond their broken lamps,
Nor lifeless, timeless, bliss.

The Chinese Yoga

When the Buddha wished to allude to the final achievement or attainment of human life he spoke of *nirvana*, a "blowing-out." This means that in that experience, there will be an absence of our familiar limitations known as body and mind. Even the mind is for us an object of knowledge. The field of our knowledge can be divided into objective and subjective. Both are within the field—both the knower and the known, the subject and the object.

Buddha's doctrine was that only in the presence of knowing are "subject and object" to be seen. Mind with its reasoning activity—its logic—generally considered as the subject, is in reality only an instrument. It does not know. Behind or beyond this mind is what among Chinese Buddhists came to be called Essence of Mind. It is Bodhi, Wisdom. If a man could put aside the error or delusion of the-self-as-mind there would be the elimination of object and subject relation from his experience, and then—*nirvana*.

It was always held that only man can perform this feat, because he—not the lower animals—has mind as *reason*. Of course, there was lower mind, or instinct, in the animals, but this was accumulated knowledge—recognition and memory. And every idea or mental picture in this store of knowledge was accompanied by feeling and therefore by desire. In modern terms we would call this collection the subconscious mind, instinct. The sub-conscious mind could not be regarded as merely a matter of bodily habit. The body is always changing its particles. The incoming particles cannot be regarded as possessing the habits which have been learned by the outgoing particles. So even the continuity of its form is carried on by the "sub-conscious mind"—not by any powers of the body. This continuity governs not only the bodily reactions to environmental impacts, but also the emotions and flow of mental pictures, or association of ideas. So there is instinct. Buddha called this complex of continuity the *skandhas*.

Man has something more than instinct. He has reason, although it must be admitted that very often he acts by instinct, and reason is often if not generally far from its maturity and power.

The height of reasoning or thinking is meditation, called *dhyana* among the old psychologists of India. In a boat, instinct would tell us to row, but reason would tell us to put up a sail, until even the putting up of a sail passed into the sub-conscious and reason led us further to install a motor.

Whatever our problem, reason will improve our reaction, but reason demands time—we must think the matter over, consider the nature of water, of boats, of many things involved, study their relations in mental pictures, and then, after this process, which takes time, the problem is solved. Meditation is the complete mental review of the materials of the problem and the study of their combination. It is applied to ordinary material problems and to the most abstruse psychological and philosophical ones.

But this does not tell the whole story of meditation. If properly carried out it ends up with intuition—something you did not know before, and have not found in the world. This is sometimes called *prajna*. This intuition is not reason, but is direct perception, and the state of the mind in which this *prajna* or intuition is in power is called *samadhi*, which literally taken means completely in agreement or order.This experience by direct perception is called in China and Japan a *satori*. But I am running ahead. Let us first look at the way in which the mind gets knowledge for us.

Mind is called "sixth sense." By mind we get to know things not available to the senses of hearing, touching, seeing, tasting and smelling. It can operate in three stages, and usually does—through testimony, reasoning and seeing for ourselves. Someone comes into the house and says there is a fire on the mountain; this is supported by reason, because there is smoke; then we can go and find the fire—and perhaps put it out. So there is testimony and then reasoning and then direct perception. This applies in religious matters. Buddha says he has found joy and knowledge; it is reasonable; we are to go and find it.

When the *dhyana* or meditation process was carried into China by the famous Indian "missionary" Bodhidharma, it came to be known as *Chan*, and a little later when it had found its way to Japan the word was further modified and became *Zen*. *Zen* is Japanese meditation-yoga.

It is not to be thought that in either India or China the results of *dhyana* were merely improved subjective experience. In India the fruit of *samadhi* was *viveka* or discrimination, which means a *new valuation*. This is stated emphatically by Patanjali in his aphorism no. ii 28, which describes the final effect of the performance of the eight Limbs of Yoga, culminating in *samadhi*. This is not a perfection of the subjective, but a transcendence of the subjective conception of the subject-object relation. Subject and object now live together in the Knowing or Consciousness in a new way. Subject-self is overcome. It was a piece of Ignorance, a five-branched tree of ignorance.

In the case of Buddha we have exactly the same teaching, when *avidya*, ignorance, is given as the final "fetter" to be cast off, as shown in our previous chapter. This was essentially ignorance or error about self or the subjective entity.

It is natural that the method of practice of the *Chan* and the *Zen* should be somewhat different from that in India, as befits the racial types of China and Japan. The method is well described in *The Sutra of Wei Lang*, translated by Wong Mou-Lam, and in Christmas Humphreys' *Zen Buddhism*, and in several books by Professor D. T. Suzuki. Before we turn to the practices of *Zen* it is necessary to say that the fundamental conceptions associated with it are also found in the old Taoism of China, coming down even from Lao Tsu, who lived about the same time as Buddha. Buddhism became blended with this. The difference was that Buddha desired not to give a name to *nirvana*, as that would almost inevitably lead to some mental idea of it, which would then stand in the way of the transcendental experience. Even the idea of transcendence does so.

In the old teaching there was *Tao*, the motionless, master of all, both the subjective and objective sides of Nature, including man. It could equally be called the absolute motion, which, passing through every point of space in every direction in every moment of time, becomes the ever-present soul of all motions, but is motionless from the standpoint of the subject-object world.

From *Tao* come *yang* and *yin*, the active and passive sides of Nature, light and shadow. In man the two elements appear as intellect and instinct. The instinct-flow is natural, outward-going, but the intellect-flow, which is "backward-going, reversed, turned round," can become so pure that it gains release, when things are recognized but not desired. *The Secret of the Golden Flower*, translated by Richard Wilhelm, gives the layout of principles, and is a splendid source-book for this study.

Introspectively, all can see that knowledge and desire go opposite ways. Desire draws man into complicated experiences, bringing problems which can be solved only by the intellect seeing things as they are, untainted by desires concerning them. The path of yoga, in this field, thus means knowing or seeing without desire. There is, of course, knowing, or consciousness, in both cases. The animal is highly conscious, but instinctual; in man the consciousness is becoming intellectual; in the *bodhisattwa* (which means one whose intellect is pure, or whose very nature is intellect) we have man on the verge of *nirvana*, or *Tao*. In all three cases feeling and knowledge go hand in hand. Where there is pure knowledge, the feeling is love—love without desire, full consciousness and approach completely without antagonism. This is the *Zen* outlook, whatever terminology of China or India, of *Tao* or Buddhism may be used. The practice of meditation in this field is "seeing without desire." And the height of it is reached when there is direct perception, intuition in which reasoning stops. There is no *desire* for logic to stop; it does so naturally when its function is fulfilled; then intuition appears.

If we compare the art of China with that of Greece we find that one is more the product of imaginative observation, the other of introspectional observation. The word imaginative here means image-making. It is less creative and more contemplative. If the poise of the Chinese has the relative proportions shown in diagram A, that of the Indo-European is relatively somewhat as in diagram B.

It is to be understood, of course, that while this rotary motion is the same for all sane minds, the standard or evolutionary status is individual. In the individual there is growth through use or exercise, whereby each of the three elements is advanced in ability. Taking this into consideration, it will be seen that the movement is spiral as well as rotary.

The difference of different minds, and races of men, is a difference in the proportions and status of these three. I have cited art here because art is yoga in action, action free from the taint of desire and utility or use. It gives us a peep-hole into the mind. So the meditation-systems of China did not develop on very introspectional lines, as meditation in Europe has done.

In *The Secret of the Golden Flower* a form of meditation is given in which a superphysical self is built. Intellect or the light of seeing is to be freed from the instinctual, is to build a body of its own. This is done by stopping the flight of thoughts—concentrate, but quickly pass into contemplation; when contemplation

It is to be understood, of course, that while this rotary motion is the same for all sane minds, the standard or evolutionary status is individual. In the individual there is growth through use of exercise, whereby each of the three elements is advanced in ability. Taking this into consideration, it will be seen that the movement is spiral as well as rotary falls into flights again, renew the concentration. This "circulates" the process—brings it into circle, not *drives* it round, but puts an end to wandering off. As in India, attention is to be given at first to the body—body comfortable, breathing rhythmic, senses quiet. Then one listens within, to the no-sound, listens to the silence. Thus within the heart another "body" is gradually built up, which is a spiritual body.

Though many details are given in *The Secret of the Golden Flower* there is no room for them here; besides, the serious student will supply his own details. It is the body or focus of knowing (Confucius), of the heart-view (Buddha), of inward vision (Lao Tsu). The intuition will come; one must hardly ask for it, and certainly not presuppose its nature. The magical material side of it will be that the new "body" will be the intuition-vehicle for living free from the space-limitation of the body, and so, being concerned with seeing and doing remote from the body, giving what may be called a practical or objective side also to the intuition, which is not one-sided but concerns object as well as subject.

Buddha said: "Nor sink the string of thought into the Fathomless." But men cannot leave it at that; they strive to realize the truth. Buddha does not object to that, but says it will not be done by thought. Intuition which is not thought will do it. But intuition comes to us; we do not make it. Is it different from the objective, or different from the subjective? We must answer, "No," because difference is a thought, a comparison, an attribute. So not by the suppression of the world or the mind is intuition to be sought. Without their absence comes this something which they as such cannot present. They would not be themselves without it. Ordinarily the mind is taken up with objective or subjective interests and activities, leaving no opening for the third. When people seek that third, intellectual desire is usually present, even if instinctual desire has been overcome. The first point of *Zen* meditation is therefore, "Drop it!" Any means which will start the process and thwart the intellectual desire will be permissible, provided it does not prevent the "Go on" or, if there is a teacher, the "Come on!" which is like that of a mother calling a young child to walk, without a word about the mechanism of walking.

Three techniques have been specially prominent in the schools of *Zen*—the wall-gazing, the sudden question (*mondo*) and the enigmatic statement (*koan*). The first is not gazing at a wall, as one might think, but gazing like a wall. You are the wall, upright to the world, set by the plumb-line of your own nose, unaffected, intent on the Essence of Mind. Bodhidharma is said to have practised this for nine years, avoiding commitments and desires, like an upright wall. He taught for fifty years in China. The sixth Patriarch in his succession was

Hui-neng, or Wei-Lang, through whom Chinese Buddhism, harmonized with the *Tao*, emerged as a definite way of life, allowing no dogmas, requiring an enquiring mind, searching within, demanding humble faith in the coming of sudden enlightenment, and—materially—a simple life of self-restraint, industry and sympathy.

Teachings of Buddha much used by the founders of the *Zen* sect were: the *Lankavatara Sutra*, the *Avatansaka Sutra*, the *Surangama Sutra*, the *Mahayana Shraddhotpada Shastra* and the *Diamond Sutra*. To these were added the *Sutra* of Wei-Lang. The whole collection is very conveniently gathered together and presented in Goddard's *Buddhist Bible*.

The teaching of meditation in the *Diamond Sutra* prescribes sitting alone, erect, motionless, quieting the mind, with attention on no definite thing, excluding recollection and imagination, abandoning all notions of an external world, turning to inner intuitive consciousness, gradually entering *samadhi*, ideal tranquility, and thus passing from vagrant thinking and even intellectual activity into the realization of insight.

It was especially among the Chinese and Japanese that the sudden enlightenment was brought about by sudden means. Intuition is by its very nature always sudden—not built up—but sudden means or methods were also now brought in, in the shape of *koans* and *mondos*.

The *koan* is a mind-baffling statement to be meditated upon. The teacher requires an answer; there is no hurry about it, but you are expected to tackle it, and to stick at it until you have a solution. The statement is of such a nature that the intellect cannot understand it, and all its efforts to do so are in vain. It is thus thwarted and nullified, and the yogi must therefore sweat and strain, so to speak, with great will power until an intuitive answer comes. It is very strenuous, and dangerous unless the *koan* is given by a competent teacher to an appropriate student. The intuition is such that it cannot be expressed in words, but when it comes there will be a lighting-up of the mind which will cause an involuntary exclamation or action, such as the laugh or the slap of the thigh which one gives when there is a sudden seeing of the point of a joke or the solution of a conundrum, and one says, "I never thought of *that*."

As an example, the teacher may say: "You have knees, you have feet. Come, let us fly." Or, a classical one, "The two hands clap with a noise; listen to the clap of one hand." There should be no agreed upon, traditional or conventional meaning to these *koans*.

They may be invented *ad lib*. A good example occurs accidentally, as it were, in the *Glorious Presence* where, after expounding the Vedantic doctrine of "Not thus, not thus" from the commentary on the *Mundukya Upanishad* where Gaudapada says: "There is no limitation, no creation, no bondage, no maker, no aspirant, nobody freed—this is the correct knowledge," the continuation is: "And no 'no,' and there we are." Another example occurred when the Sixth Patriarch wrote his first statement: in reply to:

Our body is the Bodhi-tree,
And our mind a mirror bright.
Carefully we wipe them hour by hour,
And let no dust alight.

His stanza said:

There is no Bodhi-tree,
Nor stand of a mirror bright.
Since all is void,
Where can the dust alight?

The last two lines form a perfect koan.

The resulting enlightenment is called a *satori*. This "goal" as well as the method is called *Zen*, just as in India yoga means both the practice and the attainment. Mr. Christmas Humphreys thus explains it: "Zen is not an escape from things but a new way of looking at things, whereby they are seen to be already in Nirvana." 7 We are denying ourselves, which is the great Error. Still, one must take care not to call *Zen* or *Nirvana* a state; for that conception, or any conception, is within the *maya* or error. Nor "looking."

The *mondo* is question and answer. Here there is no continued wrestling as it were in terrible unmental attentiveness, as in the case of the *koan*. An immediate answer is required, without thought. It will be noticed that this is another way of sidestepping the thought process while maintaining the attentiveness. For example, a *Zen* master once held out a stick and said, "Call it not a stick; if you do you assert. Nor deny that it is a stick; if you do, you negate. Without affirmation or denial, speak, speak!" It is not recorded what the pupils said, but I tried this on myself and out came "On, on!" And this carried knowledge, like a dream.

Life sets us *koans* and *mondos* all the time, for never do we know enough to act with full intelligence. As far as we ourselves are concerned:

All things are rushing to their doom;
Trying to slow the rush
The mind preserves their death.

The Sufi Yogas

As is fitting in the field of a religion based upon the revelations through the Prophet Muhammad, the practices (or yogas) and fulfilments of the Sufis were and are entirely saturated with the doctrine of Islam, which is resignation to God, or rather delighted union of the will of man with the will of God. This fundamental principle of acceptance of God's *will* among the religious becomes the reception of God's *being* among the mystics.

In the efforts and attainments of these mystics must be recognized therefore *two* operators—God who is trying to give himself to man, and man who is trying to give himself to God. The second of these factors, the human efforts, naturally takes on the aspect of yoga practice—purification of the self from worldly desires, mental defects and selfish motives, often by means of frequent deep and prolonged meditation, and even by physical asceticism, intended in some cases to reduce the body to submission, and in others to demonstrate submission achieved.

It was indeed from one of these practices that the very name "Sufi" was adopted—the wearing of woollen garments by these mystics and yogis, a mild equivalent of the Christian hair shirt. The word "sufi" is derived from a word meaning wool.

The foundations of the contrast between material riches and the presence of God which has had great influence in the Sufi life were laid by Muhammad himself, when he said "Poverty is my pride," and rejected the personal use of riches, as well as in the example of earlier Prophets, including Moses, David and Jesus. Many were the Sufi ascetics and mystics who gave up wealth and pursued the simple life.

It was, however, always the constant thought or remembrance (*dhikr*) of God that was considered the means to Union (*tauhid*) with Him, in which there was the passing away (*fana*) of all the human qualities or human nature, the only continuity (*bava*) being then the continuity of God Himself. Students of comparative yoga will see in this a similarity to Buddha's doctrine of *Nibbanna*, or *Nirvana*, in the achievement of which every vestige of what man can think or feel himself to be entirely disappears. This transformation of the Sufi could take place during life, but woe to the man who might say that he had become God. The true idea is quite different from that. It is a dying to self. The orthodox of Islam would never allow a man to call himself God, or permit the idea that God would appear in or through human form. All its inspirers were regarded only as Prophets, of whom Muhammad was the greatest, and the height of their message was loss of self in God. When man is lost in God, the continuity is God's, not man's.

The technicalities of Sufi yoga practice were never codified with the exactitude found among the Hindus and Buddhists, though it must be said that Sufi teachers in India sometimes adopted portions of the Hindu meditational methods, without abating the essential aim of devotional submission. The present writer became acquainted with one Sufi teacher in the north of India who had sixteen thousand disciples or followers within a radius of about fifty miles, and was using methods of meditation the same as those of one of the Hindu schools. This brings to attention the fact that although there are many "sannyasi" Sufis wandering about with musical instruments and singing devotional songs, still the bulk were and are people in ordinary occupations, as is the case with Hindu aspirants also.

Music plays an important part in the life of most of the Sufis in India, following the Mevlavi Order established by Maulana Jatal al-Din Rumi. It is not only through the eye that things can tell us of their essential being. To go along with the experiences in perfect harmony, even unity, is the height of a sort of meditation which conveys experience beyond thought and reason. Every being acts from its own character, and usually the seeing or experiencing is limited to the material gain—so a worm sees a tree in one way, a bird in another, a monkey in another, a worldly man in another. But a spiritual man must see it in another way, without the antagonism and conquesting of his reasoning mind, but with acceptance, harmony and flowing—with, in short, a sort of meditativeness which excludes reason. On this account the allegories of Love and Wine came to fill the poetry of the Sufis. Thus one can understand stanza 60 of Omar Khayyam's *Rubaiyat*:

You know, my friends, with what a brave carouse
I made a second marriage in my house,
Divorced old barren Reason from my bed
And took the Daughter of the Vine to spouse.

In this sort of meditativeness or lovefull attentiveness there is experience above reason, above expression in words. This was usual with Emerson, so he could write:

Cans't thou copy in verse one chime
Of the wood-bell's peal and cry,
Write in a book the morning's prime,
Or match with words that tender sky?
Wonderful verse of the gods,
Of one import, of varied tone;
They chant the bliss of their abodes
To man imprisoned in his own.
Ever the words of the gods resound;

But the porches of man's ear
Seldom in this low life's round
Are unsealed, that he may hear.

Moulana Rumi expressed the longing of Love in the following verses translated by R. A. Nicholson in his book *Rumi, Poet and Mystic*:

Hearken to this Reed forlorn,
Breathing, ever since 'twas born
From its rushy bed, a strain
Of impassioned love and pain.
The secret of my song, though near,
None can see and none can hear.
Oh, for a friend to know the sign
And mingle all his soul with mine!
'Tis the flame of Love that fired me,
'Tis the wine of Love inspired me.
Woulds't thou learn how lovers bleed,
Hearken, hearken to the Reed!

It is part of the technique of Sufism to be on guard not to fail in this Love, or unantagonistic looking, in oneself as in all. There is no self-fighting in this. Look with Love, and the divine "intoxication" of the Wine will come. As Rumi, again, said:

Into my heart's night
Along a narrow way
I groped; and lo! the light,
An infinite land of day.

This awareness of the real man is put in less direct terms in the poem on *Body and Soul* by another Persian poet, Enweri—translated in Emerson's essay on Persian Poetry:

A painter in China once painted a hall;
Such a web never hung on an emperor's wall;—
One half from his brush with rich colours did run,
The other he touched with a beam of the sun;
So that all which delighted the eye in one side,

The same, point for point, in the other replied.
In thee, friend, that Tyrian chamber is found;
Thine the star-pointing roof, and the base on the ground:
Is one half depicted with colours less bright?
Beware that the counterpart blazes with light!
"Beware" means, of course, "be aware."

We may find room in this short introduction to Sufi yoga for two verses, vi 17-18—very percipient—from Richard Burton's *Kasidah*:

Yes Truth may be, but 'tis not Here; mankind must seek and find it There, p. 159
But Where nor I *nor* you *can tell, nor aught earth-mother ever bare.*
Enough to think that Truth can be: come sit we where the roses glow,
Indeed he knows not how to know who knows not also how to unknow.
Cease, then, your own Almighty Power to bind, to bound, to understand.

In his book *Sufism*, Prof. A. J. Arberry gives a list of the meanings of terms used in much of the Ṣufi love-poetry, compiled from a treatise by Muhsin Faid Kashani, a Persian author of two centuries ago. Among these are the Face or Cheek (Divine Beauty, Grace, Bounty, Light, Reality), the Tresses (Majesty, Power, the veil of Reality), Mole (point of Unity), Eye and Glance (God's beholding and granting), Eyebrow (the attributes which veil the Essence), Wine (ecstatic experience), Wine-bearer (Reality, loving to manifest itself in every form), Cup, Pitcher and Jar (revelations of Divine Acts, Names and Qualities), Sea and Ocean (revelations of Divine Essence), Tavern (Pure Unity)—but see Professor Arberry's book for a fuller list and details.

Bibliography

Akers, Brian Dana : *The Hatha Yoga Pradipika,* Woodstock, YogaVidya, New York, 2002.

Allen, Marc : *Tantra for the West: Everyday Miracles and other Steps for Transformation,* New World Library, San Rafael, 1992.

Anand, Margo : *The Art of Sexual Ecstasy: The Path of Sacred Sexuality for Western Lovers*, Jeremy P. Tarcher, Los Angeles, 1989.

Avalon, Arthur and Ellen : *Hymns to the Goddess*, Ganesh and Co., Madras, 1964.

Baba, Pagal : *Temple of the Phallic King: The Mind of India*, Simon and Schuster, New York, 1973.

Basu, Manoranjan : *Tantras: A General Study*, Shrimati Mira Basu, Calcutta, 1976.

Beyer, Stephen : *The Cult of Tara: Magic and Ritual in Tibet*, University of California Press, Berkeley, 1973.

Bhattacharyya, B. : *Saivism and the Phallic World*, Oxford, Delhi, 1982.

Bose, D. N. : *Tantras: Their Philosophy and Occult Secrets*, Calcutta, 1965.

Chakravarti, C. : *The Tantras: Studies on their Religion and Literature*, Punthi Pustak, Calcutta, 1963.

Chawdhri, L. R. : *Practicals of Mantras Tantras,* Sagar Publications, New Delhi, 1985.

Chen, C. M. : *Discriminations Between Buddhist and Hindu Tantras*, Mani Printing Works, Kalimpong, 1969.

Colaabavala, F. D. : *Tantra: The Erotic Cult*, Orient Paperbacks, New Delhi, 1976.

Comfort, Alex : *The Koka Shastra: and other Medieval Indian Writings on Love*, George Allen and Unwin, New Delhi, 1964.

Cozort, Daniel : *Highest Yoga Tantra,* Snow Lion Publications, New York, 1986.

Das, H. C. : *Tantricism: A Study of the Yogini Cult*, Sterling Publishers, New Delhi, 1981.

De Ropp, S. R. : *Sex Energy: The Sexual Force in Man and Animals*, Corgi Books, London, 1972.

Devi, Kamala : *The Eastern Way of Love: Tantric Sex and Erotic Mysticism*, Simon and Schuster, New York, 1977.

Dowman, Keith : *Masters of Enchantment*, Harper and Row, New York, 1988.

Dyczkowski, Mark. S. G. : *The Canon of the Shaivagama and the Kubjika Tantras of the Western Kaula Tradition,* State University of New York Press, Albany, 1988.

Farrow, G. W. and Menon, I. : *The Concealed Essence of the Hevajra Tantra,* Motilal Banarsidass, Delhi, 1992.

Feuerstein, Georg : *The Philosophy of Classical Yoga,* Inner Traditions, Rochester, 1996.

Frawley, David : *Tantric Yoga and the Wisdom Goddesses,* Passage Press, Salt Lake City, 1994.

Garrison, Omar : *Tantra: The Yoga of Sex*, Avon Books, New York, 1964.

Goudriaan, Teun : *The Vinasikha Tantra,* Motilal Banarsidass, Delhi, 1985.

Haich, Elisabeth : *Sexual Energy and Yoga*, Aurora Press, New York, 1982.

Hopkins, Jeffrey : *Kalachakra Tantra Rite of Initiation*, Wisdom Publications, Boston, 1982.

Jacobs, Hans : *Western Psychotherapy and Hindu Sadhana*, George Allen and Unwin, London, 1961.

Jaggi, O. P. : *Yogic and Tantric Medicine,* Atma Ram and Sons, Delhi, 1973.

Kaviraj, Gopinath : *Aspects of Indian Thought*, University of Burdwan, Calcutta, 1966.

Khanna, Madhu : *Yantra: The Tantric Symbol of Cosmic Unity*, Thames and Hudson, London, 1979.

Kieffer, Gene : *Kundalini for the New Age: Selected Writings of Gopi Krishna*, Bantam Books, London, 1988.

King, Francis : *Tantra: The Way of Action: A Practical Guide to its Teachings and Techniques*, Destiny Books, Rochester, 1990.

Krishna, Gopi : *Kundalini: Path to Higher Consciousness,* Orient Paperbacks, New Delhi, 1976.

Kvaerne, Per : *An Anthology of Buddhist Tantric Songs: A Study of the Caryagiti*, White Orchid Press, Bangkok, 1966.

Lessing, Ferdinand : *Introduction to the Buddhist Tantric Systems*, Motilal Banarsidass, Delhi, 1993.

Moffett, Robert : *Tantric Sex*, Berkley Medalion, New York, 1974.

Mookerjee, Ajit : *Kali The Feminine Force*, Thames and Hudson, London, 1988.

Mulin, G. H. : *Meditation on the Lower Tantras*, Library of Tibetan Works and Archives, Dharamsala, 1983.

Mumford, John : *Ecstasy through Tantra*, Llewellyn Publications, St. Paul, 1990.

Narayanananda, Swami : *The Kundalini Shakti*, Rishikesh, 1950.

Natarajan, B. : *Thirumandiram: A Classic of Yoga and Tantra,* Babaji's Kriya Yoga Publications, Montreal, 1993.

Odier, Daniel : *Sculptures Tantriques du Nepal*, Editions du Rocher, Monaco, 1970.

Pandit, M. P. : *Gems from the Tantras*, Ganesh and Co., Madras, 1969.

Payne, E. : *The Shaktas: An Introduction and Comparative Study*, Calcutta, 1933.

Pratyagatmananda, Swami : *Japasutram*, Ganesh and Co., Madras, 1961

Rajneesh, Bhagwan : *Tantra: The Supreme Understanding,* Chidvilas, Boulder, 1993.

Rastogi, Navjivan : *The Krama Tantricism of Kashmir,* Motilal Banarsidass, Delhi, 1979.

Rele, Vasant. G. : *Mysterious Kundalini,* Taraporevala, Bombay, 1927.

Schmidt, Toni : *The Eighty-Five Siddhas*, Stat Etnografiska Museum, Stockholm, 1958.

Shaw, Miranda : *Passionate Enlightenment: Women in Tantric Buddhism*, Princeton University Press, 1994.

Singer, June : *Androgyny: Toward a New Theory of Sexuality,* Anchor Press/Doubleday, New York, 1976.

Sircar, D. C. : *The Sakta Pithas*, Indological Publishers and Booksellers, Delhi, 1973.

Tattabhusan, P. H. : *Kamaratna Tantra,* Government Press, Gauhati, 1928.

Van Kooij, K. R. : *Worship of the Goddess According to the Kalikapurana*, E. J. Brill, Leiden, 1972.

Wayman, Alex : *Yoga of the Guhyasamaja Tantra*, Motilal Banarsidass, Delhi, 1977.

Winternitz, M. : *Notes on the Guhyasamaja Tantra and the Age of the Tantras*, IHQ, Calcutta, 1933.

Woodroffe, Sir John : *The World as Power*, Ganesh and Co., Madras, 1966.

Yogananda, Swami : *Autobiography of a Yogi,* Fellowship, Los Angeles, 1946.

Zimmer, Heinrich : *Myths and Symbols in Indian Art and Civilization,* Bollingen Series/ Pantheon/Random House, New York, 1946.

Zvelebil, Kamil. V. : *The Poets of the Powers*, Rider and Co., London, 1973.

Index

N

O

P

R

❑❑❑